The
Homosexual
Matrix

C.A. Tripp
The Homosexual Matrix

McGraw-Hill Book Company
New York   St. Louis   San Francisco
Düsseldorf   Mexico   Toronto

Book Design: Marcy J. Katz.
Production Supervisor: Erna E. Helwig.

23456789 BPBP 798765

Library of Congress Cataloging in Publication Data

Tripp, C. A.
  The homosexual matrix.

  Bibliography: p.
  Includes index.
1. Homosexuality.   I.   Title.
HQ76.T75   301.41'57   75-6987
ISBN 0-07-065201-5

Contents

Preface

Homosexuality would certainly be an easier subject to describe and to analyze if it were confined to the people who practice it. But it is more than a brand of behavior that can be viewed at the level of choice or of some personal imperative. Much like heterosexuality—its mirror image in a way—it has extensive biological and sociological implications. And it has a whole history of consequences in religion, philosophy, and science. To trace these roots and to follow its repercussions through this maze—in short, to draw a picture not only of homosexuality but of its social matrix —has been the aim of this study from the start.

And yet despite my own previous work as a sex researcher and psychologist, and much help from some of the best minds in both fields, this project has taken more than ten years. It was necessary to sort out the issues, to go after special sources of information, and in the process, to stay as empirical and inductive as possible rather than reaching hasty deductive conclusions. How pleasant it would be to be able to say that all this time was spent in an orderly carrying out of various procedures that were fully planned from the beginning. But in practice, one encounters many sidetracks in sex research, some of which have to be explored immediately before another step can be taken. Other times, one must visit and revisit a particular milieu to catch its flavor, to recheck early impressions, or to travel some entirely new avenue that appeared on no map before. Such things as building rapport with a new group, gathering special samples, and making innumerable observations may all move very rapidly; but it is sometimes quite another matter to "make sense" of the results or to suspend one's judgment long enough to let them take their own shape.

It was possible, for example, to "put together" a group of 52 transsexuals in less than a week (a not-at-all-homosexual group, by the way, but one which was especially useful in tracing certain aspects of inversion). But it took more than a year to adequately understand the 8 of them whom I came to know and like very much in close, friendly surroundings; they proved to be very articulate and a trove of information. There were extended contacts, too, with many other individuals—including 12 of the 210 persons who were (or had been) connected with various branches of the federal government, and whose often firsthand accounts were helpful in rounding out much of what is cited here in "The Politics of Homosexuality."

But of course, any study of this kind—which is mainly a synthesis rather than being statistical in its own right—owes a major debt to the careful work of others who, over the years, have run the experiments and conducted the surveys that have established the baseline data which, in turn, allow additional observations to be worth something. The present study owes a special debt to the work of Frank Beach, William Young, John Money, and especially Alfred Kinsey and his associates—Wardell Pomeroy, Clyde Martin, and Paul Gebhard.

Perhaps I should add a personal note here, for it is more than that. Through a lucky connection with Kinsey in 1948, I soon became closely associated with him and his work. And while I was never a member of the Kinsey Research staff, through nine years of this association I did have a chance to make various contributions to their work and to benefit enormously from its whole tone and character. In fact, those years produced much that was influential on what is presented here. For while this study was not outlined until much later, those Kinsey years established the basic attitudes that were to guide it—and oddly enough, its research method. Oddly, that is, because it borrows little of the statistical taxonomy Kinsey was famous for. But what it does borrow are certain of the sampling techniques and styles of close-up observation he actually used in much of his background research.

The actual production of the present study owes much to the advice and talents of three colleagues—Lewis Coopersmith, Fritz Fluckiger, and George Weinberg. It was Weinberg who, in 1963–64, most urgently insisted that this project should be undertaken, and during its course he has given much aid and support. Since early 1965, Coopersmith has spent countless hours both in helping to plan the work and actively contributing to its interpretations. And over the last five years, Fluckiger—a specialist in scientific method and one of the most erudite scholars in sex research—has taken a close interest in each phase of the work; he has been a constant source of special information and guidance.

In matters of presentation, there has been a final, important arbiter. McGraw-Hill's Editor-in-Chief Frederic Hills made an exceptional contribution on two fronts. He actively helped preserve the integrity of the work (portions of the manuscript had been subjected to strong prepublication pressures which were not acceded to), and he also lent his own considerable talents. In numerous instances, Hills' grasp of the material and his remarkable power of mind and language strengthened the effort to hold to clear, simple phrasing even where complex ideas were being dealt with.

With all these contributions, then, the evolution of this study reflects a host of influences spanning a considerable portion of two decades. The aim here, much as it was at the outset, has been to combine quite a number of common and not so common observations into a new picture of sexual events—one which has been analyzed with an eclectic psychology, and with an eye to both anthropological and biological considerations. If the patterns and realizations that have finally emerged provide a reasonably complete picture of homosexuality—of its own matrix and the social matrix in which it occurs—then this book will have succeeded in its main goal.

C. A. Tripp

1

Popular and Historical Concepts of Sex

If the "sexual revolution" of the last fifteen years has demystified homosexuality and thus improved its image, it has been by no means totally domesticated. Indeed, the closer that image moves toward something that might gain outright acceptability, the more it arouses and alarms the very considerable forces against it—forces that none too patiently await their chance to relabel it as outrageous.

In any case, the new liberalism is not to be trusted. That sexual variations are tolerated and talked about more freely than they were before does not mean they are any better understood. In fact, a sudden new "tolerance" of something usually means people have rushed into a surface acceptance of it while being less inclined than ever to sift and to grapple with the basic issues. This is especially true in sexual matters, where liberation and personal freedom have become the key notions. The sex researcher finds himself in a peculiar position. He now frequently has to raise the questions as well as find the answers to them, and on both counts he runs the risk of sounding irrelevant. In "the old days" whenever he wanted to make a point that went against conventional belief, both he and his audience knew where his opposition lay—squarely within religious doctrine. His listener's initial bias could then be traced to what had been learned in Church or Temple. Often the shock of this alone was enough to open an intelligent layman's mind. Not any more. Most people now see themselves, if not as independent thinkers, then at least as being free of church dogma. Quite religious people, too, tend to be convinced they are no longer stuck in the sands of time—for, after all, who hears ancient pontifications any more?

But what has the new liberalism actually accomplished? It has done something. It has clearly brought major changes in language and in surface posture, along with the pretense that nothing anyone else does is ever an out-and-out shock, even when it is strongly disapproved of. In addition, there have been certain actual though hard to assess changes in our mores, especially in judgments of heterosexual behavior. Premarital coitus has become commonplace enough to make the adult virgin a vanishing species—and a bit suspect besides ("Maybe there is something the matter with her"). Women's magazines now admonish a wife, especially the young wife, to overcome her inhibitions: On her own accord she should fellate her husband, please and surprise him in other ways, do and request what feels good, discuss sexual reactions, and otherwise let it all hang out. Probably much of this qualifies as a show of freedom; sometimes it is exciting hot-talk designed to fan the fires of fantasy. In any case, there are indications aplenty that sharp relaxations in the mores, whether displayed in the short story and motion picture or advocated in the advice column, do not really "play in Peoria."

Both of these trends—the show of freedom and the quiet, powerful pullback—are even more apparent in views on homosexuality. In recent years, there have been strong movements to change sex laws or to remove their jurisdiction over anything done between consenting adults in private. No doubt these changes, already enacted by a number of states and countries, including Illinois and England, are a portent of the future. And yet, it is precisely in such "liberalized" regions that one begins to get a glimpse of just how thoroughly entrenched classical mores are. England, in practice, is at least as rigorous in its attitudes as it was before. Anyone involved in homosexuality there had better watch his step, and Chicago is more surveillant of him than it has been in over a century. These secondary results of liberal legislation are not to be thought of as offshoots of some temporary backlash. There is every indication they are not so temporary. Laws against homosexuality were removed from the books in Switzerland and other European countries nearly forty years ago—a change that took the matter out of the courts, but in the name of "taste and decorum" enforcement standards were actually tightened.

None of the usual ways of interpreting these situations will quite suffice. It is not correct to say that major legal changes along with the loosening and tightening of various social attitudes add up to "no change." Nor is the uneven progress of liberalization at all well accounted for by the ever-popular notion that the world is run by two factions: a group of people who are liberal, wise, and up-to-date but whose reforms are slowed by a separate group of very unliberated die-hard conservatives. The truth is that almost nobody is very "liberated." Any observer capable of seeing an inch below the surface will find a quite intact layer of "original values" in the thinking and basic attitudes of even the most urbane, sophisticated individuals. A person may enjoy acting in variant ways sexually and otherwise—and whether he does or not, he may be utterly permissive in his attitude toward someone else's doing so. But of course, this permissiveness implies the granting of a permit which, in turn, salutes the rules to which it is an exception.

Similar expressions of unchanged values are apparent in many other contexts. At upper social levels especially, the homosexual often reaps various advantages from his position. To a few of his heterosexual friends his very difference may make him more interesting; others lean over backwards to keep from being or seeming prudish. Still others are predisposed to like him for much the same reasons that tend to cause a person who is vulnerable in any way to be more likable. But in all such examples, as in the many opposite ones in which a person is damned for his difference, the basis of comparison—the assumed norm from which his variations are measured—is very much in evidence.

Why this inevitable allegiance to a centerline expectancy? Is it an automatic holdover from early training, an underlying expectation of uniformity, a moral obligation, or some other tyranny of collective assumptions? No doubt it is all of these and more—influences which to some extent harm the objectivity of everybody. With this in mind, there is much to be learned from recalling certain fundamentals in the background of us all.

Historical Perspectives

In every society there have always been customs, laws, and moral demands imposed on its individual members as the price for the privilege of belonging to it. Every society also forms value judgments which become the criteria for deciding the kinds of behavior that will be approved or disapproved. Firm regulations soon follow, one of their main functions being to establish a certain uniformity in both social and private behavior. Socially, at least, this uniformity has considerable value; it facilitates cooperative efforts of the group and minimizes a wide range of frictions and disagreements.

Approved and disapproved forms of behavior translated into concepts of right and wrong are then applied to every aspect of life. They affect the clothes one wears, the food one eats, the ways in which kindness and hostility are expressed—and, most firmly of all, the kinds of sexual expressions that are deemed acceptable or unacceptable. No doubt the rigor of sexual mores stems, in part, from the unusually high emotion that accompanies sex.

A few of the rules by which a society regulates sexual behavior are needed for practical reasons, such as protecting the weak from the strong. Often they are extensions of fundamental principles concerning the rights of others, or restraints against assault and battery. The capture of another man's mate, rape, and other types of forced relations are against the law in every society. In other instances, too, sexual prohibitions have a protective flavor and appear to be the result of social experience. It is understandable that sexual acts which lead to the discontents of incest or involve the abuse of young children have come under tight restrictions.

But the great majority of our society's sexual regulations arose without reference to practical necessity. They were products of religious philosophy and various spiritual values which came to be placed in opposition to "sins of the flesh." In the eyes of Church and Temple, sin is perpetrated whenever people "spill the seed" in masturbation, mouth-genital contacts, anal intercourse, or engage in homosexual practices. Civil courts have absorbed these regulations and, to this day, sometimes enforce them to the letter of the law. It has never been claimed that such activities threaten persons or property; nor does the law pretend that they do. They are listed as crimes against nature, as abnormal, and as perversions of nature's intent—as if there were some source other than nature from which they could have come.

The religious philosophies which underlie the sexual mores of our society were brought together and elaborated by men who believed that a life of celibacy, abstinence, and asceticism was morally superior to one containing *any* sexual expression. Although it was "better to marry than to burn," sex even then became fully acceptable only when practiced at certain times, in certain ways, in certain positions, and when certain motivations —and not others—were present. Sexual excitement *per se* was always associated with sin, even in one's sleep or one's imagination—hence, the notion that he who looks at a woman lustfully already commits adultery in his mind. Similar attitudes continue to equate sex with licentiousness—without the "right kind" of affection it is vulgar and lewd—attitudes which continue to reiterate our antisexual philosophy.

Our sex laws and customs stem from early Jewish codes which had previously come in part from still earlier Hittite, Chaldean, and Egyptian ideas. Although Jewish sex law was basically outlined in the Old Testament, it gained most of its punitive, highly restrictive character from moral arguments put forward in the Talmud, which was written just prior to and during the time of the early Christians. Since the first Christians were Jews living under Roman rule, their ideas on sexual behavior were derived from a combination of Jewish sex law and the tenets held by certain ascetic Roman cults. The later Christians proved to be even more rigorous and harsh in their antisexual edicts. Thus, broadly speaking, our mores gained their direction from Jewish history and their harshness from Christian elaborations.

This reactionary antisexual philosophy must be understood in its historical context. Very early Jewish mores apparently alternated several times between sexual and antisexual forms. But for much of the whole First Temple period (ending with the Babylonian Exile), the Jews shared many of the sexual ways of their neighbors—including various forms of sexual worship. There were such extremes as male and female sacred prostitution (fees donated to the Temple as a means of absolution), the introduction of young men to the sexual-religious exaltations of orgasm within the Temple, and ceremonial mouth-genital contacts between priests and worshipers. (In fact, ritual mouth-genital contacts were so deeply ingrained as to be among the traditions which later proved hardest to change. To this day, certain Orthodox circumcision ceremonies still include a ritualistic fellatio of the newly cut penis.[143,61]* What is important about these practices is not that they existed, but how most of them were brought to a quite sudden end.

Within about a fifty-year period during and immediately following the Babylonian Exile, conservative Jewish factions began to reformulate and insist upon a sharply ascetic philosophy. This movement has often been attributed to the desire of a scattered and "chosen" people to reunite itself by reaffirming its faith and its uniqueness. No doubt there were political and still other psychological reasons as well. At any rate, Jewish leaders became extremely antisexual and categoric in their arguments. Many new condemnations were established, mainly by classification: Innumerable acts were labeled as clean or unclean, with additional prohibitions set up against particular animals, particular foods, and against sex relations with persons of a particular social status. Prohibitions against popular sex practices understandably required powerful justification; already-established loves and hates were evoked, and logical-sounding rationalizations were used. Most sexual activities were deemed to be against God's will,

---

*Superscript figures throughout the book correspond to the numbered references beginning on p. 292.

and there were specific efforts to identify prohibited acts with the ways of now-despised neighbors. In addition, the rigors of religious classification were combined with a newly formulated purposive concept of sex. Sex, it was said, was strictly for reproduction. All other uses were proclaimed to be against nature, against God, and against the human spirit—and anyway, such practices were the ways of pagans, of enemies, and of the flesh.

Much milder forms of a purposive concept of sex had, of course, been prevalent before, and not only among Semitic peoples. The Ancient Greeks and many other societies had codes demanding marriage and reproduction. (An inability or unwillingness to have children had long been grounds for divorce.) But as long as these conditions were met, other sex expressions had been permitted, even lauded. The invention of the post-exilic Judeo-Christian tradition was to establish the claim that sex was *only* for reproduction and to label all other uses as perversions. Thus, purposiveness became the rationale for limiting sex and strengthening asceticism.

In science too, purposiveness has been troublesome. As a general concept, it originated in prehistoric times, undoubtedly when man was first attempting to find order in the universe. Aristotle used a purposive philosophy in his descriptions of animal structures and functions. And the very earliest ideas having to do with animal "instincts" focused on the purpose which various observers thought they saw reflected in the behavior of living creatures. Up through Darwinian adaptation and on into the early part of the twentieth century, biologists continued to find purpose in natural phenomena. More recently, the biological sciences—at least the stricter taxonomic ones—have tended to confine their efforts to recording observable fact, relating events in terms of cause and effect, and accepting nature as it is instead of attempting to explain it in terms of ultimate goals.[143] In psychiatry and the social sciences, however, purposive concepts of sex have maintained their hold with remarkably little change. Many clinicians and the lay public in general continue to view most sexual variations much as the early priests and rabbis did.

With the expansion of the social and political power of the early Church, sex law and custom came to be rigorously enforced by religion. But since the twelfth century, the administration of civil and criminal law has gradually been wrested from religious hands. Yet the whole area of sex, tinged as it is with moral connotations, has for so long embarrassed law-makers that the legal wording of sex is quite imprecise. Nobody knows exactly what "unnatural sex practices" is supposed to include. "Sodomy" is sometimes taken to mean a variety of sexual contacts, or only anal and not oral contacts, or any and all homosexual acts. In any case, what was originally ecclesiastic law has become our common law, and with all its vagaries it remains even more firmly entrenched in the underlying assumptions of popular opinion.

Although the taboo on homosexuality is probably still strongest where there are religious objections to it, it would be an oversimplification to think that strong feelings against this or any other sexuality are derived directly from religious dogma. Often the path is indirect. There are, after all, many non-religious people who are much opposed to homosexuality—as are many religious persons who are unaware of any specific edicts against it. Evidently, religious teachings become implicit in the customs and attitudes of a society, eventually regulating both the central tendency of behavior and the expectancy of what people do sexually. Departures from what is expected almost automatically invite disapproval and notions of "abnormality." And, as usual, once a taboo becomes established it leads to results that reinforce it. Most people who are involved in homosexuality are understandably wary of revealing it, thus the continuing impression that it is fairly rare and not a part of ordinary life. It may seem all the more irregular when judged by its most visible examples, often made up of people who do not fit into the social mainstream or who have become disturbed as a result of sharing the assumptions that underlie conventional opinion.

Highly derogatory interpretations of homosexuality owe their consistency to the mutually reinforcing overlap of moral, legal, and psychiatric viewpoints. The translation of conventional attitudes into pseudoscientific jargon appears to have been especially prejudicial. At any rate, the essentially moral assumptions have not changed much; homosexuality is still widely thought of as an aberration and a perversion of nature's intent. Many people are bothered, too, by the idea that the homosexual component in themselves or others may indicate some kind of impaired sexual identity—in men, a lowered masculinity, or even effeminacy. But perhaps the single most troublesome assumption has been that every mature person would be heterosexual were it not for various fears and neuroses developed from parental and social misfortunes.

In recent years, the actual and often complex nature of homosexual behavior has finally become approachable. It has turned out to be quite different from traditional descriptions of it. The character of heterosexual behavior, too, has proved to be something other than what is ordinarily thought. In looking at these matters, biology deserves the first word concerning the nature of sexuality in general and homosexuality in particular.

2

Biological Considerations

Are glands, hormones, and other biological components directly involved in homosexuality?—do they have anything to do with either causing or supporting it? These are questions that in one form or another began to be asked before endocrinology was born, and they persist today as they will in the future. They have seemed especially relevant whenever the stereotypes of effeminate males and masculinized lesbians have come to mind. To many people, a man's masculinity is impugned if he sexually responds to other males, and all the more so if he develops an emotional attachment to a male partner.

The aim here will be to review the basic biological issues and to show their possible relevance to sexual psychology in general and to homosexuality in particular.

The Sex Hormones

The first sex hormones were isolated and synthesized in the early 1930's. When testosterone, the most effective of the "male" hormones, was tried out on spayed animals and on men whose testicles had been damaged early in life, the results were dramatic. There were immediate increases in energy level, a vitalization of sexual interest, and various bodily changes in the direction of masculinization. Capons rapidly became roosters, geldings began to act like stallions, and so on. Human males responded with heavy beard growth, a redistribution of body fat, and a much increased virility. These experiments, of course, were all "replacement" examples in which the animals or men had suffered a shortage of testosterone which, when replaced, produced the masculinization.

Almost immediately, both endocrinologists and clinicians became interested in testing the effects of testosterone on homosexuals, effeminate and otherwise. The questions were clear: Does the seeming lack of masculinity in these men reflect a shortage of male hormone?—and what would be the effect of adding more? These questions were so compatible with prevailing notions of homosexuality that they were destined to be tested and retested over the years. Since much of the curiosity behind such questions is rooted in a set of persistent psychological associations (existing at some distance from biology), one can expect ever more sophisticated experiments to be devised in the future.

But for reasons which will soon become apparent, these future experiments will always fail. Their pattern, too, is predictable. Each new study will appear to originate with the discovery of some new biochemical substance or some new mode of measurement. Each will show promise—perhaps enough to have its day in the news media—before quietly dissolving under careful examination. Still, there is more than a negative message here. There is value in understanding the previous history of such experiments. Besides informing us of what is true and not true, hormone tests have raised and partly answered questions of major importance in human sexuality.

The first tests run by endocrinologists required difficult measurements of the hormonal steroids thrown off in the urine. The results were unreliable and, hence, statistically insignificant; they sometimes showed even higher levels of male hormone in homosexual than in heterosexual subjects.[90] Recently, endocrinologists have perfected much more precise techniques for making direct measurements of hormone levels in the bloodstream itself. When extremely effeminate males (homosexual or heterosexual) have been tested by these means, they have shown entirely normal hormone levels.[179]

But even if the results of these experiments had been positive, they would not have been applicable to homosexuality in general for reasons cited by Kinsey more than thirty years ago: The idea that definite chemical substances might account for homosexuality incorrectly assumes that heterosexual and homosexual responses are discrete and that they differ in some fundamental way.[137] On one level, it might be easy to postulate such differences—but not differences which would be compatible with how easily a homosexual response can develop and can coexist with heterosexuality.

Nevertheless, a number of clinicians have seen fit over the years to run their own experiments by administering testosterone both to effeminate and to ordinary homosexuals. The results have been consistent: When there were any behavioral changes at all, the subjects became more like themselves than ever. Their sex drives were usually increased, and sometimes their effeminate mannerisms as well (when they had any), but there were never any directional changes in their sexual interests.

From these experiments, formal and informal, it has become abundantly clear that the sex hormones play a considerable role in powering human sexuality, but they do not control the direction of it.

The Directional Controls of Sex

It can be anticipated from the outset that much of what guides human sexuality—the choices that are made and the actions that are taken—depends upon what people learn from their particular society and from their individual experiences in it. But these and other learning processes are rooted in a biological groundwork of slowly accumulating changes that have occurred over eons of mammalian evolution. The controls that have come to direct human sexuality are best appreciated if they are compared with their biological forerunners.

In all lower mammals, sexual activity is rigorously regulated by *specific physiologic controls*, a new and careful phrase (much more than a wording change) for what used to be called "instincts." These controls, in turn, are either activated or suppressed by various cues that are usually directly related to reproductive processes. In fact, the females of most species are sexually responsive and will accept mates only a few days a year when they are ovulating and are thus capable of being fertilized. The same hormones that cause females to ovulate also regulate their outgoing signals of sexual readiness and lure. Whether these signals are in the form of an odor, a color, or a set of body movements (or all of these), they are "designed" to trigger the neurologic mechanisms of a male's sexual arousal. His arousal, in turn, causes him to give forth the gestures and sounds that trigger the female's next cooperative movements, and so on.

Although the males of most species are capable of becoming sexually aroused at any time, in actuality they seldom become so unless they are receiving specific cues. In fact, among most species, an unripe female not only fails to send out arousing signals, she sends out others that actively squelch both a male's aggressive and sexual responses toward her.

In viewing the courtship and sexual intercourse of lower mammals, it may often seem they have "intentions" and that they somehow "know" what they are doing. Far from it. Virtually every movement is predetermined by keyed responses. A male usually requires dozens of cues to run through the cycle of first becoming aroused by the scent of a female, then finding her, approaching her, then chasing and playing with her, becoming further aroused, and finally mounting her. The act of mounting may itself require a number of body cues and, once accomplished, it cannot be continued without moment-to-moment signals that cause each movement and thus keep the action going. For instance, the nerve endings on the inner sides of the front legs of a male dog must be stimulated (usually by friction against the body of the female) in order to trigger pelvic thrusts—the thrusts which are required not only for penis insertion but for perhaps a score of internal muscular contractions on which orgasm depends. [13, 69]

This remarkable interlace of keyed responses, a multitude of interconnected events, proves to have both advantages and disadvantages. On the one hand, it stabilizes and guarantees an effective sexual performance by stereotyping it—in effect causing a complicated series of events to take place through having been "programmed." On the other hand, the price of a stereotype anywhere in nature is a loss of flexible adaptability. The same interconnection of sequential events that holds together a stereotyped performance may cause it to fall apart entirely when one link in the chain is broken. An animal whose pelvic thrusts depend on specific signals cannot achieve them when for any reason the signals fail. He must dismount and begin again, frequently from far back in the courtship span.

There are other examples that suggest still more rigor and less flexibility in stereotyped sexual performances. In the course of thousands of generations of a species, accidental or circumstantial events that repeatedly occur and that may have had no importance in the original sex pattern can become integrated into it, and then even crucial to its success. In a species where the male happens to bite the neck of the female as he holds on to her and balances himself during intercourse, any failure to bite her— or simply not to bite her hard enough—may rob her of the pain reactions that have become necessary to trigger the sorts of internal contractions that are required to bring the eggs into position for fertilization. Or, in a species where the male ordinarily has to fight off other males to reach a female, the mere absence of a fight before intercourse can result in impotence or sterility. (Before this was realized, zoo keepers were often surprised that ripe mates either refused to copulate or proved sterile.)*

---

*These kinds of examples show, in part, why older concepts of "instinct" are out of date, even in accounting for animal behavior. "Instinct" implies an innate, hereditary, already-put-together set of actions that are directed from within. But, in fact, seemingly automatic behavior is gradually put together at the time it occurs as a result of the kinds of controls shown. There are elements of "component learning" in the picture too. An animal that has not had an opportunity to play with others while growing up may be totally unable to carry out courtship procedures when the chance comes. Under close examination, there is no evidence for innate knowledge. What is inherited are neurologic structures which (if properly organized by prenatal chemistry) are "ready" to respond in specific ways to inner and outer stimulations.[69,13,290,291]

In short, the sexual patterns of lower mammals are exceedingly dependent upon species-developed cues. The meshing of a multitude of these cues supplies the sequence and thus the total organization of the sexual performance. As long as the sequence of cues is not broken and none of the cues is missing, the lower mammals are able to complete their often complex sexual routines the very first time they encounter a ready mate.

The picture is sharply different at higher evolutionary levels. Already at the level of monkeys and apes, sexual patterns are neither stereotyped nor guided by specific signals; they are almost entirely dependent upon individual learning. Male monkeys that have neither seen nor experienced sexual intercourse may have the capacity to respond to a receptive mate but they have not the slightest idea of how to go about it. They do not know what goes where, or how to make the bodily adjustments necessary for copulation. There may be attempts to rub the penis against a female's leg, against her side, or to insert it into her ear. Several years of trial and error may be required before such a male is able to perform effective intercourse. (His final solution to this problem may be quite individualistic, such as persuading the female to sit down on his erect penis while he reclines.) This greatly increased dependence upon what is learned is in line with progressive evolutionary changes that have gradually taken place in the composition of the brain, mainly in the development of the cerebral cortex.

The cerebral cortex is the most recently evolved and the highest developed part of the brain. It amounts to less than a fourth of the brain in lower mammals but accounts for more than 70 per cent of the brain in monkeys and apes, while in man it is expanded to over 90 per cent of the brain mass and is much more organized, too. Upon this structure depend all the higher psychological capacities of man—thought, memory, imagination, and the organization of experience. In its gradual development the cerebral cortex has taken over the management of most voluntary behavior, including sexual behavior. Conversely, with each improvement in the brain, there has been a progressive relaxation of specific physiologic control over sexuality.[69] Thus, human sexuality is exceedingly variable, deriving its directionality (espe-

/final targeting) from what is individually learned and
.iced in personal and social settings.*

, yet despite all this, the notion that physiologic factors
;how still manage to determine a person's sexual direction is
an idea that dies hard. It is sometimes suggested that people's
constitutional make-up can affect their aggressiveness—and that
in a society like ours where the sexes are expected to show a
marked difference in their aggressive–submissive balance, their
sexual choices or role-preferences might thus be influenced. In
support of this idea, it undoubtedly is true that people start off
with very different dispositions and levels of aggressiveness (sometimes evident in differences in restlessness even before birth as
many observant parents could testify). But one must be careful
not to assume that these differences are relevant to a person's
eventual heterosexual or homosexual orientation. On the contrary, there appears to be a very poor correlation (if there is any at
all) between a person's constitutional slant and the kinds of

---

*At this point, it is sometimes asked why "nature" should have been so
"careless" as not to have retained a few directional controls over sex instead
of allowing the whole matter of procreation to fall into the loose and chancy
hands of learning, particularly since in other matters evolution has been
busily improving everything else. Actually, the question itself bristles with
the most dubious underlying assumptions—that "nature" exists as an entity,
that it "knows" what it is doing, that it has any aims to be careless about,
that it "wants" to procreate in the first place, or for that matter, that it gives
a damn about what happens to any of its species. (No doubt thousands of
species have faded away and other thousands have died aborning for every
one that has survived.) But, quite aside from all these objections, it so happens
that reproductive processes have profited greatly in their escape from specific physiologic controls. The extension of the breeding potential from a few
days a year to many more for the human female and to every day for the
human male is a tremendous escalation by itself. And while individual
developmental, conditioning, and other learning processes inevitably divert
a portion of the human sexual response toward homosexuality and a dozen
other nonreproductive modes, the very same cortical faculties provide
language, expectation, anticipation, fantasy, and a whole repertoire of symbolism which, together, provide human sexuality with what is probably its
largest single leap forward: the capacity to imagine an opportunity, to plan
for it, and to be aroused by it before rather than merely after it occurs.

aggressiveness that may later comprise his social and sexual orientation. Nothing seems to equal, let alone exceed, the influence of learning and learned responses in determining what effect even constitutional factors will have. Fortunately, the soundness of this conclusion can be demonstrated.

There are a number of instances on record in which infants have been misassigned at birth to the wrong gender. Sometimes this has been the result of a newborn girl's clitoris being misjudged as a small penis. Or a boy with undescended testicles and a small penis may be thought to be a girl, and raised accordingly. (A person's gender-identity so quickly becomes entrenched that these errors of assignment cannot be successfully corrected after about the time a child begins to talk. But, in practice, such errors are not usually discovered until puberty brings on voice changes, menstruation, beard growth, or breast development.) Yet these children have characteristically grown up to be ordinary men and women *according to their sex-of-assignment.*[184,187] Sometimes their accomplishments are incredible: genetic females growing up as males, thinking of themselves as males, marrying and having regular intercourse with their wives (via a thumb-sized clitoris) and, where no plastic surgery has been involved, even overcoming the psychological hazards of being males with breasts.[186]

But the point is much larger than matters of identity and adaptability; it has to do with the essential power of training and expectation. Of the more than twenty adults who have been misassigned to the wrong gender and later carefully studied, not a single one has stepped outside of an entirely "heterosexual" life[186]—though, of course, they could not have been so flexibly redirected had physiology been paramount.

Having established that the direction of a person's sex life is determined primarily by his learning and by how he reacts to a host of experiential events, it is useful to return briefly to constitutional factors. For while the latter are not controlling, they are present and can still wield certain kinds of influence. People vary enormously in their cortical capacity to organize the effects of their experience. And matters of disposition and temperament unquestionably affect the ease with which individual experience stamps itself into a person's total register. (Thus there are sizable differences in how easily people can be conditioned in any direction.) But perhaps the most clear-cut instances of the effect of constitutional factors (factors which are probably neurologic at bottom) are to be found in the highly individualistic ways people have of responding sexually—quite regardless of the kind of partners they have come to require.

For maximum effect, many people want their sexual arousal to be built up slowly and gently; others feel teased by anything other than a rapid, straight-to-the-target arousal. Thus direct genital stimulations may be preferred—or only tolerable at the end of a long series of foreplay procedures. Some people want their build-up, once started, to proceed to the point of orgasm without interruption; for others, interruptions are enjoyed and may be prized as a way of protracting the contact and of repeatedly starting all over again. In the course of an affair, many people find they have a much more intense interest in the partner during the chase than in the final sexual contact; others are bored by the chase and may not develop much interest in any partner until after an overtly sexual contact has developed. Or in the initial stages of a relationship, one or both partners may be unaware of having any sexual response to the other, only to have it suddenly loom large before them. Although this element of surprise may be the product of circumstance, it just as often seems to be quietly stagemanaged at some subterranean level of awareness. In fact, an element of surprise appears to be an integral component of all exciting sexual situations, one that is observable far back in the mammalian species.

The cortical organization of human sexuality is such that it eventually becomes keyed to specific cues, or to whole contexts of association. Thus, after much individual conditioning everyone tends to develop a personalized pattern of sexual behavior that, in some ways, is as specific for the individual as are the group patterns of lower animals. Or to say it another way, people and lower animals both end up with sharply specific sex patterns, though in man these vary enormously from one individual to the next.

Just how specific a person's sexual pattern is may be hidden from easy view by the fact that it can be expressed in such different contexts. A person's interest in a particular partner may be founded, as the storybooks say, on a thoroughgoing love and admiration, or it may be called forth by as little as a partner's evident readiness to respond. A particular element in a partner's personality or physique may be sufficiently admired to trigger a person's entire battery of sexual responses. Or only a fragment of what is admired may be combined with certain kinds of irritating qualities in the partner to arouse motivations of sexual conquest. Or with little concern of any kind for the partner, a person may be strongly motivated in a sexual situation by the possibility of acting out a primal scene, or of watching himself in action in his mind's eye.

The capacity of human sexuality to become focused-in on local details of a sexual situation is of particular importance. The highest sexual response of many people depends on their hearing harsh words, or only gentle ones, or on hearing nothing at all as they carry out their activities in total silence. Many people reach a full response only after receiving evidence of their own attractiveness from a partner; others respond more to a partner's disdain, obliviousness, or protests. More than a few individuals are sexually responsive to pain, to rejection, or to other evidence of a partner's real or symbolic hostility. On close examination, nearly every adult's highest level of response is limited to particular kinds of partners, and to relatively few situations that fulfill specific personal demands—demands that are decidedly fetishlike in character.

This tendency to focus on particular erotic details does not stop with a person's selection of partners and situations. It continues throughout intercourse, as if to refine and to intensify his sexual response by concentrating it into a "hot spot" of attention. In fact, as a person builds up to his highest level of response, he narrows down still more to particular points of interest rather than spreading his attention diffusely over all his partner's assets at once. From moment to moment he may move his attention from one point to the next, and rapidly so. (To later have a global picture of what went on, he must reconstruct it from a series of mental snapshots made during the event.) Thus, even partners who are in love, and who are therefore attracted to many qualities in each other, reach their most intense arousal as each focuses in on a particular trait of the partner—perhaps a particular element in the whole situation or on a particular body part. During mouth-genital or mouth-body contacts, it is the microcosm of, say, an erect nipple, the curve of a breast, an engulfed penis, or some other detail that becomes the focal point—in a sense, the momentary symbol of the whole person.*

If we now step back for a broad perspective, the evidence suggests that a focusing-in of sexual attention may be one of the central mechanisms in the whole process of human sexual conditioning. Young children show an utterly polymorphous sexuality. Before puberty, boys respond with vigorous erections to a great variety of stimulations, often to situations which arouse any kind of intense excitement. These may include everything from fast rides, getting mad, and seeing big fires to reciting before a class or getting home late—in short, to any combination of fright, anger, or pain that raises tension and excitement. With the coming of puberty and an increased sex drive, this diversity of response quickly begins to narrow down, first to general sexual situations, then to more specific situations, then to people, and finally to particular kinds of people. Under the spotlight of attention and affection, this narrowing-down proceeds to ever smaller and smaller segments of time and detail—moments of intense arousal fixing their focus on a particular person, on particular traits that epitomize that person, then on to one trait, a particular detail that stands for that trait, and so on. What started out as a generalized sexual response to fire engines and to cataclysmic events may wind up with its entire investment focused for an

---

*Early sex researchers believed that only men focus-in on specific details within a sexual situation, and that women stay conscious of its ensemble. When this is true, it denotes a sharp difference in the partners' arousal levels. Both sexes focus-in when highly aroused. And a person of either sex becomes "ensemble-conscious" when—and only to the extent that—he or she stands apart from it.

instant on the way the light falls into the dimple on somebody's cheek.

This final result—the selection of a particular partner whose smallest details may be so invested with meaning as to bring a person's sexual response to fever pitch—represents more than a culmination of individual development. It can also be seen as the culmination of a trend in evolution. In the evolutionary course of the mammalian species, as the control of sex has gradually moved from glands and reflexes to the heights of cortical management, an immense diversity of sexual expressions has unfolded into a panorama of possibilities. Yet for reasons which are probably neurologic at bottom, the most intense and therefore the most effective sexual experiences always require a high degree of directionality. In achieving this directional focus, each individual gradually loses his initial diversity of response as his sexual interests become ever more narrowed down to specific channels of expression.

For most people in our society, the heterosexual-homosexual alternative amounts to a fork in the road where the routes soon diverge too far apart for a person to jump from one to the other— let alone to travel them both. In effect, a choice must usually be made, but it is seldom one which can be genuinely biased by deliberate intent or by individual decision. It is a choice that stems from what will later be shown to be each individual's elaborately evolved sexual value system, a set of values that soon begins to eliminate the weaker alternatives while guiding a person none too gently toward the kinds of partners, the kinds of situations, and sometimes even the kinds of acts that have become the salient imperatives of his highest sexual response.

3

Inversion
and Homosexuality

Only in popular thinking are homosexuality and inversion synonymous. For several decades biologists and experimental psychologists have recognized that these are distinctly different phenomena, though they may or may not occur together. Homosexuality refers to any sexual activity between members of the same sex. Inversion, on the other hand, implies nothing about the sex of the partner; it refers to a reversal of the commonly expected gender-role of the individual, whether animal or human. For instance, a female dog that mounts other females, or males, or even the leg of her owner is inverting her behavior from the usually submissive-receptive mode of her female role to the specific and much more assertive behavior characteristic of males.

In the past, homosexuality and inversion were universally thought of as identical. The main image seems to have been that when two men have any sexual contact, at least one of them (or both if they interchange roles during sex) would have to be sexually submissive, thus inverting his expected male role. In addition, the stereotyped notions of homosexual men being effeminate and lesbians being masculine have reinforced the idea that inverted gender-roles and homosexuality go together.

But there are serious contradictions in equating inversion and homosexuality. In the first place, there are several homosexual practices—mutual masturbation, for instance—in which both partners are equally active and neither demonstrates any role-inversion. Then too, many effeminate men and aggressive women are primarily, if not entirely, heterosexual. Moreover, there are many entirely homosexual men and women who never invert their expected gender-roles in either their social or their sexual behavior. Thus, it eventually became necessary to recognize inversion as a behavioral entity in its own right—a behavior found throughout the mammalian species and one which is almost as frequent in heterosexual as in homosexual relations.

In man, inversion is not only prevalent, it is widely recognized as a necessary part of any well-balanced relationship. Heterosexual men and women often freely invert their primary gender-roles—for example, in intercourse that is initiated by a woman who sometimes stays dominant both in her position and in guiding the action throughout a sexual contact. Or regardless of who starts sex, the partners may momentarily alternate roles as the initiative is passed back and forth. Certainly there are times when the partners are equally active. More often, an aggressive-submissive balance is maintained, but continually shifted between the partners as either becomes dominant in terms of body positions, pelvic thrusts, or orifice insertions (via tongue or finger). Sometimes roles are interchanged as if by tacit agreement. Or once the first arrangements are established either partner, by shifting role, may suddenly produce an element of variety, of surprise, or of role-competition that whips up new excitement.

The importance of inversion is perhaps best illustrated if we subtract all its elements from heterosexual intercourse and then see what is left. What remains is primal-scene sex in which the male is always "male," is always aggressive, and is always intrusive toward a female who is always passive and who merely submits. Yet despite this image of coital incompetence, inversional forms of sex are steadfastly avoided by a sizable portion of the population, especially at lower social levels. In fact, the lower the social level, the stricter the adherence to primal-scene sex.[142]

In both heterosexual and homosexual relations, many men feel their manliness would be jeopardized (in their own eyes and in the eyes of others) if they inverted their dominant role, even for a moment. Women often have equivalent concerns about maintaining their femininity. The underlying assumption seems to be that a person's sexual identity is less stable and less genuine if it wavers and that a man's virility, in particular, is thrown into doubt if he gives up his dominant role in a moment of inversion. All such ideas are sharply contradicted by biological evidence.

Inversion has proved to be a frequent occurrence in every carefully observed mammalian species, whether in captivity or free living. This reversal of gender-role is no mere shift in an animal's aggressiveness. Often it is a precise performance of complex actions that are characteristic of the opposite sex. Among rodents, for instance, the male role involves a whole sequence of special actions. The male not only mounts the female and inserts his penis with pelvic thrusts, he then immediately throws himself back from her (before orgasm), bends forward to fellate his own penis, and then remounts her. This cycle is repeated many times before finally ending with his ejaculation. When an aroused female inverts her gender-role (which, when she is in heat, she may do simply on finding another partner of either sex in front of her) she repeats the entire male cycle. She not only performs the mounting, the pelvic thrusts, and the sudden backward disengagement, she also bends forward to fellate her nonexistent penis before remounting. Conversely, when the male inverts his role, he not only permits himself to be mounted, but may go into full lordosis (a crouching action), raising his hindquarters and putting his tail aside, exactly as does the female. From such examples it is obvious that the neurology (the whole sexual substrate) of each animal contains the full neuromuscular program for performing both sex roles.

In some species, such as dogs, where sex may be playfully protracted over a period of time, the female often attempts to arouse a distracted (or exhausted) mate by licking his genitalia, mounting him, and otherwise taking the initiative. In this example, her inversion might seem to be only a teasing activity. But on close examination, the evidence suggests that her inversion is, in fact, an alternate sexual capacity capable of being a full response in itself. A female dog that is coming into heat will readily mount a human arm or leg—indeed, she may carry this to the point of reaching a male-like orgasm[265] even though she (like the females of most other mammals) does not achieve orgasm in ordinary intercourse.[142]

Often the circumstances in which animals invert their sex roles suggest that they would "prefer" their primary gender-role if opportunity permitted. But just as often this is not the case. A male that has recently copulated with a female, by this very fact, may be especially ready to invert to a female role when approached by a sexually aggressive mate of either sex. Does this mean that his inversion is the product of his retaining a sexual interest at a time when, by a kind of embarrassment of riches, he is faced with opportunity but is not yet ready to re-respond in his usual fashion? Yes, at least in part. A temporary fatigue of the primary role is, indeed, one of the conditions which can be especially conducive to inversion.

However, other evidence suggests that the inversional alternative is so powerfully established in mammalian biology that it can sometimes induce a sexual response when the primary role is totally dormant. For instance, cows that are *not* in heat (and are therefore unready to accept any male) will often vigorously mount other females that are in heat.[11] Such examples indicate that inversion, far from being merely a "convenience reaction" to permit a frustrated individual to achieve sexual outlet, can in its own right facilitate arousal. Or to put it the other way around, the internal and external factors which invite inversion often manage to stimulate a not-otherwise-arousable individual into being sexually interested and active.

Notable, too, is the fact that there is little connection between inversion and whether the context in which it occurs is heterosexual or homosexual. Where an animal's inversion produces a sexual contact with a partner that just happens to be of the same sex, the relationship is technically—but not always very convincingly—homosexual. The partners may merely be matching their sex roles and may not even be aware of each other's gender.* And although humans are certainly aware of whether a partner is male or female, they are free in either case to invert their sex roles. They may do so to satisfy an inner urge, to accommodate a partner or, as some people like to say, "just for the hell of it."

All examples cited thus far have involved sexual intercourse. In these, inversion may last anywhere from a few moments to the few minutes that intercourse may require. But in man, inversion may extend far beyond intercourse—and beyond sex itself. Obviously, a person not only has an expected gender-role in sex, but a whole socially defined gender-role to live up to. In our society, as in most, men and women are expected to express their particular gender in their attitudes, their body movements, in the clothes they wear, and in a variety of other ways. In fact, every item of social behavior that is attributed to one sex and not to the other automatically becomes part of an expected gender-identity, and by this very fact becomes eligible for inversion. Thus, what are thought of as effeminate gestures in men, masculine mannerisms in women, all examples of transvestism (wearing the clothes of the opposite sex), and other gender crisscrosses become uniquely human forms of inversion.

But why should a person ever *want* to invert his gender-identity? The motivation is just as often to amuse or to control an onlooker as it is to satisfy some urge within himself. A stereotype among male comics—as popular with audiences today as it has been for centuries—is to occasionally dress up as a woman or even to more or less constantly use feminine gestures and reactions. Many comedians, from Charlie Chaplin and Jack Benny of yesterday to the latest television comic, keep their gestures at a

---

*Often the reverse is true, too. Two animals of the same sex may be specifically attracted to each other, leading to a sexual arousal that can only be expressed by one partner (or both, alternately) inverting its role. Such examples contradict the popular belief that animals never prefer a same-sex partner. In fact, both elaborate homosexual courtships and ongoing homosexual relationships have been observed among lions, porpoises, porcupines, monkeys, and a variety of other animals—all while in the presence of heterosexual opportunity.[11,142]

halfway-house between male and female. Thus, an audience is invited from the start to take them not at all seriously—and in comic situations, to root for the underdog who seems so vulnerable to attack and to the shocks of everyday life. Evidently, there are simplistic amusements in a pretended inversion, too. People in tribes and cultures the world over are greatly amused by the buffoon who caricatures members of the opposite sex.

At the other extreme, as in religion, inversion can be a deadly serious business designed to master the minds of men. In Christianity, for instance, the fates themselves are seen as prone to a pendulum-like inversion: The meek shall inherit the earth—The last shall be first and the first last—He that finds his life shall lose it and he that loses his life shall find it. A person is promised high moral status for inverting even his most reasonable hostilities: Love thine enemy—Bless them that curse you—Do good to those who hate you—Pray for those who spite you. And still higher rewards are promised for one who, by inverting his own behavior, virtually forces the other fellow to invert his: Do not resist abuse but turn the other cheek—If a man takes your coat, give him your cloak also—If a man forces you to go a mile with him, go two. In a hundred ways and in most religions, a person is told to go north in order to arrive south. One of the central ·mechanisms in all these examples (as in all inversions of aggression) is clear: It is to dominate by submitting.

Physically too, inversion in various forms is extremely prevalent in religion, especially monotheisms. In these, the god is never conventionally heterosexual. He may be hermaphroditic, or fat enough to look pregnant, or dress in womanly robes. Usually he is a bachelor god who has no truck with women except for an occasional Immaculate Conception. (Virtually all of the many gods born on earth have been sired by such means.[32]) In a sense, his dual sexuality is reiterated by his high priests who, like himself, tend to be all-powerful potentates in female garb who are able to be both masculine and maternal at the same time. Wherever priests and shamans have not been bachelors, they have often had both male and female wives, an especially frequent arrangement among the indigenous tribes of Siberia and North America. Or the holy ones may simply be what has to be recognized as primarily homosexual, as were the shamans in many societies, and as rabbis often were in the days of sacred sodomy. [61,47,37]

The fact that inversion in one form or another is more often present than absent in religions the world over suggests that it is determined by a variety of motives. Often there is the implication that a religious figure gains exceptional powers from possessing both male and female attributes. Armed with these, he is certainly less subject to mundane, colloquial comparisons, and his magic is made more mystical, too. In folklore as well as in religion, men dressed as women tend to be seen as benevolent figures, while women who have somehow got hold of maleness are usually seen as witches, sorceresses of the devil. In either case, any would-be challenger is hard put to wangle against the wand-waver.

Much of this—the bamboozlement of onlookers and the attainment of special powers from various male-female combinations—is also implicit in many forms of transvestism that are not at all mystical. Transvestism may or may not be as exhibitionistic and as closely allied to homosexuality as public opinion supposes. Certainly there are homosexuals who cross-dress to shock people, to amuse themselves and others, sometimes to make a living as professional female impersonators, or to gain attention for still other reasons. The homosexual who cross-dresses (more often as a lady than as a plain woman) "plays" with the square world, confounds even the viewer who knows he is a man with one surprise after the other, and invites any hostile critic to focus his anger on a false target. As a "drag queen" he not infrequently revels in the accusation that he is impossibly effeminate. Since this is an image over which he has control, he can turn it on and off at will and in a moment invalidate the charge. As for the impersonations themselves, these vary all the way from being as transparent as those of a television comic to being so convincing that he must deliberately introduce flaws into his performance to cue in observers to the fact he is really a man.

It is useful to recognize certain connections—and yet distinctions—between men in drag, stage-type female impersonators, and male transvestites. All engage in cross-dressing. All impersonate women. All, technically speaking, are transvestites, and all engage in more than a momentary inversion. But they differ considerably in their motivations and in what their cross-dressing means to them. Ordinarily, the rare homosexual who wants to dress in drag wants only to amuse or to baffle other people and would not bother to cross-dress without an audience. This much might be said of the female impersonator too, though the expertness of his performance (whether professional or freelance) generally denotes a higher personal investment in acting out the role; he performs as much for his own enjoyment as for audience reactions. The ordinary transvestite has a still greater investment in his own performance and may have no interest whatever in other people's reactions. In fact, much male transvestism is practiced entirely in private, either while at home alone or by wearing only the underwear of women.

A fact well known to sex researchers but mindboggling to the layman is that most transvestites are clearly and exclusively heterosexual. In fact, a recent study by Wardell Pomeroy has shown that homosexuality is even less prevalent among transvestites than it is in the general population.[218] Much the same can be said for transsexuals too (i.e., persons who carry transvestism to the point of wanting to actually change their sex, as Christine Jorgensen first did), in that they rarely have any interest in homosexuality. (Not that the heterosexuality of transvestites and transsexuals is exactly equivalent. It can and has been argued that while transsexuals are seldom homosexual, they are so uninterested in sexual activity and tend to be so focused-in on matters of role and of gender-identity that they really do not fit either heterosexual or homosexual descriptions.[218]

But still, if a man is intensely interested in things feminine, why should he want to dress and often to act as women do? The reasons vary greatly and help make the whole range of transvestism and transsexuality an extremely diverse group of phenomena. Sometimes it is as if a man's overriding fascination with women and with everything about them causes him to devalue maleness and to want to suppress it in himself. Or without actually putting down maleness, there is often a kind of utter disinterest in it, coupled with a fascination for what is womanly—

womanly as opposed to ladylike. Both the heterosexual transvestite and the transsexual characteristically have more interest in the housedress than in the flowing gown, and have virtually no interest in the showy, cosmetic femininity with which the female impersonator in his high heels, frills, and jewelry reaches an image of high style. (A top-level female impersonator could not only enter a Miss America contest, he might very conceivably win it.) But for the transsexual male, the achievement of a solid, womanly femininity is all important. When he buys a delicate negligee he handles it and puts it on with the reverence and the awe of an underprivileged housewife who has been working hard all day—a far cry from the attitude of the female impersonator who approaches the same garment as if he had just been brought home in Cinderella's coach after an evening of being the belle of the ball.

Part of the transsexual's fascination with femininity is quite conventional. In all ordinary heterosexuality (and in homosexuality, too) a person wants to add something of his partner's attributes to himself. The essential puzzle in transsexuality is not so much why the additions are attractive as why a person carries them so far and wants to subtract, even blot out, the components of his own gender. In these spectacular manifestations of inversion, a person is ready to renounce not only his gender-role, but his whole gender-identity as well. Logically, one might expect that men who actually want to change their gender would have some starting advantage—perhaps a body build or a shortness of stature to make it conceivable, or at least a touch of effeminacy at the outset. But not only is this seldom the case, the fates seem to have a penchant for exactly the opposite trend, as one towering male after another from the ranks of policemen, doctors, truck drivers, and athletes puts in for a sex change.

The perils and pains that the transsexual is ready to undergo in his change can stagger the imagination. Physically, there are protracted hormone treatments, a one-by-one wiping out by electrolysis of hundreds of thousands of hair follicles on his face and body, an amputation of genitalia, and a surgical reordering of internal body-structures to permit the insertion of a vagina constructed of his own tissues. Plastic surgery on his face, neck and

Adam's apple may also be required. Nor in the details of how he conducts himself is his task a pushover. Usually, with no original effeminacy to help him along, he must struggle to learn every gesture, every body movement and every voice inflection while, at the same time laboriously eliminating all the male equivalents as he proceeds toward a goal that often disqualifies him for his present occupation as it opens the door to his longed-for chance to be happy in, say, a secretarial job, the underpaid skills for which he has yet to learn.

Before all this is seen as too wildly artificial, it might be well to remember that everyone's gender-identity, at some private level of reality, is treasured beyond all measure. The transsexual—in a sense like everyone else—is struggling to honor something there, something that by a process of inversion has replaced his first completed program of identity.

But if the transsexual must point by point strain to change so much of his behavior, what part of the task is inversion doing? Where is that automatic role-switchover that so characterizes inversion in its momentary forms, and that is so phenomenally demonstrated by the female impersonator who, as if with one stroke of a brush, can paint himself indistinguishably into a portrait of femininity? At first glance, it is tempting to say that people vary in their acting talents, in their capacity to "feel" a role, or that previously learned male components are stamped in at different levels. But it is important to understand that the female impersonator has certain advantages in reaching for his particular goals. He is mainly interested in an outer image of femininity. The showy, highly animated, largely cosmetic qualities of the femininity he wants to duplicate are the surface opposites of the rugged, straightforward masculinity our society upholds for males; opposites are clear cut and relatively easy to copy. The transsexual, on the other hand, sets himself the far harder task of achieving a highly authentic, womanly femininity. And while his efforts are labored as he struggles to change his body and his social mannerisms, at some deeper level his inversion is indeed spontaneous and often produces an astonishingly valid feminineness long before he looks the part.

Starting as he often does with a quietly adequate masculinity, the transsexual's inversion utterly transforms any of his competitive and conflict-ready qualities into a kind of lenient forbearance, an unfeigned modesty that is often a model of womanly grace. More than this, there is usually a remarkable pleasantness in his personality, a niceness and a pliant, lamblike gentility that make him appropriately duteous, malleable, and subservient.

These qualities are often startlingly evident when the transsexual comes up against authority figures—the police, lawyers, physicians, or sex researchers. He may encounter the police when a neighbor recognizes him as the same person in different garb (perhaps by noting his goings and comings, or by a distinguishing facial feature), thinks he is up to no good, and reports him. At the station house (to which he has been promptly brought by the baffled policeman who was sent to investigate the case) he may at first be subjected to piercing questions. But the tone of the questions quickly mellows, for the transsexual is characteristically polite and nonresistant; he tends to have a quiet honesty about him and is never sarcastic. In fact, the gentle manners of this person who looks, walks, talks, and acts like a woman virtually defies his being seen as a man, even when the facts are known; he is obviously not a "drag queen" nor is he antisocial in any respect. Although he may be frightened by crass questions and formal procedures (it is against the law to seriously masquerade as a member of the opposite sex), his whole bearing is much more that of a woman in distress than that of a man who has been caught pretending to be something he is not.

The transsexual's behavior with various professionals is even more revealing of a certain womanly forbearance. In the course of trying to understand himself, obtaining necessary services, or of merely contributing to science, he may spend many hours taking tests, answering questions, and receiving sex researchers in his home—sometimes only to later find himself written up as being crazy, as possibly having a brain defect, or as the victim of some other dire malady. His attitude may then be one of caution and regret, but it lacks the biting anger and disgust which, by contrast, many homosexuals have voiced after having cooperated with judgmental professionals. His equanimity in the face of sovereign abuse is itself eminently feminine.

The transsexual's abiding patience is particularly impressive when he is himself a doctor, a lawyer, or a psychotherapist—and is thus an authority in at least one of the fields from which he may seek either aid or a second opinion. A transsexual psychiatrist who cooperated with the present study and who came to be known in depth over a period of many months had always had (when seen as a woman) a quietly delicate, often humorous way of describing himself and of gently countering any point he considered wrongly taken. But when seen as a man he was much less deferential, to put it mildly. In this cast, he was sharp-minded, exquisitely articulate, and formidable indeed. In a still polite but utterly masterful way, he was able to integrate and to apply modern conditioning theory to the variables of gender-identity with a sweep, a clarity, and a refinement of concept that soared beyond anything presently contained in the formal literature on the subject. Then does this mean he was merely acting a part when, as a woman, he was demure, always gentle, and capable of adroitly imbuing every conversational challenge with charm and humor? Hardly. The transsexual's whole bearing is much better described as a behavioral set than as an acting job. At the deepest levels it can have the spontaneity and the bone-marrow authenticity of a genuine femininity—a most impressive inversion.

In looking back over all these examples, it is notable that each contains at least one surprise to common logic. (As several investigators have remarked, inversion seems itself inverted.) It is remarkable that the transsexual, having a genuine womanliness in many of his basic reactions, should have to struggle so hard to attain the surface femininity that the female impersonator finds so easy. It is perhaps even more surprising that transvestism and transsexuality seldom involve either homosexual or effeminate men—that both of these categories are primarily peopled by heterosexuals, and by curiously conservative ones at that. One might expect that at least the ranks of female impersonators would be dominated by effeminate men, but neither is this the case. Convincing impersonations require great control, the capacity to perfectly shape all gestures and voice inflections; the best female impersonators can turn their femininity on and off at will and do not "live it" in their everyday lives. And, by common sense, one might suppose that since effeminate men invert much of their social behavior, they would be more inclined than other men to invert their gender-roles during sexual intercourse. Wrong again. There is considerable evidence to suggest that effeminate men are particularly hesitant to be sexually submissive; it is as if whatever motivates inversion concentrates itself upon a single level of expression. Conversely, it is the sure-footed, securely aggressive males who most readily invert their expected roles, both in heterosexual and homosexual relations.

Nor should one be too quick to conclude that the "rules" of inversion are set by sociologic influences—a child's upbringing and the like. Inversion gains its basic backing from strictly biological sources. But here again, the fact is the reverse of what common sense might expect, for inversion is tied to the robustness of the sexual drive. Among the lower mammals, individuals differ in the frequency and intensity with which they invert their sex roles. But as Beach first noticed, the individuals that most easily invert their gender-roles are the ones that "invariably prove to be unusually vigorous copulators" when exercising their primary roles.[8] Thus, exactly in contradiction to the fears that make many men afraid to invert their masculine dominance in sexual relations, the biological capacity for inversion implies a distinctly high rather than a low virility.*

Of the several reasons for presenting this outline of inversion, the most urgent has been the need to straighten out the convolutions which have tangled most interpretations of homosexuality. The popular tendency to equate homosexuality and inversion has been the most troublesome. It not only has attached too much inversion to homosexuality, it has attached much too much homosexuality to inversion. Colloquially speaking, homo-

---

*The fact that inversion "rides on" and requires a very strong sex drive has been experimentally substantiated. When male animals are castrated they soon begin to lose their virility, but they even more rapidly lose their capacity for inversion. The administration of small doses of male hormone will then reawaken ordinary sexuality, but inversion does not reappear until a robust virility has been fully re-established.[6,7,11]

sexuality might still be called inversion in the sense that nine-teenth-century writers had in mind: simply as a reversal of what one expects a person's sexual choice to be. But at higher levels of semantic precision, serious complications arise. It *is* true that certain kinds of inversion (e.g., effeminacy) are more fre-quent in homosexual than in heterosexual contexts, but it is also true that the most extreme as well as the most generalized forms of inversion are predominantly heterosexual phenomena. Thus inversion has come to be recognized as an entity in its own right, a basic capacity for behavioral reversal that pervades not only sex, but religion and philosophy as well.

In sexuality, inversion varies all the way from a momentary reversal of a person's expected role to the more or less continuous reversals seen in effeminacy and transsexuality. Momentary inversions (including those that last for the duration of a sexual contact) are so much a part of both heterosexual and homosexual relations as to be taken as a matter of course. It is their near-total absence (as among lower social level males) that seems irregular. At the other extreme, it is tempting to rate as super-irregular all those extraordinary ongoing inversions, be they effeminacy, transsexuality, loving thine enemy, or any constant application of the Christian ethic. But in our present early stage of psychologi-cal research, it seems wiser to try to comprehend the breadth of human variations than too quickly rush in to judge them.

4

The Origins
of Heterosexuality

From the moment it is realized that there are no instincts to guide human sexuality, the whole problem of the origins of heterosexuality looms as a major puzzle. Where does heterosexuality get its backing, particularly to become an exclusive preference? The magnitude of this question is not instantly apparent, since on the surface, nothing would seem simpler. Most people see their heterosexual responses as innate and automatic, but trained observers understand that people are specifically heterosexual because they have been geared by their upbringing to expect and to want to be. One reason most people are heterosexual (as opposed to polysexual) is that their religious and social traditions directly support family living and the kinds of mateships that comprise it. Certainly there is nothing mysterious in how family life communicates itself as a model to be followed by each new generation. Nor does it seem necessary to spell out the innumerable ways in which people in our society are informed of heterosexuality, have their expectations and overt experiences channeled toward it, and are warned against deviating from it.

On the other hand, all this training and expectancy falls far short of explaining exactly how a person develops an intense interest in the opposite sex. He or she obviously does much more than follow social expectations. A person usually comes to view particular kinds of mates as intensely and personally meaningful.

Part of the emotional intensity involved in being attracted to a partner can be traced to the real or imagined rewards of sex, rewards which can imbue a partner or a whole situation with value. But not even this powerful effect accounts for the breadth of attraction between heterosexual partners; they often fit each other in a multitude of ways which go far beyond anything erotic. What is more, they are often attracted to each other when they are *not* compatible, when they *do not* particularly like each other, and in a variety of other circumstances in which conflict reigns. In fact, on close examination there turns out to be a remarkable amount of conflict in most relationships, including the best. It is not for nothing that a great many societies have axioms denoting the battle-of-the-sexes and complaining, not always humorously, that the trouble with women is that a man can live neither with them nor without them.

The very fact that heterosexual attractions survive the formidable conflicts inherent in them only intensifies the question of what, exactly, motivates men and women toward each other. The whole matter is best approached by confronting its broader aspects: Where does heterosexuality stand in the history of man? How does it look cross-culturally? What works for it and against it—and anyway, what are the alternatives within and outside of it? There are plenty of other questions too, many of which are crucial to the issues at hand—questions concerning the interrelationships between heterosexuality, family living, and something which has come to be known as the male bond. In one form or another, homosexuality often plays a significant role. Where does it fit into the picture?

At first glance, it might seem that the continuation of man depends on a clearly predominant heterosexuality and that homosexuality, especially if it were rampant, might threaten the survival of the species. Not only is this not the case, something close to the opposite is true. Societies which choose to actively suppress homosexuality tend to do so with broad-based moral tenets which at the same time cut into heterosexuality much further than could any of its competition. Furthermore, those societies which are most lenient toward homosexuality and practice it most, be they primitive tribes or the most advanced civilizations, are precisely the ones with the highest birthrates and the most serious problems of overpopulation. The North African Moslem cultures are the best-known examples, though they are not the most extreme.*

It has sometimes been suggested that since the physical and dispositional compatibilities of opposite sexes are so excellent, everyone would become conditioned to respond to the opposite sex if boys and girls were given free access to each other during their formative years. Much evidence suggests that early sexual experiences can, indeed, influence a person's sexual tastes and, under certain conditions, set a pattern. Cross-cultural comparisons have indicated that the smoothest heterosexual adjustments by far are made in those societies in which boys and girls are permitted premarital sex-play with each other.[69] Likewise, whenever early homosexual contacts are made rewarding either by being condoned or by being made interesting behind certain kinds of taboos, they tend to continue with vigor into adulthood.

Nevertheless, the utmost caution is required in evaluating the conditioning effect of early sexual experiences. In our society, at least, there is a very uneven correlation between what people do in their early sex-play and what they will eventually prefer. Most early homosexual play turns out to be inconsequential. Nor do early failures and traumatic experiences seem to have much effect in swaying the course of either heterosexual or homosexual patterns. Most people who become primarily homosexual remember feeling this motivation before having any chance to try it out. Others have accumulated considerable heterosexual experience before discovering their homosexual responsiveness.

Similarly, in comparing whole societies, there may be much or

---

*A number of sex researchers from Havelock Ellis to Kinsey have estimated that homosexual activity outnumbers heterosexual activity in Arabic countries. Contrary to what might be expected, societies with even higher homosexual rates have still higher birthrates for reasons which will be examined in Chapter 5.

little correlation between early sex practices and how people later respond as adults. As might be expected, some of the most homosexual societies are those in which such practices are condoned. Yet in a few societies in which young men *must* engage in homosexual practices, say in the course of puberty rites, homosexuality in other contexts later disappears as if by magic.[279,168]

One of the main conclusions to be drawn from all these contrasts is that early (or any) sexual experience, by itself, carries little weight; what counts is the context in which it occurs. Wherever sexual activity of any kind is merely casual, dutiful, or is seen by the partners as a kind of play, it is not inclined to arouse much emotion. And without emotion—even a sense of drama—neither a person's partner nor what they do together is likely to become imbued with much importance.

Conversely, a sexual situation becomes exciting and meaningful when there is a certain tension between partners who perhaps admire each other. Or quite without admiration, an erotic interest may build from a note of either foreignness or antagonism between partners who then use sex to reduce their distance, to bridge the gap between them as they explore and savor the exotic. Sexual attraction clearly thrives on a degree of tension and distance between partners.

In what might at first seem to be a contradiction to this tension requirement, there are a number of sexually permissive societies in which boys and girls—and later, adults as well—are allowed to make any and all sexual contacts with nearly any willing partner short of direct incest. But even here, there is little tendency for the easiest contacts to be the ones most frequently chosen. On the contrary, the most valued relationships, and certainly the most intense ones, are between partners who cannot instantly take each other for granted. Elaborate courtship procedures may be a preliminary requirement. Or the socially approved way of announcing one's sexual choice may carry considerable tension in itself: The boy or girl (whichever is expected to make the advance) may begin by scratching or pinching the partner, often severely. Among the African Mbuti where girls are expected to make the first move, they indicate their partner-selection, be he only their choice for that day, by roundly beating the lucky fellow, sometimes inflicting permanent bodily damage.[267]

Among a great many peoples, a man is expected to beat his wife regularly; any failure to do so becomes Exhibit A in a woman's complaint that her husband no longer loves her. Similarly, at lower social levels in our own society, wife-beating has a long tradition—as does the abuse both partners are ready to heap upon any well-meaning outsider who would come to her defense.

More often than not, barriers in the form of various resistances to a lover are placed within the sex act itself. Choroti women spit in a lover's face during coitus.[69] Apinaye women bite off bits of a man's eyebrows, loudly spitting them aside[207]; Ponapean men do the same to their female partners, pulling their eyebrows out by the roots.[69] Turkese women poke their fingers into a man's ears. Trobriand Islanders, who are particularly nonrestrictive in permitting sexual liaisons, bite each other on the cheek and lips till blood flows, snap the nose and chin, tear each other's hair, and otherwise lacerate their lovers.[168]

Thus it is no accident, but something within the scheme of things, that the societies which are highly permissive in their sexual mores are the ones that routinely employ severe biting, scratching, hair-pulling and other assaults. Conversely, societies which expect sexual expressions to be gentle and affectionate are, across the board, highly restrictive in sex, especially in terms of partner accessibility. The whole issue of sexual "resistances" will be analyzed later. For the moment, it is important to realize that every society makes its lovers run a gauntlet, but that each, by its mores, makes the barriers of different stuff and erects them in different places.

Despite all that can be said in favor of easy sexual contact— such as how it helps establish a sexual pattern—much can also be said for the frictions that whip up erotic intensity: the alienations, the antagonisms, the embattlements of contact that on a dozen levels set the gap for the spark of sex to jump.

Evidently, a breach between men and women has been useful in other matters, too. The sexes have been differentiated far beyond what biology alone would necessitate, not only in nearly every tribe but in all advanced civilizations. Part of this separation has been fairly well rationalized in many societies by divisions of labor and by other practical considerations; most of the rest is a product of hidden psychological motivations.

The extent of male-female separations and the depth of them in the history of man are staggering. They are worthy of a partial review, not because they are fodder for feminist complaints, which they are, but because they hold the key to more than one sexual paradox. In many subtle ways, the psychology behind them powerfully insinuates itself, though not always for the worse, into the fortunes of heterosexuality.

In most early societies, men and women have had living arrangements which have called for their spending most of their time apart. More often than not, the sexes have been separated in their sleeping arrangements too, either occupying entirely different quarters or being apart under the same roof. Sexual intercourse has usually been relegated to brief periods quite outside any context of companionship. Nor did the invention of marriage and the nuclear family do much to bring the sexes together. For a man and woman to belong together has not usually implied an extensive mutual sharing of experiences; mutual sharing implies a degree of equality which is itself ruled out in most societies.

Just how women came by their low status and have chosen for the most part not to protest it are in some ways obvious and in others quite obscure. No doubt the strength of males and its usefulness in making a living, coupled with the lower aggressiveness of females, have had much to do with status arrangements. But before this usual explanation is carried too far, it should be remembered that in a number of societies strength and endurance are not put to the test, or are tested more on the backs of women than men. Furthermore, their differing status is hardly ever spelled out in terms of male superiority; the emphasis is usually on female inferiority, or on the dire dangers and foibles of women.

Most tribal peoples have associated women with blood due to their menses, a sign of harm if not a lethal liquid. Certain of these connotations have been carried over into the highest civilizations, though here a more frequent complaint has been the charge that women are unclean, the dispensers of defilement.*

---

*The charge of being unclean has stemmed primarily from fishlike vaginal odors. Sometimes these have been given positive connotations, as in concepts of mermaids and sea-nymphs. But these are playful creatures washed

Even more widespread has been the charge that a woman, by her submissiveness, takes more than she gives in sex, saps a man's strength, and weakens him before the hunt. Almost the world over, to associate with her before a battle invites the losing of it. Or to have her on board ship or mixed in any venture of chance jeopardizes luck, if indeed it does not guarantee disaster. Nor do the gods much like her. Their holiness is generally defiled by her presence when she is passive, or threatened by her witchcraft when she shows spunk. There is hardly a religion in which she has anything approaching equal status, and in many she is entirely ruled out of this secret rite of men. [275]

Sometimes women have won secondary gains from their lowly status. They have had the good fortune to have nearly always been considered poison in any cannibal's diet. (Montezuma ate only young men of the sort he also preferred in bed[284]; less aristocratic cannibals were simply afraid of womanly flesh, for as everyone knows, you are what you eat.) While many peoples have thought that Nature herself deemed women the burden-carriers and the gatherers and preparers of food, many African tribes have held the belief that cattle will sicken and die in a woman's presence; here the result has been that men have had to do all the milking and get behind the plough as well, lest the ox die. [165] Women have often had their status raised as a result of their childbearing-magic being thought to have a beneficial effect upon agriculture and the multiplication of underground tubers. Of course, they must then tend the fields and dig for those tubers, but at least they are worthy of being treated fairly well.

One might expect women to have fared better with the coming of civilization, but just the reverse has been the case. Civilization invariably dissolves the somewhat democratic communality of tribal life. People then fall into sharply differing social levels,

---

clean by their environment. An aggressive woman is a fishwife. Men who prefer the company of women or who enjoy mouth-genital contacts with them are "fish-eaters" in many languages. The pornographers of ancient Peru carved statues of the penis as a little man holding his nose inside a vagina[79]; the theme is rampant in the bawdy humor of every continent and has taken on ponderous proportions as it has invaded one religion after the other in the form of charges of defilement.

where one power structure after the other in religion, politics, and law separate the factions still further despite all claims of an even hand. Higher premiums than ever are placed on authority as opposed to mere labor, on steadfastness as opposed to emotionality, and on power in every form. (The fact that upper-level women may have a higher standing than lower-level men amounts to little, since the paper money of class status is hard to spend outside the realm in which it is issued.) The "weaker sex" is called just that at every level.

Plato classed women with children and servants, repeatedly stating that in all the pursuits of mankind the female sex is inferior to the male. Euripides has his Medea say, "Women are impotent for good, but clever contrivers of all evil." To the Hindus, "Woman's mind is hard to direct aright and her judgment is small." Buddhists complain that women embody all the snares which the tempter has spread for men and that, besides being dangerous, they hold the lures of infatuation which bind the mind to the world.[220] The Chinese have a saying that the best girls are not equal to the worst boys.[244] Islam pronounces the depravity of women to be much greater than that of men. And Mohammed, though quite a ladies' man himself, said, "I leave you no calamity more hurtful to man than woman. . . . Oh assembly of women, give alms, though it be your gold and silver ornaments, for verily ye are mostly of Hell on the Day of Resurrection."[151]

The roots of our society are replete with the same ideas, and worse. The Hebrews held women to be the source of evil and death on earth: "Of woman came the beginning of sin and through her we all die."[75] The Bible states that for this sin God deemed that forevermore, as a punishment, she shall be subservient to her husband.[83] St. Paul clarified the issue for Christians by proclaiming that Adam was really innocent and not deceived, but that his woman was and thus was the sole transgressor.[260] Tertullian carried the issue a step further, complaining that by inventing death, Eve caused not only all men but even the Son of God to die: "And do not forget that each of you [women] is an Eve; you are the Devil's gateway and the unsealer of the forbidden; you accomplish the work which the Devil alone is not valiant enough to do."[257]

Under Christianity the onslaught against women gained so much momentum that at the Council of Mâcon held near the end of the sixth century a major issue raised was whether or not women are human beings. After careful deliberation, and then by a narrow margin, it was decided that they probably are human, since the good Lord spun the first one out of Adam's rib.[95]

But being human was not enough to make a woman acceptable to Jehovah any more than to most other gods. The Christian fathers let her into the church provided she entered by a side door and wore something on her head to keep the eyes of God from being defiled as he looked down upon the congregation. She eventually had to wear gloves too, for at the Council of Auxerre it was decided that a woman should not touch church furnishings, and under no condition receive the Eucharist into her naked hands.

In a sense, these were relatively liberal arrangements, for women were not allowed to enter the major temples of the Hindus, Buddhists, Mohammedans, or most other religions. A Hindu statute proclaims that should a consecrated image be touched by a dog, a woman, or any other lowly beast, its godship is destroyed; it must be thrown away and the ceremonies begun afresh; women can worship an idol, but only if they stay back from it.[270]

This hygienic distance was so important to the Christians that while they would accept a glove-thickness to protect church ornaments, no woman was allowed to be near the altar during Mass. And a woman in a choirloft was enough to despoil a whole church—an idea that led directly to the practice of obtaining soprano tones by castrating young boys.[75] Outdated stuff? The last dictum against women in the choirloft was issued by the Vatican in 1971.

A question might be raised as to whether religious examples of the demeaning of women are really generalizable to their status in everyday life. It has sometimes been suggested that the standards applied in the presence of the gods are always extra-ordinary —and that in nearly every society, women in the home and in other situations of informality have received more respect. Furthermore, say the apologists, excluding a woman from public gathering places, keeping her off the street when she is alone, or having her hide her face behind a veil (as she must in many societies) are for the "respectable" woman's own good. And the "proof" of this is that established women in every society (wives, mothers and eligible daughters) have readily accepted these restrictions, have helped enforce them, and have appreciated being set apart from "bad women." Of course, the very existence of the concept of "bad women," for which there is no male equivalent, is itself a reiteration of the charges against them.

Among the attempts to de-emphasize all this and to claim that it is no longer so important is the kind of observation first made by Westermarck: that as each civilization ultimately reaches maturity, it tends to relax its strictures against women and to elevate them to a level of equality. It is forever fashionable to say that superstitions belong to the past, that moderns are liberals and, anyway, that things are fast changing.

Much could be said for each of these arguments, and for Westermarck's eloquent formulation, but it is best not to be blinded by them. Ancient fears and prejudices have a way of reasserting themselves in each new generation. Certainly most of the really serious charges against women live on—weaving themselves ever more subtly into the very fabric of modern mores on which the claims of emancipation are writ large.

For instance, the "castrative" blood-fears of tribal peoples are reflected in men's continuing hesitance to have sex with a menstruating woman. There are jokes aplenty concerning the perils of being "caught" by a woman, and of how she otherwise dampens a man's freedom. Intellectual slaps persist in stereotypes of the dumb blonde, the dizzy dame, the crazy broad, and the hysterical scatterbrain—or something of the reverse should she turn into a shrew, "wear the pants," or become a bag, a nag, or a hag. In English, as in many other languages, there are more negative words for women than for any other entry.

All the highest civilizations have retained at their peak essentially the same and the original complaints against women, no matter how well disguised behind a façade of respectfulness. The underlying attitudes are evident not only in wit and proverb but most sharply of all in the charges hurled at women in moments of anger—charges, as before, that they take more than they give when they are passive, or when they are not, that they are bitches, witches, or phallic females. Thus, all too clearly from the distant past the jungle drums continue to beat out the message: that women are dangerous; that they threaten male dominance in a hundred ways; that a man's blood flows into a woman's womb leaving only water in his veins, as Masai tribesmen put it; that she has an adverse effect upon the accumulation of wealth and upon victory in all forms; and besides being either fearful or exhausting even when she doesn't intend to be, she is by her very nature devious, tricky, and worthy of being watched.

Most of these complaints ultimately boil down to two basic charges: that in one way or another a woman can easily threaten a man's virility, and that in getting what she wants she can be devious. Although these concerns are widely different—the first being a subjective feeling and the other quite tangible when true—it can be shown that both stem from problems in the aggressive-submissive balance between the sexes. A few of the more superficial stresses between the sexes are sufficiently beyond culture and training to clearly appear in prehuman examples. Female monkeys, for instance, are less combative than the males, less straightforward in competing for bits of food, often play tricks to win an advantage and can be downright devious and sly in doing so. The males are more simple-minded, in a sense more prone to brawn than to brain. But it soon becomes apparent that these differences are tied more to the role an individual plays than to its gender: In a situation in which a mature female monkey is dominating a young, smaller male, it is she who is straightforward in expressing her aggressions, while he tries one trick after the other to get what he wants.[287,292]

Thus, in the usual aggressive-submissive balance between the sexes, it is not surprising that there are often elements of truth in the charges brought against women. The wonder is that she is not always devious since there are only two sure-fire ways out of the trap. Either she can develop a certain directness of manner (which easily impinges upon her image of femininity), or somehow find most of her personal satisfactions within the narrow confines of her expected role—a role derived partly from nature and the rest from social demands.

On the other hand, the strain between the sexes gains much of its impetus from male dominance and from what goes on in the minds of men—in effect, the psychology of their role. At first glance, it might seem that the advantages implicit in a man's superior status, coupled with the trappings of a personal adequacy, would give him security in his position. Perhaps it does wherever men are careful not to press their margin of advantage too far. But most societies expect extra high levels of adequacy in men, a kind of bravado, and otherwise encourage their dominance. From this high peak of primacy, men often find their virility tenuous, imagining as if by some pervasive paranoia that they can lose it in any but the most carefully balanced interactions with women. Certainly an exalted status in any aspect of life suggests to its beneficiary that by an easy shift of events the tables could be turned and, indeed, the first could become last and the last first.

Thus, in dozens of tribes and civilizations the world over, especially those that laud men most, women are imagined to have that curious combination of traits: a draining overdependency, and yet secret powers of their own. Perhaps this is the place to remember that most by far of the world's demons have been depicted as vampires and she-devils capable of reversing the primacy of men. Similar fears, in less mystical form, continue to exist in daily life too, where nearly every man has virility concerns that cause him to find a woman's oversubmissiveness a champion turnoff lest it bleed him dry, and her too high resistance an offense to his status and to his ego. Thus, workable heterosexual relationships require a fairly critical balance between the contrasts that separate the sexes and the mutualities that help make their interactions feasible and rewarding.

Despite the ease with which the most glaring imbalances in the status of the sexes can be traced to the male ego, it has not operated alone. A considerable body of evidence suggests that both sexes have always conspired to affirm the primacy of men and the subservience of women. Undoubtedly, their aggressive-submissive relationship has taken its cue not only from their physical and temperamental differences but from the symbolic connotations of sexual intercourse: For the most part, and in most ways, both sexes want the male to "be on top." Thus, despite the many legends about Amazons and the first incorrect reports on a few scattered tribes, not a single genuine matriarchy has ever been found, nor has ever been known to exist.[1]

It would be a mistake to think that because this pattern of dominance and submission has often been painfully exaggerated, it has merely been a loadstone in human relations. On the contrary, this arrangement has been basic in bringing the sexes together and in making their interactions work. The most stabilized mateships invariably display a clear-cut dominance pattern. And there is much evidence (human and animal) to suggest that without an element of dominance males tend to have potency problems.

But if the secret of heterosexual compatibility lies in a certain natural dominance-difference between the sexes, then why has nearly every society widened the breach and increased the stress between men and women to the point of threatening their communication with each other? Part of the answer is unmistakable: Something within the sexual psychology of man requires a higher level of stress between the sexes than biology alone supplies. Thus, it is no accident that combative elements are injected into heterosexual intercourse precisely in those societies in which sexual permissiveness threatens to equalize the sexes. Evidently, people are ready to pay whatever price they must in order to keep a certain disparity, a "resistance," or distance between the sexes. Later it will be shown that sexual attraction thrives when and only when the partners are in some sense alienated from each other.

Still, if most men and women in any society are conditioned to want and to respond to conventionally defined versions of each other, and if they are then able to find mates they consider appropriate and desirable, why do they not enjoy each other's company more? In a great many societies there are separate huts for men and women, not only before marriage, but after as well. And there are very few societies in which married partners both live in the same quarters and also spend most of their free time together.

Many explanations have been offered for this separation of spouses: that men and women have sharply differing interests; that wives in Greek and Roman times were less educated than men and thus were boring to be with; that until recent times athletic events and even the theatre were too bawdy for female eyes and ears (Shakespearean drama, like most, was written entirely for male audiences); that men need recreation, yet it was too unsafe for women to venture away from home even when escorted; that in Victorian times and to no small extent today men and women want to cluster into separate groups because they want to be uninhibited, need relief from domestic confinement, or "live in different worlds." But a far more powerful reason than any of these, or than all of them put together, resides in a whole psychology of males: their tendency to bond together.

The Curious Case of the Male Bond

Men everywhere have tended to cluster and affiliate with each other into tight-knit cliques, and into larger groups. Many observers have attributed the formation of such groups to what the members then do with their affiliation—be this hunting, the waging of war, or the exercise of political power. Thus, the whole bonding tendency of males has been interpreted as purposive: that men must form close alliances if they are to be effective in working together.[258] Perhaps so; but it can be shown that the male bond is just as pronounced in situations in which men are relaxing as it is when they are engaged in some project.

Practical excuses for male bonding, real or contrived, are seldom lacking. Tribal peoples of every ilk explain to themselves and to visiting anthropologists that their men must affiliate to maintain high standards for the hunt or for various emergencies. Thus, their young men are admitted into the adult group only after they have been subjected to painful initiations which supposedly imbue them with the stoic fortitude they will need in their manly tasks. In our own society, college fraternities pretend connections between their initiations and various high aims—as do the Rotarians, Elks, Freemasons, and dozens of other special or secret societies from the Rosicrucians to the Ku Klux Klan.

The call of some outer need, be it for vigilantes to enforce justice or for men to man a volunteer fire department, easily becomes a rallying point for the male bond to express itself, just as it does in men's clubs and in a variety of other all-male institutions. In corporate settings, no less than in athletics, one hears of teams, teamwork, and the team spirit.

There are more than a few examples in which the male bond exists almost as tangibly as if one were able to touch it, though the membership itself may be totally changeable and expendable. Within the military services, for instance, the Fighting Sixty-Ninth, the Flying Tigers, and other heroic subdivisions operate and are thought of as bonded groups, though their ranks may be largely wiped out and suddenly refilled with entirely new recruits. Nevermind that such titles of glory and tradition may be encouraged by an Upper Brass that finds them useful; the new recruits find them personally useful, for the male bond thrives especially well in an atmosphere of heroic magnitude.

The male bond also thrives on individually instigated deeds of derring-do and in surroundings of lesser accomplishment. What a man did alone, what he almost did, and what he plans to do all pervade the talk sessions at fishing and hunting lodges, the golf clubhouse, and on the courthouse steps. Neither the quarry, the action itself, nor any particular happening has as much value as does the mutual sharing of it with other men. A man's wife is no substitute; she may fully congratulate him, but nothing she can say or do will reverberate inside his pridechamber as will the reliving of an experience in the minds of other men.

In most societies, the male bond involves a considerable amount of bodily contact. Americans, and to a lesser extent Europeans, are quite unusual in their avoidance of intimate physical contact. Both the amount and the kinds of such contacts in other parts of the world are thus a surprise and a shock to Western eyes: Men more than women tend to hold hands or place an arm around a friend's waist or shoulder as they walk along. And the detailed view an anthropologist gets is even more striking. In a number of tribes, the standard greeting is to reach out and gently grasp a stranger's penis, or to cup his testicles in hand.[237] In others, (e.g., the Cashinahua) friends lie together in hammocks during the day, casually fondling each other's genitalia while talking (though it is considered embarrassing if one's friend, or the anthropologist, gets an erection).[136]

In perhaps three-quarters of all societies, the sleeping arrangements are such that men lie closely intertwined, legs and arms
thrown over and around each other; even tight clasping and
kissing are not at all unusual. Jules Henry has well described the
Brazilian natives with whom he lived:

> Kaingáng young men love to sleep together. At night they call
> to one another, "Come and lie down here with me, with *me!*"
> Then there is a shifting and squirming so that [the friend] can
> lie down where he is bidden. In camp one sees young men
> caressing. Married and unmarried young men lie cheek by jowl,
> arms around one another, legs slung across bodies, for all the
> world like lovers in our own society. Sometimes they lie caress-
> ing that way in little knots of three or four. Women never do
> these things. [103]

Whether there happens to be a taboo on overt homosexuality
or not, the sleeping regulations remain about the same. In the
Malay Archipelago, it is all right to crawl inside another man's
sarong for an all-night, skin-to-skin contact provided there is no
overtly sexual gesture. Among the Mbuti of the Congo (who also
ban homosexuality), it is all right to tightly clasp a sleeping-
partner between one's legs, even to place one's arms and legs
between a partner's legs and to sleep cheek-to-cheek besides; but
it is improper for one to clasp the other too tightly if their chests
are touching. (Yet even when a regulation of this sort is
breached, the partner merely moves an inch or two. Evidently,
here, as in most other events in human relations, a fairly clear-
cut implication of deliberate intent, real or imagined, must
accompany a violation for it to cause offense.) [267]

These body-contact examples are hardly homosexual in an
erotic sense, least of all in the eyes of the participants. Nor would
it be correct to view them as any garden variety of "latent homosexuality" (since that might imply a greater tendency for them to
become overtly sexual than they in fact have). And yet, the male
bond clearly carries a considerable charge of affection—an urge
for contact which is unquestionably bent more upon seeking a
personal intimacy than a group solidarity.

Even in our society, the male bond is replete with barely disguised sexual connotations. The hazings and initiations in college fraternities may involve considerable nudity, the spanking of naked buttocks, tying various objects to the penis, and vows of togetherness that sound like marriage ceremonies. And more than a few erotic elements are present in the traditions of giving a man a stag party the night before his wedding, of affectionately bearhugging him before sending him off none too promptly to his heterosexual venture, and of expecting him to later return as a father bearing cigars.

Among native peoples, initiations into manhood more often than not involve circumcision or other specifically sexual manipulations. (If these tortures were merely to test the fortitude of the young men, as is frequently claimed, then of course it would be easy enough to find nonsexual sources of pain.) Sometimes the sexual elements are even more apparent. Dozens of societies initiate their young men into manhood by demanding that they sexually submit to their elders—frequently stating outright that this is necessary in order to inject boys with the juices of manhood.[69,281] All these examples—and the sheer breadth and variety of them throughout every known society—should wipe out even the most recalcitrant doubts concerning the homosexual components that exist in man and in his male bonds.

And yet, the male bond as it is ordinarily composed eventually manages to bolster rather than to compete with heterosexual interests. Exactly how it does this is a matter of far-reaching importance. According to a classical view based on "man's basic bisexuality," the male bond "uses up" the homosexual components by satisfying them, leaving men with purified heterosexual appetites. There is nothing particularly wrong with this somewhat simplistic bipolar explanation, as far as it goes. Certainly there are plenty of everyday examples of men congregating, gradually tiring of their own company, and then vigorously seeking out women. Quite apparent, too, is the reverse cycle in which men tire of the company of women (especially wives) and rush back to the comforts of their male bonds.

A similar pattern is apparent on a far broader scale in cross-cultural examples. With hardly an exception, the most vigorously and consistently heterosexual societies are precisely the ones which use the most blatantly homosexual forms of male bonding. Here again it is as if a more or less direct expression of homosexuality (in a localized or institutionalized form) is the most effective way to satisfy it or to compartmentalize it, thus clearing the decks for heterosexuality.

But such an explanation amounts to hardly more than a descriptive dualism, and a fairly crude one at that. The impetus behind the homosexual urges contained in the male bond remains unexplained, and virtually none of heterosexuality's powerful pull has yet been accounted for. It is necessary to deal not only with these questions, but to see exactly how the differences between men and women become exaggerated, and how they facilitate the attraction of opposite sexes.

Ego-Modeling and Its Consequences

The routes by which a person reaches an individual gender-identity and models his ego toward it are in some ways obvious and in others quite obscure. Boys and girls of course begin to be channelled into sharply differing gender-identities practically from the day of birth. The very names given to boys have a crisper sound than the phonetic softness of girls' names. And from infancy the sexes are fondled somewhat differently. Later, how they are dressed, the kinds of toys and games they have, and a variety of other distinctions encourage boys and girls to develop contrasting attitudes toward themselves and others.

By the age of five a boy usually has many clear ideas as to what is and is not gender-role appropriate for males. In fact, by then he is well on his way toward policing his own actions, avoiding those he sees as belonging to girls, and perfecting boy-like attitudes. The intensity with which young children do this became clear in an unpublished study done in the early years of the Kinsey Research. Scattered among the questions put to the children were a number containing gender-violations such as, "Does your father use lipstick?" The answers were not only negative but were delivered in a tone of disgust, even ridicule: "Of course not! Don't you know lipstick is for girls?" It soon became abundantly evident that the gender-differences perceived by children are intensely felt, and are held in sharper emotional focus by them than by adults.[140]

As boys grow older, they tend not only to associate but to become allied with each other. Both as an individual and as a member of his peer group a boy seeks to model his ego, building into his personality and into his self-image the kinds of attitudes and reactions that are seen as appropriate for males. These affiliations with other boys, and the ego-modeling efforts to which they are devoted, reach such a peak in the years near puberty that even to associate with girls is thought to be unmasculine, even sissy. Incidentally, this denigration of girls is astonishingly cross-cultural; it is evident not only in every branch of Western society but is nearly universal. It is a first and a most vigorous expression of male bonding.

After becoming affiliated with each other, young boys tend to be far more rigorous with themselves, more single-minded, and more alert to what is gender-appropriate than adults would demand.* There are rewards of high respect for the boy who is good in the ballpark, or who is adept at any other activity deemed masculine. And there are excruciating penalties for one who stands apart, cries easily, or makes himself an unforgivable sissy by spending his time with girls and sharing their interests.

Thus, an early version of the male bond is heavily involved in helping a young man establish his personal identity. He uses his male alliances to compare himself with others and to explore his own potentials. As he develops particular abilities, he can compete for the rewards of special recognition. But it is one of the lasting marvels of the male bond that it permits a person who has

---

*It has become apparent that the early psychoanalysts in particular seriously overemphasized the part played by parents in a child's identity formation. Part of this emphasis may have stemmed from the fact that most early analysts were Jewish, Jewish family life being unusually close knit and powerful. In any event, the Kinsey Research found that the attitudes children develop in their formative years tend to be determined more by the peer group than by the family, as evidenced by the fact that when the two sets of standards do not agree, children tend to adopt those of their peers. Perhaps a child can take for granted a degree of acceptance by his parents, come what may, but his acceptance by peers depends on his thinking and acting as they do.

only a few skills (or possibly none at all) to identify with the pooled talents of the whole group, quite as if he himself possessed them all.

After puberty, a boy's ego-modeling efforts begin to expand beyond a personal emphasis on building his identity. More than ever, he may feel the need to prove his masculine adequacy, perhaps in team sports or in other activities in which he is closely allied with a few boys and competitive toward others. But he also has an appetite for new kinds of status and accomplishment, especially those associated with his widening social opportunities and expectancies. His newly emerging self-assurance (or a need to appear assured) enhances the value of whatever looks like adult action and independence, as heterosexual exploits certainly do.

At this point, a boy may or may not have any specific sexual interest in girls, but he can easily see advantages in this direction. Girls represent, at the very least, a new challenge and a new audience. Even showing an interest in them can be a passport into the stereotypes of adulthood, a sign of independence and grownupness. Any success he has with them is a badge of progress and a mark of status, whether it actually reinforces his heterosexuality or not.

Quite aside from these and other social encouragements that set the stage for heterosexuality, it is apparent that the sexes are often destined on more fundamental grounds to find each other attractive. There is a mutual fit in their differing modes of being dominant and submissive—especially since the ego-modeling of boys and girls encourages them to develop one-sidedly in complementary ways, each becoming systematically incompetent at the tasks and talents ascribed to the opposite sex. A boy's one-sidedness is particularly confining; the highly valued manly traits that comprise it are thought to be quickly undermined if he retains any "feminine" traits. To round himself out and thus correct his cultivated masculine eccentricity—that is, to regain much of what he has systematically eliminated from his personality and to savor softness in a hundred ways—he needs the company of women. Conversely, a woman's cultivation of less robust qualities tends to leave her short on the kinds of stability and symbols of security which are the specialties of men, and that are obtainable from them.

Certainly there is nothing new in the basic idea of complementation. In the fifth century B.C., Socrates based his eulogy of love on the observation that each partner, being less than self-satisfied, strives to get from the other what is needed and admired. The basic concept is intuitively understood by everyone. It is implicit in the nursery rhyme of Jack Sprat and in the adage which predicts a marriage will work "if the dents in her head fit the bumps on his." Nor does the idea of complementation become difficult—in fact, it is made easier—if it is viewed as a person "importing" what is needed from a partner while "exporting" what the partner needs.

This import-export view of what goes on in a mateship quickly begins to open up new vistas in complementation. One begins to see that the heterosexual male, in his best relationships, imports far more from his mate than is commonly realized. He can import or use not only her differing viewpoint—including her often more gentle way of looking at things—but since she, unlike himself, has the social permission to be fragile and in some ways childlike, he now has the excuse to gratify these qualities in himself. He may fill his house with labor-saving devices and cushion his life with a hundred comforts "for her sake"—indulgences which, if demanded purely for himself, could look self-pampering, if not downright "soft." Emotionally, too, he has much to gain. When he is with a woman he can afford to be impressed by a sunset, to speak of children as "cute," and to laugh and play in ways that would otherwise embarrass him.

What a man "exports" is also very important, not only because it can be valuable to his female partner but because it can be very valuable to him. Many a man enjoys flaunting his sweep, his dash, or some less obvious version of his maleness before his hopefully appreciative female partner. Looking at himself through her eyes (whether correctly or not), he can revel afresh in his own prowess. Thus, part of what a man imports from a woman is her admiring view of him, and part of what he exports to her is used by himself to validate his own self-image. (Women accomplish much the same for themselves when they use, and enjoy watching themselves use, whatever version of femininity they have made their own.)

All of this in its more blatant forms is clear to the casual observer. Anyone can see that a man who is displaying his dash and adequacy to a woman or who is otherwise showing off before her is bolstering his male image as well as trying to cash in on it. But a moment's reflection will also make it clear that this whole aspect of male behavior works in the opposite direction from complementation. Most of what a man imports from women is complementary in that it corrects for (and thus reduces) his masculine eccentricity—but to the extent that he revels in his own exports, he manages to hold on to that eccentricity.

The most important issue here—and it is a matter of far-reaching significance—is that despite the many advantages of complementation, there is much in people which struggles against it. Men, especially, tend to impose sharp restrictions on their appetite for complementation, seeking only particular kinds of complementary interactions with their partners while avoiding all others. The net result is that most people in most societies (today as in the past) achieve only fairly coarse forms of complementation with their partners—as opposed to delicate, highly personal interchanges. Even where great affection prevails, many couples mesh mainly in terms of their physical fit and in fairly crude versions of dominance and submission. Men more often than women are content with these scant arrangements.

Is all this because men are callous brutes who know no better? Or is it, as the voices of Women's Liberation would have us believe, that extensive and delicate meshings require an equality of status and a mutual respect which most couples do not have? It is sometimes suggested that wherever the sexes are sharply polarized, the gap between them is simply too wide to be well bridged. No doubt one could find examples to fit each of these observations. But in all such interpretations there is the underlying assumption that the sexes want, and would profit by, a more extensive complementation if only they were not too clumsy, too ignorant, or too trapped by their training to achieve it.

Before approaching a more sophisticated interpretation, it is worth remembering that delicate complementations entail costs and risks that many people experience as threateningly undesirable. Besides the strains inherent in making close emotional contacts with the opposite sex, there are dangers in overcloseness: To really understand a woman and be understood by her, a man often feels he has to make serious compromises in his general posture. To give up more than a fraction of his autonomy and to move in the direction of softness may strike him as a watering down of the purified maleness he has gone to some trouble attaining. And with continued closeness there is the risk of having too much of a woman's outlook become his own.

Many men stifle these risks at the outset by holding on to a certain coarseness and avoiding all delicately intimate contacts with women. Other men solve the problem by going ahead with a very close contact, fully enjoying its refreshment, as their somewhat burdensome masculine eccentricity is complemented, but then returning immediately to their male friends with whom they rejuvenate their male outlook. Thus, a major continuing motivation for the male bond is apparent: It is the ballpark (sometimes literally) in which a somewhat bent masculinity is bolstered and restored to its original shape.

Incidentally, from this vantage point it is also clear at last how the male bond manages to deliver its considerable force to heterosexuality. Its homosexual component is ordinarily much too far from anything erotic to offer sexual competition to heterosexuality. But by supplying relief—in a sense, putting gas back in the tank—it satiates male needs and refreshes a man's appetite for a forceful return to heterosexual contacts. Many women intuitively understand this refueling operation, and although they may miss their men who are "off with the boys," they use the time themselves to recuperate, correctly sensing that they are the ultimate benefactors of men's diversion from them. Their hunch is right, as is the hunch of other women who feel a pensive disquietude with men who have no close male ties.

Of the two broad examples of complementation cited above, the first, in which men make little effort to "tune in" to women (staying to fairly coarse forms of complementation), may seem far inferior to the other. And in many ways it is. Certainly, men who are anywhere near this alternative hear many complaints. Women keep reminding them that they want to be loved for themselves and not merely thought of as "sex objects." Their wives often hold lifelong complaints of being emotionally deprived and of not being understood—"It's as if we live in different worlds; he just doesn't understand me at all."

But for a variety of reasons, the whole question of what kinds of complementations make the best mateships is by no means as unequivocal as one might think. Relationships in which coarse complementations prevail certainly are short on intimate communication and, besides this lack of emotional delicacy, they can present profound sexual difficulties for women who are not "easy responders." And yet, the not-very-intimate relationship tends to have great staying power, and often an earthy vitality that is somehow constantly renewed as if by its own disparity.

Nor, by contrast, are the many advantages of delicately balanced complementations—advantages of compatibility and of mutual understanding—always quite as wonderful as they might at first appear. As the partners make the necessary compromises to achieve an excellent high contact with each other, they win intimacy and a genuine closeness, benefits which contribute to the comforts of daily living and to their ability to get along with each other. For a time, their sexual compatibility soars as well. And there can be no doubt that delicate and intimate heterosexual relationships tend to improve the status of women as well as the kindness with which they are treated. But all this blending and complementation not only does not contribute to the lastingness of sexual attraction, it soon begins to dissolve it. Thus, in well-balanced ongoing relationships, the compatibility of the partners tends to progressively improve while their erotic zest for each other markedly declines.

Almost as an apology for what happens to people's sexual response to each other in close ongoing relationships, it is often pointed out that love of a different kind grows deeper. Undoubtedly it does. But it is worth emphasizing that the benefits of a smooth togetherness are bought at the price of dwindling erotic tensions—a descent which can easily threaten the whole enterprise. Conversely, a genuine closeness is notable by its absence in the most intense forms of erotic interest, including the high romance that can so disconsolingly occur between utterly mismatched partners. Thus, it is in new relationships and in marriages torn by fights and clashes—that is, where complementations and the details of compatibility have *not* been worked out—

that the highest erotic excitements flourish. Throughout a multitude of examples it becomes apparent that the comforts of a personal closeness, and the stuff of sexual attraction are at cross-purposes.

With this disparity clearly in mind, if we look again at the history of heterosexuality, many of its most glaring peculiarities begin to fall into place. That previously mentioned inclination of sexually permissive peoples to pinch, to pummel, and to otherwise abuse each other during coitus, besides heightening their tension, puts the partners on guard—in effect, stirring up sexual excitement by transforming their familiarity and any affectionate closeness into a coarser, more zesty form of dominance and submission. In other societies, tension between sex partners has been assured not by inventing frictions and alienations, but by seeking them readymade: In tribes which practice exogamy, wives must come from other tribes (via capture, purchase, seduction, or exchange); it is as if the women at home are too close and too familiar to be sexually interesting.

At first glance, the picture looks very different in our society, where traditions of romance and of love-and-affection emphasize a likemindedness of partners and urge that sexual contacts should not only be free of any brutality, but should be a symphony of togetherness and of gentle communication. But all this "coming together" of the sexes is *after* the price has been paid. It is after a long period of holding the sexes apart, and after teaching them that sex itself is something bad that only love can redeem. The key element in all this pretraining is the establishment of a barrier or some other form of resistance between the sexes. This is the breach between lovers that makes high romance possible, and which keeps it going for its short life before familiarity dissolves its crucial contrast. The manufacture of resistance is exactly what the sexually permissive societies are up to in their fierce coital encounters, and it is the motive in many another variation from wife beating to all the other coarse forms of complementation. Thus, it is apparent that people in all societies struggle in one way or another to maintain a partially alienating resistance between the sexes; what vary are the choices of what that resistance should be, and whether to place it before, during, or after the partners get together.

From this vantage point it is evident that the many derogations of women are more than merely the incidental offshoots of male supremacy and female "inferiority." They also qualify as contrivances that sharpen the breach between the sexes, increase the tension (resistance) between them, and add spice to their relations. A familiar counterclaim is that the sexes have been overly separated and that, far from being enjoyable, the breach between them has often interfered with the attractions of heterosexuality. It would be easy to find examples to substantiate this result as well, but the two views are not actually contradictory. Sexual attraction requires a certain "optimal distance" between the partners, a degree of resistance which can be destroyed by too much disparity as easily as by too much closeness.

Despite all the social and sexual biases which can affect the derogation of women, it is a matter of far-reaching importance that at the level of individual psychology a woman's status is highly variable. It is determined more by how she conducts herself than by other people's predispositions toward her. To take an extreme example, not even in the most chauvinistic societies is a wife a drudge on her wedding day, or for some time following. It is as if she only slowly works her way down to this level (admittedly with the help of social pressures) by allowing the forces of familiarity and subservience to plod toward their destination. Nor in any era has the individual woman suffered low status whenever she has been "willful" or has simply had the power—be it political, financial, or social—to express her independence or even her own choices. To merely exercise a choice between suitors has usually stirred chivalry or something close to it. And any more energetic expression of determination, be it balk or bite (sometimes mere pluck), has usually cut unchallenged through the highest barriers of male supremacy. Men are less able and much less inclined to cope with a willful woman than with a man who oversteps his station.

Perhaps the general observation to be made is that nothing so insures a woman against becoming overly subservient as does her exercise of choice—a degree of independence, no matter how she manages to obtain it. Thus, even courtesans and concubines have usually had more wealth, more freedom, and more respect of the sort which a personal formidability entails than have the wives of the men who have supported them. Where does such a woman gain her leverage? Is it that she is partially unrelinquished and holds the option of saying yes or no? That may be part of it, as is her power to dazzle and to mystify a man. But the essence of her grip is in her basic posture, one which makes her approachable and yet allows her to stay unconquered in a sense, never to be taken for granted or to have her appeal worn thin by the overcontact that invites fatigue. She knows how to be temporarily submissive without being constantly subservient, let alone subjugated. Nor do men want her to be humbled and subdued. That is the fate of women with whom they have too much contact, a too-easy access, and from whom they want to pull away, frequently with that ancient complaint that they are being bled dry.

Much of this is relevant to what women face in modern societies: the problem of maintaining a fairly critically adjusted, mutually satisfying middle-course in their relations with men. Whenever any woman gives up too much of her individuality, becomes overdependent, or stays within the narrow confines of a domestic treadmill from which she mainly sings a song of sameness, undue subservience and emotional neglect will be her lot as surely as it ever was. At the other extreme, too much independence can blot out the image of ultimate submission that sexual allure requires. The woman who demands her way can usually have it, but seldom her appeal at the same time. For reasons that are rooted at least as much in biology as in social tradition, the sexual arousal of most men depends on their being dominant over a partner whose submission is neither too easy nor too hard to obtain.*

In looking back over the origins of heterosexuality, it is evident

---

*These observations have proved hard to absorb. People either tend to believe they "know all this already" or to wash away the implications by quickly attributing most dominance-submissive phenomena to mere sociological influences. Thus, it is sometimes said that men and women could or should be equal in most matters including decisional authority, with male dominance relegated to overtly sexual situations. Such arguments may make sense on ethical grounds but are sharply at odds with certain biological traditions. It is a matter of profound significance that all sexual attractions depend upon resistance barriers and that a man's attraction to a partner (and thus his arousability) is almost invariably keyed in to dominant and not to democratic motifs.

that an array of directives fills the vacancy left by the evolutionary disappearance of sexual "instinct." And quite an array it is, for nothing in human society varies more than do the means by which individuals come to find each other attractive. In theory, the undirected urgency of the male sex-drive, led by nothing more than free experimentation and differences in the aggressiveness of the sexes, might be enough to lead most people toward heterosexuality in each new generation. But, in practice, few societies permit free experimentation, and no society either leaves sexual matters to chance or is content to rely merely on the persuasions of advice and expectancy. Every society encourages its members to see particular modes of behavior and particular bodily features, and not others, as sexual.

And yet, the effectiveness of this social conditioning varies considerably. Many people have their sexual interests channeled toward the opposite sex virtually by suggestion alone; it is what they have seen on every side and have come to expect. Early try-outs may hasten the process and deepen the channel. Other people (a few males and a great many females) only slowly develop a specifically *sexual* attraction to their partners, with or without try-outs. Still others, by some combination of fantasy and expectation, come to eroticize ideal versions of possible partners long before actually encountering any. Males, with their more urgent sex-drive, are especially inclined to eroticize real or imagined partners in advance by trying them out in masturbatory fantasies.

Thus it would seem—and it is true as far as it goes—that a specific heterosexual motivation can start with social suggestions which lead to real or imagined sex experiences, events which then simply condition men and women to respond to each other. But it has become apparent on close examination that one more ingredient must always be present as a catalyst. A person's sexual motivation is seldom aroused and never rewarding unless something in the partner or in the situation itself is viewed as resistant to it. This resistance may be in the form of the partner's hesitance, the disapproval of outsiders, or any other impediment to easy access. Even the five-year-old boy and girl who go behind the barn for sex-play are aware of some of the social divisions that separate them as well as certain violational aspects of what they are doing. Zest begins here, not twenty minutes later with what may or may not "feel good."

After puberty, as was shown, it is often the contrast between the sexes that makes them need and want each other as they seek to repair their individual biases. Certainly the boy who has developed the masculine eccentricity he and all his friends have helped him reach (and the girl who has bent and narrowed her talents to the recommended extremes) may feel the one-sidedness that a heterosexual complementation can correct. But here again how, exactly, does this hunger become eroticized?—as opposed to merely sponsoring a close friendship, as indeed it often does. Once more it is apparent that an erotic attitude does not develop toward a fully accessible partner (even one who is wonderfully complementary), but is aroused like a cannibal's appetite when a desired but somehow remote partner cannot "be had" by other means. And as anyone can see, sexual motives are especially stimulated in a person who feels an urgent need or an intense admiration for the qualities he sees in a partner and wants to "import." Certainly there is much in sex that has to do with wanting, taking, conquering, or otherwise possessing a partner, sometimes one who has as little as a single highly desired quality.

It is memorable, too, that despite all that has and could be said about why men and women generally need and want each other, there is also much in people which makes them want to hold on to the undiluted purity of their hard-won gender-eccentricity. Men are especially inclined to want to keep their one-sidedness, their distinctively male outlook, come what may. From here they may be titillated, bedazzled, or profoundly intrigued by the ways and attributes of women. Certain of the contrasts they are responding to comprise the complementation that many men seek; other men are drawn to women and are fascinated most by the sheer strangeness of the creatures. That women are not very different from men in many ways while being unfathomably different in other ways only makes the canyon of alienation seem deeper than ever, yet narrow enough to be tantalizingly bridgeable. This, indeed, is the gap for the spark of sex to jump. But it is more than that. It is the gap, the optimal distance between partners, that pervades all sexual attractions and without which they cannot exist.

The fact that sexual motivations founder or simply prove impossible once a fairly critical distance between partners is violated in either direction turns out to be the key to many a locked-up secret in human relations. Evident at a glance is why the male bond is not susceptible to becoming overtly sexual. The closeness of it, its likemindedness, and its camaraderie offer too little gap for sex to bridge; whatever erotic voltage does get generated tends to be immediately short-circuited into friendship. Evident, too, is why friendship, familiarity, and eventually even intimate complementations are antithetical to sexual interest: They all lack sufficient gap, sufficient resistance. Sexual zest does not arise from the comforts of similarity and agreement. Even after it finds its natural origins it is put to sleep by the music of high accord and, in that atmosphere, local injections of novelty and newness do not arouse it for long. With no outside source of resistance, sexual attraction requires the sharper zap of clash or of foreignness—a note of antagonism set in a disparity of outlook or of rank. Consequently, a certain enmity between the sexes, be it expressed in the downing of women or in the nearly universal battle-of-the-sexes, has always been central to their attraction.

Thus, there is method in the madness by which men have invented ways of maintaining distance from their women. These have most often involved keeping the sexes apart in divisions of labor, in their daily living, and in their status levels as well as in the use of relatively coarse forms of complementation. Where people have yearned for a more intimate closeness than any of these systems afford, they have often been able to achieve it for short spans of time bounded by an increased distance at other times. Such a combination is evident in courtship, in love-affairs, and in various arrangements of having a mistress or lover. It is also evident in a great variety of ongoing relationships in which intimacy is interrupted by frequent quarrels, by time away from home, or by contact with other partners. Conspicuous by its absence is the love-story dream: the ongoing, sexually vivid, delicately intimate monogamous tie. It exists—like mermaids, perpetual motion, and heaven itself—in the human imagination.

Then does this mean that the highest levels of intimacy and of complementation between men and women are either fleetingly transitory or can only be had at the price of discord? It very nearly amounts to this. In the mores of our society, sex has been invited and expected to pay the whole penalty: The standard recommendation that partners should remain strictly monogamous over the years makes no provision for the fact that their sexual interest in each other—dissolving at the rate at which intimacy is achieved—dwindles toward zero. Not that this decline is always lamented. Many people are philosophically prepared to renounce the drama and excitements of sex, especially when these are gradually replaced by a gentle, comfortable compatibility.

But many other people are wary of the risks entailed in any such compromise and in the conventional alternatives as well. They, too, value ongoing relationships but they are neither ready nor willing to sustain the usual penalties. They particularly do not wish to have their sexuality strangled by a rigorous monogamy or paid for by frictions, by the consequences of surreptitiousness, or by interpersonal distance. Instead, they try to design their own individualized solutions to these difficult problems. In an atmosphere of emotional continuity they may grant each other a certain autonomy and independence (often more symbolic than real), including a degree of sexual freedom. Their rule may be to never mention an outside contact, or to always mention it or share it in some other way. These arrangements also have their pitfalls and usually require a good deal of "fine tuning," especially in the beginning. But when they work as they often do, they tend to work very well, indeed, for an open hand can hold the most intimate, the most binding, and the most lasting ties of all.

5

The Origins
of Homosexuality

Much of what was found in the origins of heterosexuality reappears or has near-equivalents in the origins of homosexuality. Again the central questions concern how and why people become sexually attracted to their partners, what the import-export arrangements are (i.e., how homosexual complementation works), how the distance-resistance phenomena fit into the picture and, perhaps most important, exactly how same-sex attributes become eroticized. But there are notable differences, too. Since the homosexual alternative in our society lacks any guidance from social expectancy, its origins are more scattered and diverse. By comparison, heterosexuality is much more organized because, of course, it is always institutionalized—that is, guided by expectancy, religion, stated regulations, and the like.

Actually, much could be gained from making heterosexual-homosexual comparisons in a society which institutionalizes both. But homosexual findings made in these settings are usually cast aside as being too far afield to be relevant to anything in our society. In fact, even fairly sophisticated observers continue to believe that while homosexuality may be "normal" in a society which approves of it, it still should be regarded as "deviant" (the new word for "abnormal") when it occurs without direct social support. Sometimes this belief is rationalized on numerical grounds, though it probably derives most of its impetus from a curious faith in the power of conventional stereotypes, or from a desire to justify the mores.

Of course, it *is* true that the specific origins of any sexuality are not likely to be entirely identical in any two societies or even in two individuals. But there are a few basic motivations that do manage to stay the same across cultural lines, even when a particular item of behavior may look entirely different. For this reason, it seems useful to delay the specific analysis of homosexuality in our society, and to look first at certain of its broader and sometimes its most peculiar aspects in distant places.

A Rapid Cross-Cultural View of Homosexuality

High, low, and intermediate rates of homosexuality are found among people who live in hot or cold climates, who are rich or poor, light or dark, educated or not—and quite irrespective, too, of whether they live in a stone-age society or an advanced civilization. Nor does the basic family structure seem to make any difference. Whether fathers live at home or are mainly absent and, in either case, whether they are attentive to their sons or virtually ignore them matters not. What does matter is the conceptual framework in which sex is cast—but even here, it is best to "float loosely" over a dazzling array of variables before too quickly concluding what goes with what.

In general, it can be said that where homosexuality is lauded, or even merely approved, it tends to be prevalent, and that where there are strictures against it, it is less prevalent. Evidently, then, laws and laudations do have their effects—but not quite in the neat, systematic fashion one might suppose. The very lowest and also the very highest rates of homosexuality occur among peoples who have no rules whatsoever either for it or against it.

Take the case of low rates with no rules. Sometimes the homosexual potential is superseded from the very beginning by an overriding, highly effective heterosexual conditioning, achieved either by marrying off five-year-olds, or by otherwise sponsoring an overt heterosexuality among infants. More often, a pervasive heterosexuality appears to stem not so much from early practice as from the kinds of especially intense expectancy and conformity that are often implicit in small tribal societies. But on close examination, it usually turns out that even here a homosexual potential is clearly evidenced, though being drained off by large amounts of affection and body contact between males. These substitutional forms can be extensive. As mentioned before, it may be the style for boys and young men to sleep skin-to-skin, sometimes freely caress each other, walk everywhere arm-in-arm, and otherwise express a great deal of affection[222,103] —or even for adult males to while away the time of day lying together conversing and casually fondling each other's genitalia.[136]

Where homosexuality is neither short-circuited by these means nor brought under strict taboos, it is often institutionalized in laudatory forms. The Kiwai of New Guinea require their young men to be sodomized during puberty rites "to make them strong." The Papuans and Keraki do the same "because the juices of manhood are necessary for the growing boy."[281] Homosexual practices carried out with at least this much veneration have certainly not been limited to "primitive tribes"—remember that even the Hebrews practiced religious fellatio until after the Babylonian Exile. And yet, the pressing implications of such practices have usually been ignored in favor of thinking of the examples purely as religious peculiarities rather than seeing them as expressions of sexual desire. In partial support of the curious notion that mere custom is involved, it does seem to be true that whenever a society passes a law that says every man *must* engage in homosexuality and that he really ought to practice it until he is married, he gladly does all this and, later, gladly gives it up. But in societies in which homosexuality has larger aspects of free choice (even though it may be recommended only for unmarried males) there is strong evidence that it rarely if ever disappears later, rules or no rules.[51,40]

Nevertheless, there continues to be a widely held impression that the homosexual alternative is somehow fundamentally recessive and that, at least as a preference, it can neither predominate in quantity nor "stay put" in time without specific support from either religious demands or conceptual sources (such as the male-ideal of the Greeks). To put the matter straight, it is worth considering one of the South American examples in which all the men in an entire tribe maintain an ongoing, predominant homosexuality without the aid of a single formal concept to support it.

Among the eastern Peruvian natives (a totally isolated branch of the Amarakaeri) visited by Tobias Schneebaum in 1956-57, homosexuality was dominant to the point of heterosexual contacts being relegated to only two or three ceremonial occasions a year.[234] During these special times, heterosexual acts were quickly completed at the end of a long drinking bout with no evidence of affection between the intoxicated partners. Except for these special occasions, the men spent each night intertwined with each other in body-piles of six or seven individuals. (The women and children huddled together in a different way in a separate part of the longhouse.) Sexual activity regularly occurred between paired males who also appeared to be affectionate during sex; but since the men were not "possessive," there was a certain randomness of partner selection from one night to the next. (Homosexual activity sometimes occurred in the daytime, too, but then only privately in the bush.) Nothing indicated any religious or conceptual backing for these practices, although a rudimentary "idealism" might possibly be inferred from the fact that none of the contacts ever involved more than two partners at a time, and that the men were acutely age-conscious: All intercourse was anal with the older partner taking the active role, yet the same man would freely be submissive when with a partner even slightly older than himself.[235]

The breadth of this homosexual conditioning is comparable to the extreme heterosexual conditioning seen wherever infant marriage is practiced. And yet there are important differences. Here, the young males have no overt sexual conditioning until after puberty—and, in fact, not until then are they permitted to join the male sleeping piles. A further detail of special interest to sex researchers is that while the puberty rites in this society do not involve sexual acts, they verge on being a mirror image of ordinary homosexual puberty rites: They take place adjacent to and just previous to the ceremonial heterosexuality, and within the same drinking bout.[235]

Worth examining, too, is another whole class of more familiar examples which carry important implications for certain events that occur in our society—examples of *berdache* as practiced by various North American Indian tribes. As the Indians explained it, when a young boy was noticed as being effeminate, he would immediately be labeled a *berdache* (man-woman) and from then on, he would be treated and trained as a female (usually of somewhat higher than average status)—behaving as a woman, sexually and otherwise, with men who could win his-her favor. (In some tribes he "belonged" to chieftains; in others he was free to share his favors.) The Indian informants in most tribes said nothing of any other kind of homosexuality—and, in fact, consistently implied that their *berdache* training programs only built up what was already evident in a few young children. (Until quite recently, even anthropologists sometimes reported homosexuality as rare in these tribes "since there were only a few *berdache* with whom the other men had sex"—once again reflecting the naïve notion that homosexuality exists only where there is role-inversion.) But on closer examination, it often turned out that effeminate males were far too rare to satisfy the market, with the result that in many of these societies the *berdache* were chosen in considerable numbers at birth—boys to be raised in the style of women, yet interestingly enough, with some care to preserve various male qualities.[30,37,52,106,149,268]

There have been literally dozens of variations on this theme—with and without there being childhood training, with and without the role-shifts being self-chosen and, in both cases, with those shifts being a part-time or an all-the-time affair. Among the Siberian Chukchee, for instance, it was the custom for a man to have several regular wives along with one male wife who dressed and acted like a woman in all duties—but for the husband to merely look the other way when "she" (while still married to him) took a mistress and was very much a man in the other household.[29] Other variations have included such oddities as a man's male wife scratching "herself" in order to "menstruate" real blood or else feigning pregnancy instead—later going through the contortions of labor, sadly placing the "stillbirth" (usually feces wrapped in leaves) in a burial urn, and then holding a funeral at which the disappointed father would wail in mourning.[52]

In standing back and looking at all these examples, what can one conclude is going on in them and what do they mean? What is *not* going on is more immediately apparent. There is no attempt in any of them to actually fool anybody. Even the transvestism is no more than a thin veneer—usually with a good deal of overtly homosexual action such as reaching under a *berdache's* garment and making such comments as, "Oh, you have such a nice big vulva . . . and now it is getting even bigger." Then why all this masquerade? Is it merely a way of injecting an element of distance and allure (even heterosexual allure) into a playfully bizarre scene? Or is it a way of allowing the dominant male to retain the trappings and security of his heterosexual pattern while departing considerably from it (and perhaps allowing the submissive male to savor the oddity of his inversional role)? No doubt these and other interpretations will fit. But it is important to give at least a nod of recognition to sheer ignorance and surprise: When a man, for whatever reason, is hit by a sharply activated homosexual desire without his having any notion of how such a relationship could exist on its own, he is almost forced to squeeze it into fitting the standard male-female format he knows, and thus "heterosexualize" it. In any case, one of the results of heterosexual and homosexual activities being "packaged together" in people's minds (be they Indian braves or quite a few men in our society) is that the homosexual potential is then exposed largely without inhibition to whatever ambient motives there are for its support. From such indeterminable settings it may emerge only rarely, take curious routes to the surface, or boom forward to find expression in almost any man.

Observers who first begin to look at the cross-cultural aspects of homosexuality are often inclined to account for part of it with standard notions of proximity and availability. Where women are in short supply or are overly segregated, it may be tempting to believe that men are more or less forced to turn to homosexuality. But to the extent that such a correlation exists at all, it has to be read the other way around: The fact is that women are seldom in short supply in the first place unless homosexuality happens to be high. The same kinds of male glorification that drive homosexuality up also tend to lower the value placed on women, which, in turn, may lead to both a deliberate and an "accidental" infanticide of newborn females, as was true in Greece and Rome. (There may be more to it than that. Anthropologists have recently found that among certain highly homosexual peoples in the Southwest Pacific the actual ratio of male births is itself above average.[51])

As for the effect of an extreme segregation of the sexes, the results are so varied as to suggest that this is only one influence among many—if, indeed, it is ever to be taken at face value. In Moslem societies, for instance, a sharp separation of the sexes often appears to increase the amount of homosexuality; in Hindu societies it definitely does not. Such contrasts are at least as marked among tribal peoples, where the very lowest rates of homosexuality often occur in conjunction with the highest degree of female segregation.

The "segregation" of males is another matter. As noted before, men in every society tend to cluster together in various kinds of male bond arrangements. Just how this bond happens to be "hooked up" helps decide whether homosexual contacts will be encouraged, discouraged, or virtually snuffed out. In our society, the talkative, backslapping, walk-around-nude-in-the-locker-room type bonding tends to wipe out any basis for sexual interaction—no gap, no barrier, no mystery, no hide-and-seek, and thus no sexual interest.

But astonishingly, just this brand of bonding sometimes does prevail in a society in which the men have a high degree of homosexual response, amounting to a clash of styles which immediately threatens to ruin either their camaraderie or their sex. To remedy this situation, various "barriers" are inserted into the system, frequently at precisely those points—and nowhere else—that sex is expected to work. In a society where the main gathering place is a men's hut, and where homosexual relations between men and boys are prized, the boys may not be allowed in the hut at all, or they may be let in but never intimately approached there ("I'll see you in the bush tonight").[51] Or intended partners of any age may banter in the ordinary way in the daytime provided they become a little remote toward evening, and perhaps have sex only in the dark without conversation. Or it might be permissible for them to do and say anything at night when they are alone provided they never mention it to each other in the daytime. (These latter codes are not unfamiliar in our own society, and are stereotypes among rough-riding cowboys and lumberjacks.) In several African tribes, it is all right for two men to masturbate each other in broad daylight, even while not particularly secluded, provided they say not a word and are careful to avoid eye-to-eye contact during sex. But judging by the frequency of various distance-producing systems, most highly homosexual societies find it easier to adjust the tone of the male bond in the first place, rather than later trying to insert gaps and barriers into it. Not much adjusting is necessary. They can keep all the clustering, provided they go easy on too much casual nudity and avoid a certain overfriendly familiarity.

Beyond all "distancing" arrangements, there is much evidence to suggest that a society's concept of maleness and the values it attaches to it are what most control the amount of homosexuality. It is not quite possible to say that the degree of male emphasis or the height of male ideals are what count; in one version or another male values are upheld in every society. In fact, quite a strong case could be made for the probability that manly virtues of some sort are about equally emphasized in all societies, and that in this respect there is not much difference even between tribes and civilizations. But there are large differences in the kinds of qualities expected of males and the amount of individualism men are expected to show. Where male aspirations are cast in a noncompetitive mold, homosexuality tends to be low, but where perhaps the very same aspirations are rated individually with a consequent emphasis on such concepts as the winner and the hero, the homosexual potential is readily activated. For instance, among native peoples who live by hunting, if it is customary to share and share alike with little tendency to rate whose marksmanship is better or worse than that of somebody else, homosexuality is *always* low. But if it is customary to celebrate the expert hunter—perhaps count his trophies and compare them with those of the next man—then an enviable, individualized maleness is lionized and homosexuality can be high to very high. In fact, these trends are so pronounced that even in "heroic" societies which have instituted the strongest possible codes against homosexuality, there is more of it by far than in "non-heroic" societies which may not have even bothered to formulate any rules against it.

But there is another question here. Since there are so many different ways for maleness to be lauded, and so many odd ways for the homosexual potential to find expression, what really causes homosexuality to be low where it is low? As indicated before, there are a few societies (very few) in which it is simply drowned out by an overriding early-practice heterosexuality; or a considerable homosexual requirement may be "used up" in one of those completely nonerotic forms of body-contact. But what about the other societies in which homosexuality is indigenously low without any such special handling? In most of these, hetero-sexuality is quite rigorously programmed (often by arranged mar-riages) but is fundamentally stabilized by nothing more than a firm social expectancy. It is a system which easily produces a high heterosexual uniformity, especially in small tribal societies where there is considerable communality and not much individual diversity. And yet, any such vague handling of the homosexual potential leaves it far from dead.

For instance, there are a number of these societies in which homosexuality is (or was) known to be relatively rare, sometimes very rare, and yet if an adroit homosexual foreigner should come along and introduce "the practice" to a few men in their teens and twenties, it may catch on like wildfire—or, as is more often the case, it may simply be quietly and quickly accepted by seem-ingly any man.*

Sometimes the word will spread through a tribe or town with

---

*The homosexual visitor may be an explorer, an anthropologist, a trades-man, or whatever. In the days of British colonialism there were countless representatives from the Foreign Office. Not infrequently, men drawn to exotic travels have not only been homosexual but quite adept at making their approaches; thus, their rebuffs as well as their different kinds of ac-ceptances have been informative to sex researchers. It is notable, too, that "traveler's reports" at this level have tended to be remarkably reliable and free of contradictions.

many other men soon indicating a sexual interest in this or in any later traveler. This interest, by the way, is seldom based on experimental or sexual-release motives, as one might think. On the contrary, the native novice tends to be remarkably flexible, reciprocal, and quickly affectionate, regardless of whether affection is part of the heterosexual pattern in his society or not. In other locales, there may be no "spreading effect" whatsoever—merely a kind of naïve readiness to accept and return the sexual attentions of the visitor.

For reasons not fully understood, when homosexuality or some newly introduced version of it does catch on, it can be absorbed in quite different ways. It may be "added on to" the mores, or integrated into them. In Malaya, Burma, and Thailand, for instance, it is quite unusual for young adult males to have any sexual interest in each other, and yet many find foreign males, especially Caucasians, almost irresistible. In other social climates, the Japanese course of events is evident. Homosexuality is certainly not new in Japan; in primitive forms (purely anal, nonaffectionate relations between males of unequal status) it has appeared in Japanese scrolls for at least four hundred years. But this hardly compares with the Japanese escalation in quantity and quality (including ongoing relationships between equal-status males) which has taken place since the American Occupation. In fact, the Japanese have so embraced every newly introduced form of homosexuality that many members of the younger generation think "gaybar" is a Japanese word, without the slightest notion of its origin.

If these and similar examples were considered alone, it might be tempting to conclude that while the homosexual potential may not be well developed in a particular social milieu, it is always quite ready to be activated. But whether this will be true for any significant number of individuals depends in part upon whether certain underlying concepts of sex and of self are "right" for it. Let that adroit explorer or even the most experienced consul try his hand in any Hindu society from India to Bali, and unless he happens to find the rare exception, he will get nowhere at all. And yet, if he moves perhaps only a few miles away into Moslem territory, he will find he is himself fairly deluged with propositions. Not that this difference stems from the *sexual* mores.

Hindu strictures against homosexuality are no more pronounced than those of the Moslems, but the basic philosophy is sharply different. Much in the Hindu mentality is pitted against the attainment of personal aspirations, whether via sex or any other means. (A man is encouraged to see himself less as self than as part of a cosmic consciousness.) And in the absence of any tradition for individually developing and for greatly admiring such things as same-sex attributes, the homosexual alternative is left without what is often its crucial catalyst.

In looking back over these various examples, one can readily see that our society combines certain highly contradictory elements. From its Greco-Roman heritage, it has derived a brand of individualism and of personal striving which is very conducive to homosexual motivations—and from later sources, a philosophy and rulebook which are antihomosexual in the extreme; even affection between males is suspect. In view of the amount of homosexuality that exists anyway, it is sometimes suggested that our moral strictures are not very effective. But they are remarkably effective if one takes into account what they are up against: In America, for instance, at least fifty out of a hundred men admit being, or having been, sexually attracted to other males, and yet few of these "give in" to their response and only three or four turn out to be homosexual in the usual sense.[142] Given this heterosexual success of the mores, the exceptions are what need to be accounted for: By what manner of individual psychology does a person in our society become predominantly or entirely homosexual?—is something the matter with his background, with his personality, with both, or with neither?

Unfortunately for present-day understanding, these questions began to be elaborately answered by Freud and other founders of psychiatry at a particularly critical time in history, the early years of this century. It was a period in which there was a new awareness of homosexuality yet hardly any notion of its extent and variations. Little was known of learning processes and cross-cultural comparisons, much less biology. Notions of instinct had not yet been challenged, let alone displaced. In what later proved to be quite troublesome, scientific curiosity had a boundless appetite for systematic explanations along with an unguarded acceptance of purely deductive logic.

Freud was good at both. After discovering that young children are not sexless, he postulated a whole series of theories having to do with various phases of development and the specific motivations by which a child shapes not only his sexual interests but his whole identity as well in an attempt to win approval and ward off danger—or as Freud really put it, to seduce his mother and wipe out his father. Whether fantastic or reasonable, these notions were an exercise in a kind of primal-family determinism which could be applied to local acts or to whole sets of motivations. An end result was seen as evidence of a previous aim or of a person's desire to repeat a pattern, frequently without the slightest reference to individual learning. Thus, kissing was seen as an extension of breast-feeding, neatness an extension of toilet-training, miserliness a desire to hold on to one's feces, and ambition in all forms an expression of penis-power; the list was unending. The phenomena of homosexuality were approached in the same way with elaborate new conjectures concerning identity, oedipal motivations, and various fears.

These ideas deserve a passing mention for several reasons. They were not only quickly accepted by psychiatry (where they still dominate formal theories), they also proved to have a lasting popular appeal—ideas that can be stated without reference to their phantasmagoric underpinnings, and which have interchangeable parts that can be rearranged to "explain" any instance one might encounter. Thus, it is still widely believed that a boy turns out to be homosexual when he identifies with his mother and becomes effeminate. Or, if he identifies with her without becoming effeminate, then he must be trying to take her place with his father (either to win his father's love or keep the hostile fellow appeased). Or, by identifying with his mother, he later wants to repeat the joys he experienced with her by choosing boys whom he can treat as his mother treated him. Or without identifying with her at all, his wish to have sex with his mother becomes transformed into a wish to enjoy the kind of sex she enjoys. Or maybe he is really heterosexual after all, but is in love with his mother and wants to stay true to her, so he gives up all other women. Or simply by loving her too much he can have his sexuality prematurely aroused at a time when it has nowhere to go but toward other boys. Or if she is a mean mother, he comes to hate her, ever afterward disliking and distrusting all women. Or whether he loves her or hates her, on discovering she has no penis he develops a "castration complex" that forces him to turn to other males in a need for sex-with-safety. . . .

In fact, the castration-complex seemed to so neatly explain the "fear of heterosexuality" it became—and remains—a centerpin in psychoanalytic theory. Homosexual men are said to be afraid of losing their penis in contact with partners who lack one, and by a certain agility of logic, lesbians are said to fear the "castration" of being penetrated. According to an especially outlandish version of the castration-complex, a man can become homosexual because he unconsciously imagines there are teeth in the vagina, and so, unaccountably, he chooses to place his penis in a cavity where there are real teeth.

Over the years, the curiously impersonal, cartoon-like quality of these notions has been softened by injecting humanistic and reasonable-sounding motivations into them. Special emphasis has been placed on various sorts of inadequacy-feelings. With these kinds of revisions, the basic ideas have persisted in psychiatry and have more than ever filtered down into popular thinking, where they continue to satisfy the curiosity of the unwary. Thus, it is still widely believed that homosexuality stems from "identity problems," from a fear of the opposite sex, from various infantile "fixations," and most palpably of all, from parental influences. A weak father is occasionally blamed, but by far the chief villain in the play is the dominant, the smothering, or the close-binding mother.*

---

*The dominant-mother theory has come into such extraordinary prominence as to deserve a special note. For good reasons, sex researchers have never accepted the notion, but it has had quite a run in both armchair psychiatry and low-grade popular sociology—perhaps helped along in recent years by the fashionable tendency to attribute any individual's plight less to factors within himself than to some outside authoritarian oppressor. The dominant mother seemed to fit the shoe. With or without that weak father at her side, she was first credited with causing most male homosexuality. Later, she was implicated as well in the origins of schizophrenia. After that, she was cited as largely responsible for alcoholism, and soon she

Actually, none of these theories would have held up even if they had been more carefully formulated. All were doomed from the outset by their underlying assumptions. By viewing homosexuality as a result of a damaged or blocked heterosexuality (a kind of choice-by-default), the whole thrust of the inquiry became focused on the real or imagined negations in a person's life. It was a pointless effort at best, since all sexual attractions are based on positive motives: the real or imagined benefits a person hopes to gain by a sexual conquest or by "possessing" the partner. Once the whole question of homosexuality is properly raised in terms of its own motivations, one at least has a chance to pursue its very considerable variations.

Even when viewed from a distance there is an astonishing diversity in homosexuality, beginning with how it first presents itself. It may arise at such an early age as to appear to have been inborn or, as a conscious urge, it may occur for the first time well into adulthood. At almost any age it may take shape only gradually, often as a result of increasingly effective try-outs. As an ongoing pattern it may seem to start suddenly with a single impressive experience. Much more often, a homosexual response turns out on close examination to have been well established long before becoming overt. Sometimes it appears to have a certain dispositional support; more often it does not. Very young boys frequently associate what is male with what is sexual in such a way as to arrive at a powerful homosexual thrust before realizing

---

was named as a major cause of drug addiction. Still later it was "discovered" that her loud ways interfere with the appetite of young children, causing underweight—or else that she tends to force-feed her offspring and thus is responsible for overweight as well. In fact, in the study of not a single negatively defined behavior has she been found either absent or innocent. Apparently she is a hazard to success as well: A recent study of medical students "found" that not only dropouts, but unhappy adults as a group, had "smother mothers." Thus, the whole issue has become ridiculous on its surface; underneath, it is a technical monstrosity. Certainly the mother-son closeness that sometimes occurs in homosexuality is far better interpreted as the product than as the cause of the disposition which supports it.

that heterosexual possibilities even exist. Not that these and a host of other sexual starts are the only beginnings of homosexuality; it can begin from sources far away from sex. In fact, eroticism often arrives as a late guest at its own banquet: A high degree of affection or rapport between two people, especially if they see each other across an otherwise unbridgeable barrier of age or of status, can easily generate sexual feelings.

A boy who for any reason develops an intense admiration for another male may soon find his adoration drifting toward the erotic. Certainly there is much in our society that encourages a boy to especially appreciate male qualities and male accomplishments. He is supposed to strive for these in his ego-modeling, and does, but he can also develop an intense admiration for the seemingly wondrous attainments of a usually slightly older male model, too. A high-intensity admiration very easily becomes eroticized, especially when it is focused on a particular individual—a result all the more likely when a youngster is sexually precocious or has still other reasons for welcoming a sexual contact.

It has often been thought that boys who have "identity problems" or who feel inferior in some sense are the ones who are inclined to admire the masculine attainments of others enough to eroticize them. And by extension, a host of other insecurities, as well as low aggressiveness in general, have been thought relevant. Sometimes these descriptions do fit, though by no means as neatly or as often as one might suppose. Certainly the "down" qualities of timidity, squelch, and self-criticism are not very reliably transformed into the "up" stuff of aspirations, admirations, and the like. Thus, no correlation at all has been found between timidity and homosexuality. In fact, the aggressive swashbuckler is considerably more inclined to become involved in homosexuality than is the timid bookkeeper. Nor does low self-esteem or being a "loner" imply any trend in sexual orientation. And yet, in various combinations these qualities can be relevant, especially when they are at odds with other aims a person may have. Evelyn Hooker has noted (with a careful eye to aspirations) that a boy who sees himself as set apart from a nearby peer group often views other boys as having a certain prized alliance—a situation that can breed envy, desire, and the invention of an erotic solution to his problem, particularly if he finds an especially admired group member with whom a sexual bridge is possible.

The results, however, can be the same without any social misalignment. Even a boy who is near the top of his group and knows it, especially if he is somewhat idealistic, is quite capable of having his aspirations continually soar ahead of his own achievements. Much like a musclebuilder who is fired ever more by each bit of improvement, it is as if his whole concept of maleness and the very encouragement he gets from what he has already accomplished lead him to constantly raise his sights. In the spirit of this abounding appetite, he may be quite ready not only to glorify an admired male, but to search for one and often, then, to engineer a sexual contact.*

On the other hand, a homosexual value system can begin to take shape in an entirely different way—i.e., without the presence of "ideals," high aspirations, or envy in any form, not at first anyway. The whole orientation can start from almost purely physical associations. Young boys are often fascinated with the anatomy and functional capacities of male genitalia. To explore these and to indulge in homosexual play—especially when it is stealthily done or when it involves a courtship-like overcoming of another male's hesitancy—can make the homosexual alternative exciting. In fact, the "chemistry" of such situations can be so enticing that no overt sexual experimentation is necessary: An imaginative and sexually precocious boy's fantasies of what he would *like* to do or to explore with a specific male can be

---

*Technically speaking, there is no difference between the origin of homosexuality in the case of this "champion" and in that of the frail fellow with the inferiority feelings. In both cases, male attributes have become eroticized through an extreme admiration of them. Moreover, there is nothing definitive about either the level of a person's achievements or the height of his aspirations alone. What counts is the *perceived distance* between them—in a nutshell, the distance he sees between where he is and where he would like to be in terms of accomplishment, image, or whatever. Thus it is the contrast implicit in this distance which determines a person's appetite for same-sex attributes and, consequently, his readiness to admire them, to eroticize them, and to import still more of them.

sufficient, and in some cases may even generate more excitement than would an actual try-out.

What is more astonishing, the first step in the whole process can take place in the total absence of any partner, real or imagined. A considerable body of data indicates that boys who begin masturbating early (usually before puberty) while simultaneously looking at their own genitalia can build a crucial associative connection between maleness, male genitalia, and all that is sexually valuable and exciting.[78] These associations amount to an eroticism which is "ready" to extend itself to other male attributes, particularly to those of a later same-sex partner. This associative pattern sometimes manages to preempt heterosexual interests, not only by coming first but by vitalizing a nearby thought-chain most boys entertain to some extent: that since girls have no penis, they are sexless and thus sexually uninteresting.

This whole line of development in which maleness is the target as well as the gun of sex is no mere invention of armchair theorists. Its reality is supported by an impressive amount of parallel evidence. As a group, males who have a high homosexual proclivity more often come from a sexually precocious segment of the population than from slower-maturing segments.[142,82] And not only do homosexual males tend to arrive at puberty early, they tend to start masturbating much earlier (and continue it more extensively the rest of their lives) than do males who are less early and less active sexually.* Conversely, males who belong to that portion of the population which arrives at puberty relatively late tend to be less active sexually and are extraordinarily prone to being entirely heterosexual. Perhaps this connection

---

*Before the sexual precociousness of homosexual males (as a group) was tabulated by the Kinsey Research, Freud and a number of later psychoanalysts had noticed it, but by not knowing its correlates, they misread it. Freud attributed this precocity to the sexual overstimulation the child receives in the oedipal situation. Irving Bieber and his followers not only assumed the same overstimulation, but attributed it directly to the sins of the close-binding-intimate mother.[28] Anyone who wishes to continue entertaining such notions must now be prepared to account for how anything a boy's mother can possibly do to him can physically bring him to puberty early and generally give him a larger-than-average penis size.[125]

between late maturation and heterosexuality is due in part to the fact that the active sexual conditioning of late-maturing males takes place at a time when they and their peers are de-emphasizing male values. But before placing too much stock in such neat sociologic explanations, it is worth remembering that the same basic trends prevail among lower mammals.*

But exactly what does all this mean? It does not quite mean that early sexual associations and excitements, by themselves, can produce a fully motivated homosexuality. And yet, there is every indication that these early biases wield a powerful if not always decisive influence. At the very least, they ripen an individual for the ideational and experiential impressions he may later weave into a homosexual value system. To eroticize male attributes already alerts a boy to a hierarchy of male qualities and invites him to make the kinds of comparisons in which his own assets may seem outpaced and outdistanced by those of a particularly admired partner.

At first glance, this might again suggest that "inferiority feelings" are a source of homosexual motivations. But it is important to understand that these feelings are themselves derivative: Erotization always tends to raise the value of the items it touches, not only by exalting them, but by keeping a person's aspiration level soaring ahead of his own attainments. Often the result is to make a person feel a sharp disparity between what he has and what he would like to have. Even the confident and utterly secure male

---

*It is worth noting in passing that the early Victorians, long credited with not knowing anything of importance about sex, had a theory of homosexuality which was quickly thrown out of court by the first sexologists but which now appears to have contained more than a smattering of perspicacity. They believed that masturbation and homosexuality were somehow linked and that both were related to a boy's being "oversexed." Their formulations were crude and were no doubt derived more from irrelevant moral assumptions than from empirical observation, but a few of the connections they drew between early masturbation, sexual precocity, and homosexuality have now been fully substantiated. Thus, for a boy to reach puberty early, to begin masturbation even before that, and to look at his own genitalia in the process are among the highest known correlates of homosexuality.[142,82,264]

who has eroticized male attributes is ready to improve what he has by sexually importing refinements and additions from an admired partner. Thus, in a sense, it hardly matters what a person thinks of himself; an exalted ideal is never fully satisfied by one's own achievements.

At the opposite extreme from these examples in which eroticism develops first and then finds its target, there are instances in which a boy develops an intense personal attraction to a particular male—often a stranger or near-stranger with whom he has no thought of sex. He may have a fierce urge to know and to be close to a particular teacher, a young policeman, one of his father's friends, or an older boy in another class at school whom he has not yet met. (Young lesbians sometimes have equivalent responses, except that it is rare for a girl to select a stranger as the object of her affections, and rarer still for her pursuit of the target-female to gain much momentum before there are grounds for an emotional rapport.)

It might "make sense" to suppose that such powerful attractions are forthcoming only from disturbed or socially displaced children, as is sometimes the case and as psychiatric reports routinely assume. But in general, it is far from accurate to picture these youngsters as timid waifs, self-critical and isolated from their peers while being neglected at home. On the contrary, they are often especially facile socially and may be unusually well related to their peers and parents, frequently using this very security and sociability to launch a vigorous campaign of pursuit, a veritable seduction of the target-male.

And yet, in an up-close examination, it is hard to classify these examples as either sexual or nonsexual. Often such a boy has little or no previous awareness of sex (let alone try-outs), nor does he usually anticipate anything sexual at the outset. His later descriptions place the emphasis elsewhere: "I just wanted to be near that guy and maybe put my arms around him; I had no idea of what, if anything, was supposed to happen next." "I remember being amazed at the time that I didn't know what I wanted; it was a terrific urge to maybe crawl inside him in some way." (Does this latter detail reflect a certain male proclivity to penetrate the partner? Perhaps so; women often describe themselves as having wanted to "become part of" or to "belong to" their partners.) A scene almost classical in form is, "I finally managed to land in bed with my brother's friend when he spent the night; fortunately he reached over and made a move—bang! it was like getting exactly what I wanted without knowing I had wanted it." A notable feature is that with an uncanny regularity the target-male turns out to be homosexual himself, quite regardless of whether either person knew it at the time.

Particularly powerful attractions of this sort can well up instantly, as if out of nowhere, and sometimes may drive a person to overcome almost insurmountable barriers. Here is an example which, though exotic in certain ways, is not at all rare in its outlines: A boy of fourteen was riding his bicycle down the street of a Far Eastern capital, when an American diplomat passed in a limousine. Their eyes met for a moment. The boy felt such a strong desire to know the man, he sped after the car. It pulled up at the embassy, which happened to be only two blocks away. He waited for hours to see the man who, it turned out, did not remember having seen him before, but they exchanged a few words as he got back into the car. The man later described feeling a certain urgency in the boy, "and something in myself, but it didn't amount to much." (He did not think of himself as primarily homosexual at that time and had never had the slightest sexual interest in young males. The boy was completely inexperienced sexually, "but I did have trouble keeping my eyes off one of my teachers the year before, though in my country it is very impolite to stare.") The boy waited nearby to see the man the next day, and the next, and the next after that. As the man later described the breakthrough, "I had to take the little bastard out for ice cream to get him off the embassy steps." Of course, there was more to it than that, but even when he took the boy home the first time, matters were still not settled; one of the first questions to the youngster was, "What exactly do you want?" to which the boy replied, "I don't know; I just want to be with you, to be near you and maybe to touch you if that's all right." By that time it was indeed all right, but things still moved at a snail's pace to hear the boy tell it: "I wanted to spend the night and did, but there I was with an erection in my head [and nowhere else] for hours before I finally got this American speed demon to take me on a guided tour."

In this example, as in so many others, it is as if the young, inexperienced homosexual has a ready-made appetite, a worked-out value system which is neither fully eroticized nor consciously realized until an appropriately complementary partner is suddenly encountered. And yet, the speed and precision with which the target-male is chosen often seem downright intuitive—or in the not-necessarily-better language of psychology, the process might be described as a lightning assimilation of minimal cues in which the qualities of the partner, his appropriateness of fit, and his readiness to respond are all correctly assessed.

Much less mysteriously than this or than any of the value-based origins of homosexuality, a homosexual pattern is sometimes established on a "practice first" basis. At an early age children often discover that homosexual contacts are possible and that they work. Sometimes a boy's realization that he is violating social rules adds spice to his homosexual experiments. More often, the context is the other way around: Young children have usually heard warnings about heterosexual contacts and little or nothing about homosexuality. Thus, in a spirit of conformity (rather than with the spice of being violational) a young boy may become repeatedly involved in homosexual activities without a clear knowledge that they are anything special, that they have a name, or that they are strictly forbidden. In fact, a certain childhood naïveté about homosexuality is so frequent that sex researchers have consistently found young boys to be more free in discussing their homosexual than their heterosexual experiences.[142]*

Shortly after the turn of the century, widespread recognition of frequent early-adolescent male homosexuality led to the notion that perhaps this is a phase that *all* boys go through, and that a lasting homosexuality is simply the result of a person becoming

---

*In theory, one might expect these observations to apply to girls as well as boys, but in practice, they do not. It is almost unheard-of for young girls to become involved in casually begun, purely experimental homosexual try-outs.

"fixated" at this level. (A prominent psychoanalyst once confessed to Kinsey that he thought himself to be somewhat peculiar in that he could find no trace of homosexuality in his own childhood.) The idea is still bandied about, though it can easily be shown to be spurious. Even the relatively prevalent adolescent homosexuality of the Victorian era was not high enough to substantiate it as a phase. And, of course, if it were a phase it would be cross-cultural, which it is not. Furthermore, the whole "fixation" theory is utterly embarrassed by the considerable number of adults who have both heterosexual and homosexual motivations, and who thus cannot be labeled as either fixed or unfixed. Therefore, the only aspect of the whole issue which is still worth serious consideration is the extent to which early homosexual try-outs are able to establish ongoing motivations.

Certainly most adolescent homosexual activities are inconsequential. The masturbatory sessions of groups of boys (to see who can reach orgasm first or ejaculate farthest) as well as most one-to-one contacts amount to hardly more than explorations in erotica. Even homosexual males describe these kinds of experiences as having been impersonal and unimportant. Of the remaining much smaller number of instances in which early homosexual experiences do lead to ongoing patterns, a few qualify as a kind of simple, direct conditioning; others are not so simple.

There are adolescents (and a few late-arriving adults) who begin having homosexual experiences which at first may have little appeal and only gradually become meaningful. (The same could be said for the way many people develop heterosexual tastes.) This is the conditioning-by-experience which public opinion anticipates in its attitudes toward the seduction of minors. And the same idea is reflected in the homosexual adage, "Today's trade is tomorrow's competition" (*trade* being a man who lies back to be fellated without otherwise paying any attention to his partner or admitting any specific homosexual interest). It is as if sexual practice by itself can establish a pattern which then becomes self-motivating.

Sometimes the whole pattern takes shape more rapidly. There is an occasional adolescent who, because of his training or disposition, has hardly thought of sex—let alone experienced it— before becoming involved in repeated homosexual contacts, perhaps with the boy next door. Arriving at sex from this particular background, he may be especially impressed by his first experiences. It has sometimes been argued that for such events to have a pattern-setting impact there must have been a preliminary groundwork for it: Perhaps the boy has already eroticized maleness, or perhaps something in his life-situation makes him especially receptive to the kinds of intimate affection sex can offer. Certainly these explanations apply in particular instances, but in others, nothing fits quite as well as the observation that it was the impact of these first experiences that imbued the events with lasting significance. In fact, it is not unusual for a man's strongest sexual response (women appear to be less conditionable in this regard) to be narrowly limited to persons who closely resemble his first partner—perhaps in age, body build, or disposition.*

Since a single impressive experience sometimes appears to be pattern setting, a number of sex researchers have left room in their thinking for the possibility of "one shot" conditioning. Its existence is almost certainly more apparent than real, but it may be worth one more look. The basic idea is the same as before: "If specific presupports for homosexuality are minimal, and if the experience itself was what started the ball rolling, is it not obvious that the impact of that experience was what gave it lasting significance?" Not quite; the impact itself cannot be taken for granted. There is considerable evidence indicating that for even a first sexual experience to be all that impressive, a variety of conditions have to be "right" for it—conditions which usually entail at least the elements of a value system, plus a person's being ready and willing to cooperate with his partner in maintaining that critical distance which effective sexual interactions always require. In

---

*A note of caution is in order here. The outstanding traits of a partner can take on value and meaning without having had anything to do with why that kind of partner first came to be chosen or preferred. Sexual conditioning is replete with instances in which a particular item—perhaps the perfume or shaving lotion a person uses, or a melody associated with a love affair—takes on lasting significance without having had anything to do with the original choice.

fact, a person's own actions and his readiness to take them are usually far more important than his conscious motivations; the male prostitute may be motivated by money, or think he is, and still turn out to be "tomorrow's competition."

That homosexual practices, freely engaged in, can result in an ongoing homosexual appetite has often seemed especially evident at lower social levels. Many observers have attributed this to the looser if not delinquent morals of uneducated, often poverty-blighted adolescents who easily turn to homosexual activity for convenience or money (and who, indeed, are likely to retain a homosexual appetite for the rest of their lives). At first glance, this interpretation seems all the more appropriate in, say, southern Italy and Arab countries (an observation that led a whole genera-tion of sexologists to believe that hot weather is a major cause of homosexuality). It is true that many people at lower social levels (and many Latins and Moslems at higher levels) hold quite permissive attitudes toward a boy's (or even a man's) homosexual expressions. Homosexual "play" tends to be seen as just that, or as really nothing at all, so long as his general behavior is clearly "male." And the same mentality—a decidedly "export" view of male sexuality—is easily able to embrace numerous other ration-alizations that take the curse off homosexual contacts by attribut-ing them to some temporary duress, be it a shortage of women or a desire for financial gain.

But when one takes a closer look at the examples, the homo-sexual motives usually turn out to have far more specificity and more importance to the individuals than can be accounted for by "loose morals," money, or mere sex pressure. Often there is more than enough picking and choosing of partners, even an idealiza-tion (if not of the partner, then of maleness itself), to indicate the presence of a quite definite sexual value system. In particular instances, this value system stems most directly from repeated early experiences. But since the cultures and social levels at which loosely begun homosexual practices are the most prevalent are also the ones which laud male values to the sky, we are again faced with the probability that values more often lead to experi-ences than vice versa.

At any rate, there is a note of irony in the fact that regardless of how easy or hard it may be for a homosexual pattern to become established by overt experiences, its least effective starting sources are precisely those about which the public is most anxious and on guard. Neither "child seduction" nor the kinds of instances law courts describe as "impairing the morals of a minor" seem to have much effect. Child seduction, though it can be traumatic when parents make an issue of it, is virtually powerless to start a sexual pattern. (Kinsey attributed its ineffectiveness to the fact that direct conditioning of this sort simply requires a stronger sex drive than most young children possess.) Sexual experiences around the time of puberty can be more influential, but even so, it is hard to find instances of people having developed homosexual tastes through casual or "accidental" experiences. On close examination, it usually turns out that the die was already cast by then and often that the "victim" was the provocateur. This latter detail is of more than passing significance when it is realized that a person who merely participates in a sexual activity is much less subject to being conditioned by it than is the instigator.

The various examples which have been cited here amount to hardly more than a cross-section of the major influences which can sponsor homosexuality; the list is by no means complete. Notably lacking are most of the combinational origins, combinations that can be quite intricate. The history of a person's sexual conditioning often reflects such an intertwining of attitudes that have led to the build-up of his particular sexual value system and reinforcements (including try-outs) that have established its feasibility, it is no simple matter to assign appropriate weight to these broadly differing inputs. Nor is it necessarily true that whatever came first was most important, or that any particular element in a different context would have supported the same trend. A composite of influences tends to work as a unit, gaining most of its power from how the components fit together and interact.

Moreover, a person's final sexual pattern usually extends far beyond the components on which it was first based. An early pattern, once organized, tends to extend itself. One man whose homosexuality began as little more than an exciting eroticism and another whose homosexuality began on a high plane of emotional attachment soon develop tastes which become indistinguishable: Both men then require partners with whom they can find a blend of emotional and sexual responses. Much the same can be said for the eventual similarity of other starting differences. There are those shy and conflicted youngsters whose self-attitudes have caused them to greatly admire more adroit members of their sex, and there are those self-assured youngsters whose high aspirations or whose very success in perfecting particular aspects of maleness have caused them to develop exactly the same male admirations—admirations which at high levels of intensity almost automatically become eroticized. Not only are these different starting points all but indistinguishable later, people can end up with exactly the same conflicts, or lack of them, and with the same intense focus on same-sex partners even when it was the erotization which occurred first—as, indeed, the highest correlates of homosexuality (early puberty, high sex-drive, etc.) suggest is often the case.

A larger observation is that no single element in homosexuality, no one original influence, is by itself likely to be definitive. The final existence of any sexual orientation depends upon the extent to which its various parts have reinforced each other in producing a structure, a system of values, a pattern of responses. The directionality of the whole system and much of its force depend upon the effectiveness with which it purifies its aims and wards off competing alternatives.

Just how a budding sexual value system drowns out competing alternatives is central to the whole question of how exclusive orientations arise. Part of the way in which a sexual response becomes polarized is crystal clear. As soon as a person starts to develop a sexual interest in the qualities and traits of one sex, he usually begins to view the analogous features of the opposite sex not only as different but as dissonant. (The very difference between the sexes invites a pivotal choice: Society itself defines males and females as opposites, and by the time a person eroticizes one of them, they are opposites indeed.) To the man who has begun to respond to, say, the muscularity and assertiveness of males, the female's roundness and submissive allure may not only leave him cold, but arouse distinct aversion-reactions.*

Not surprisingly, there is much within the primary or positive side of a value system that not only dictates what will be attractive, but serves to stabilize it. Once started, an organized preference quickly begins to extend itself throughout a whole inventory of gender-related items. For the homosexual man, male movements, male attitudes, particular bodily features, even such things as the timbre of certain male voices frequently begin to be integrated into his image of what is erotic. In this sense, his trove of sex-related items is expansive—expansive both in the number of attributes he rates and their meaningfulness to him. But with this refinement, anyone's aversion to the not-chosen items also tends to expand, resulting in fewer and fewer partners who are able to qualify as desirable. Thus, the homosexual's aversions come to include not only the "contradictory" traits of the opposite sex, but many traits he sees as undesirable in males (perhaps too fat or thin, too old or young, too aggressive or shy, or whatever), so that all women and most men are soon out of the running.

Of course, the heterosexual male extends and narrows his value system in exactly the same way, focusing his sexual interest so sharply upon particular kinds of women that no males and relatively few females qualify. (The man who says he is turned on by "all women" really means all whom he considers; he is simply not considering most who are, say, between the ages of eight and eighty, nor most within any other wide range of variation.)

The whole process by which people develop polarized sexual interests is so clear and accounts for the narrowed tastes of so much of the total population, the question is not why this narrow-

---

*There are rare instances in which a person develops strong aversions to more or less all members of one sex from having had numerous negative (not usually sexual) experiences with them, thus facilitating sexual interests in the other sex. This is an unusual sequence not only because sexual motives require a positive valence, but because to hate something still does not cause a person to love its opposite. There are all sorts of "woman haters" who have not the slightest sexual interest in males.

ing occurs but why it does not always occur. And yet, obviously, not everyone's sexual responses become narrowly polarized—witness bisexuality.

The Bisexual Puzzle

Most people do not believe that bisexuality really exists. Nobody questions that there are people who have sex with both men and women. Nor is there much hesitancy to grant bisexuality in some distant time or place, perhaps in some native tribe or in Ancient Greece. But within our own society, a genuine bisexuality is hard to fathom. Usually its homosexual element is either explained away as substitutional or is taken as evidence that the individual is, in fact, homosexual and that his heterosexuality is merely a pretense. Even courts of law make these interpretations.

The reasons are not hard to find. Most people are themselves one way or the other. A person is intuitively aware of what is involved in his own value system and is sufficiently invested in it to find the differing preferences of others hard to understand. But the thought of someone actually sharing one's own preferences without also sharing one's aversions strikes most people as utterly inconceivable. The homosexual is likely to be particularly dubious of bisexuality, for he is aware that many people whose tastes are not different from his own nevertheless marry or otherwise go through the motions of heterosexuality for defensive or for other extraneous reasons.

Nevertheless, after all counterfeit examples are cast aside, there still remain several kinds of genuine bisexuality. There are males who are able to respond equally well to both sexes by using virtually no value system at all. They tend not to become invested in the personal aspects of any of their partners. For them, male-female differences in body shape and in personality are of minimal importance; their own sexual performance and a partner's readiness to cooperate are what count. (Sexually they are exporters, not importers.) A few sex researchers have described these males as simply ready to "stick it in anywhere"—an observation that is less than perfect but which might well suffice for certain lower social level males and for a few others whom Kinsey has described as having a minimal psychological investment in any of their sexual activities.

Most other people who respond about equally well to both sexes have developed a double value system: They rate and choose their male and female partners by applying quite separate sets of criteria. But of course, this explanation hardly more than restates the question of how double value systems come about. Sometimes the answer is obvious: A person whose sexual conditioning has been determined largely by early sex experiences with both sexes simply develops positive sexual associations to each. A precise analogy is found in language-learning: A person who learns only one language while growing up tends to carry an accent and various imperfections in any others he later learns. But the child who grows up in a polylingual home easily develops separate phonetics and even separate thinking contexts for each.

There are still other persons who are bisexual without having had both sexes validated by early experience. More often than not, they are highly discriminating in choosing both their male and female partners, a clear sign they are using two value systems. In fact, their separate systems are made all the clearer by their near-universal tendency to point out that although they enjoy their contacts with both men and women, "You must understand, the two experiences are *entirely different*." (Often the two experiences are kept different by a selective inversion: A man may always be aggressive with women and submissive with men—much as Julius Caesar was said to have been "every woman's husband and every man's wife.") Is it that the bisexual is selecting particular qualities in particular partners which complement different components in himself? Undoubtedly so; but the question at the moment is not what motivates two value systems, but how anyone manages to tolerate the contradictions between them.

For instance, if a man is especially responsive to women who have smooth, round bosoms, and yet by another set of values he has a homosexual requirement which may put him in bed with a man who happens to have an especially flat, hairy chest, how is he able to "look past" that chest? (A double value system permits a person to "shift gears" from one sex to the other and to respond to their differing qualities, but a direct reversal of a fetishlike item of preference is ordinarily too great a contradiction for even the wondrous attainments of bisexuality.) He is able to look past it because, while he has no interest in it, neither has he developed any particular aversion to it. It is as if he "selects out" what he wants from women and from men without allowing the unwanted aspects of either to get in his way.

Evidently, then, most bisexuality depends upon a person's ability to respond to *particular* male and female qualities—an ability which can be maintained to the extent, and only to the extent, that the central items of erotic significance do not arouse a negative valence (an aversion) toward their implied opposites. In a person who has highly specific tastes (and is not just an "exporter") it is a remarkable achievement, particularly when it is realized that the exclusive orientation of everyone else is based on a single value system which has been stabilized by an almost inevitable build-up of aversions to whatever is perceived as contradictory to it. Thus, the entirely heterosexual man who happens to be especially responsive to, say, a woman's softness and gentle allure may already be quite turned off by thin, assertive females; to him, the very thought of an intimate sexual contact with a hard, angular male is a symphony of horrors.

From this vantage point, it is clear that exclusive heterosexual and homosexual responses have much in common. Both are polarized toward their respective targets and away from their undesired alternatives. And both are equally dependent upon the formation of strong aversion reactions. The persistent effort to attribute exclusive homosexuality to various fears and fixations is almost as wide of the mark as to say that people are exclusively heterosexual because they are afraid of persons of their own sex. Of course, everybody has a certain fear of making sexual contacts which have been validated neither by practice nor desire and, in a sense, all exclusive orientations are "fixations." But it is more useful to realize that the nature of sexual targeting is such that most people eventually want particular kinds of partners and not others. It is a matter of no small consequence that the integrity of a person's sexual orientation and much of its urgency depends upon this directionality—the channeling of sexual interests toward discriminative choices, while leaving one anywhere from oblivious to actually repelled by all other alternatives.

In looking back over the origins of homosexuality, there are so many ways for it to begin and so many interrelated concepts to keep in mind, the diversity is formidable. Fortunately, there are a few commonalities which bring a certain unity into the picture. A homosexual motivation is essentially the same whether it has been stabilized into exclusivity or is part of bisexuality. It always means that a person has eroticized and come to desire same-sex partners (or that he has admired and desired such partners to the point of eroticizing them). In effect, this desire means that the person wants to import admired same-sex attributes and thus that he has a felt-shortage of them. Sometimes this felt-shortage implies an actual shortage, as in the case of certain effeminate males. But what about the large majority of homosexual men who have an abundant (often superabundant) masculinity; how do they manage to retain a felt-shortage of it and thus a desire to import still more? No doubt a behaviorist would point to the power and the durability of early conditioning, but there is more to it than that. Once a value system or value-laden motive of any kind becomes established, it can easily propagate itself—much as a person's struggle for power or for money often tends to whet rather than to satiate the appetite which began it.

Nevertheless, the basic principles of complementation still apply. Nobody wants to import more of exactly what he already has. The homosexual, like everyone else, usually manages to develop his own assets to the point of becoming reasonably satisfied with them; what he wants to import are the differing qualities which have made his partner attractive. Thus, the items of highest import-priority are characteristically those which a person has never tried to develop on his own. The boy or man who has made athletic prowess his long suit may find himself drawn to the bright scholar or the kid who plays the hot piano— and vice versa. In less obvious examples, the contrast between partners may appear slight to an outside observer, but it is always there and constitutes the basis of the attraction. Notions to the effect that the homosexual is looking for some "narcissistic" reflection of his own image are as mythical as was Narcissus himself.

From this vantage point, a last and somewhat troublesome question presents itself. When it is remembered that one of the main motives for heterosexuality is the complementation it affords, the relief it gives a man in rounding out his masculine eccentricity, how can the homosexual comfortably forego this correction, continue to produce his own brand of maleness, and import still more? The general answer is the same as before: By having eroticized it, he has a near-insatiable appetite for it. But this does not necessarily mean he will be comfortable with the excesses of an accumulated masculinity; he might or he might not. At one extreme, there are a few men who soon let up on producing their own maleness once they adopt a mental set for importing it. The result can be a flagrant effeminacy looking for all the world like the exceedingly rare dyed-in-the-wool variety.*

Ordinarily, however, homosexuality neither generates nor springs from anything approaching an outright effeminacy. One frequently seen balance is that of a man who keeps producing his own male qualities and still avoids the sharp edge of masculine eccentricity simply by not taking on the bravado stereotypes many heterosexuals find reinforcing. The result can be a somewhat gentle, often gentlemanly but still quite robust maleness. It may or may not appear "soft," depending on its details and what it is compared with. Not infrequently, it has the effect of seeming to

---

*On some hard-to-specify personal level, there appears to be a general tendency for people to "go out of production" on what they import and to increase their production of whatever they export. It is not yet known exactly what kinds of internal and external circumstances cause this tendency to become exaggerated, to disappear, or to reverse itself, but it is as erratic in heterosexuality as in homosexuality. It has been found, for instance, that a man who lives with his wife and more than one daughter, but who has no sons, is inclined to be exceptionally aggressive.

raise the social level a notch, or of lowering the aggressive level by more than a notch. Still, it is not all that obvious, especially to the untrained eye.*

Far to the other extreme, there are a number of utterly masculine, sometimes supermasculine homosexuals whose toughness at least equals anything to be found in heterosexuality. Consider, for instance, such gunfighters and roustabouts of the Old West as Billy the Kid and Wyatt Earp, innumerable American lumberjacks and cowboys, special types such as Kitchener, Lawrence of Arabia, and many another warrior he-man who has swashbuckled his way through life. There is little question how such men manage to tolerate the extreme masculinity involved in producing, surfacing, and importing every aspect of maleness they can both muster and lay claim to. They are obsessed by everything male and utterly eschew anything weak or feminine, particularly any notion of importing it. Unquestionably they represent the epitome of what can happen when an eroticized maleness gains the full backing of a value system that supports it.

And yet curiously enough, most personal reports on such men suggest they have considerably more balance and pliancy than one might expect. Sexually, they differ enormously from those heterosexual males who rigidly hold on to "being male" by always being dominant with their women. Nor do they share the mentality of the lower-social-level bisexual for whom sex is mainly something one exports. On the contrary, those he-man homosexuals appear to be remarkably affectionate, even tender, in their partner-contacts—qualities that are underlined by the uninhi-

---

*The Kinsey Research interviewers had very trained eyes, and a policy of trying to guess whether or not homosexuality would be in a person's history before asking any questions relating to it. They were able to guess only 15 per cent of the men and 5 per cent of the women. As a measure of behavioral inversion (such as effeminacy) these figures are actually too high, since the interviewers were also taking into account signs of attitude and manner of dress as well as any and all other cues. But as a measure of fleeting and very subtle degrees of obviousness, the figures are a bit too low; each judgment had to be made fairly quickly and thus without benefit of what an extended contact might have revealed.

bited ease with which sex roles are interchanged. In their private relations, a submissive turnabout is not threatening. No doubt it is what it is to most men, only more so: a mode of increasing contact, something that "feels right" at the time and that somehow balances out both their previous and their soon-to-be-resumed excesses of riding the high horse.

After so much mention of unusual personal adaptations, ranging from the extremes of effeminacy to the extremes of toughness, it is important to emphasize again that the great majority of people who are involved in homosexuality are somewhere in the middle of this spectrum, and are not perceptibly different from their heterosexual neighbors. But what about their actual differences, differences from each other as well as from everybody else? Certainly these exist on every level and between each and every individual, but they defy any definitive description. In the final analysis, perhaps one should be content with two or three unifying observations: Homosexuality in all its variations always means that same-sex attributes have become eroticized, have taken on erotic significance. No matter how or when this takes place, each individual perceives a disparity between his own qualities as they presently are, and as they might be with certain additions—thus his struggle to bridge the gap. In all their essentials, the sought-after rewards of homosexual and heterosexual complementations are identical: the symbolic possession of those attributes of a partner which, when added to one's own, fill out the illusion of completeness.

6

Sex
Techniques

Quite a strong case could be made for saying nothing at all about the specific sex practices of homosexuality. It may well be true that most people either already know or could easily imagine all they care to know about these matters—particularly since the "main event" in most sexual contacts has much more to do with the stuff of intimacy and closeness than it does with the nitty-gritty of who puts what where. And yet, as soon as one begins to move into the psychology of sex and into new territories of observation—the intended destinations of this chapter—slight misconceptions about overt activity can lead to serious errors in interpretation. Even for a reader and writer to have different images in mind can be confusing. For these and other reasons, it is important to understand from the outset certain physical aspects of sex and of its surface psychology.

Homosexual relations are widely thought of as mainly mouth-genital contacts and anal intercourse. Apparently, the "penis insertion" characteristics of these actions are irresistibly analogous to the penis-vagina relations of heterosexuality. Certainly oral and anal techniques are common in homosexuality, but in large segments of its population there is a distinct, often exclusive, preference for various forms of mutual masturbation and femoral (between thighs) intercourse. Not that to realize this would necessarily change anybody's impression of homosexuality. No doubt most people will always conceive of male sexuality in general, and male homosexuality in particular, in terms of phallic actions. Certainly this focus invites the kinds of misconceptions which, in turn, tend to obscure the meaning homosexuality has for those who practice it. Thus, a concentration on phallism has made it almost impossible for many people to even conceive of lesbianism—"After all, what could two women do together?" And to various heterosexual men and women who are too inhibited to make oral and anal contacts, the notion that these techniques epitomize homosexuality has helped make it seem especially carnal and "abnormal." These and similar ideas have led to a widely held impression that homosexual practices lack precisely those kinds of affection which, in fact, are usually the main motives behind them.

Homosexuals, too, are often prudish, or for other reasons have a narrow view of what is sexually acceptable. The person who prefers mutual masturbation or a technique involving extensive body contact not infrequently insists that he really isn't interested in other practices—and that most of his partners aren't either, since he "hasn't had any complaints." He may express amazement that other men have a reputation for all sorts of sexual acts he has never encountered and never wanted. Although his attitude may in part be a defense of his own preferences, a more complex psychology is also involved. In most sexual contacts there is a tendency for the choice of activity to be determined (not exactly "chosen" or demanded) by the partner of least flexibility—so easily, in fact, that persons restricted to only a few techniques seldom do hear complaints. Those with greater flexibility are simply more accommodating.

Then, too, people often intuitively (and unconsciously) select each other according to tacit agreements in their fundamental attitudes—attitudes that turn out to have "matched them" sexually in the first place. In fact, a person who prefers particular sex techniques and abhors others may go for years without encountering a single partner whose sexual preferences clash with his own, even though he may never have discussed preferences ahead of time. Thus, a genuine conviction, rather than mere rationalization, often underlies a person's claim that this or that sexual preference is not only his own but is shared by "most people."

Men from lower-social-level backgrounds are more inclined than others to restrict themselves to active anal intercourse in homosexuality—and in heterosexuality, to narrowly adhere to phallic techniques. This preference, often a demand, is in line with several of the lower-level male's biases—a fear of seeming or being less masculine if he is at all submissive, a hesitance to use mouth-contacts or even to depart from the "missionary position."

At middle and upper social levels these strictures are rare. Indeed, here it is not unusual to find men who, though decidedly dominant in other aspects of their lives, prefer to be seduced or otherwise play a submissive role in sex. Sometimes this desire is so out of line with what a man expects his preference ought to be that he is embarrassed by it—the kind of thing his most trusted partner cannot safely mention. Other men readily accept this desire in themselves, thoroughly enjoy reversing their roles, and derive a measure of excitement from the incongruity.

Sometimes contradictions within a person's role-preferences appear to systematically balance out each other. A man who enjoys being aggressive and managerial in most aspects of his life may take a special delight in throwing over this role and becoming submissive—even subservient—in sexual situations. Although a readiness to shift roles is nearly universal among the uninhibited, it seems to be greatly heightened by any forced exaggeration of one side. The married man with a homosexual requirement who forces himself to "live beyond his heterosexual means" often prefers to be submissive in his homosexual contacts; it is almost as if he "corrects for" what he has too much of at home by a certain overindulgence in the opposite.

These same kinds of reversals are just as frequent in lesbian relationships. A woman who has been sexually submissive for years in a heterosexual role may be especially interested in taking the initiative when she is with female partners. And among entirely homosexual women, those who are most assertive throughout courtship are often the ones who are most inclined to abruptly reverse their whole style in the bedroom, suddenly expecting to "be made love to." In fact, this particular kind of reversal is so prevalent among lesbians that it is very frequently a matter of wariness or complaint.

In a sense, these few examples are teasers. They may serve to point up some of the surface complications that are involved in any examination of sex techniques, but to the sex researcher they are much more than that. All such observations, each with its curious bits and paradoxes, fairly bristle with questions—questions that are worth raising mainly because they touch on so much that is common to us all.

All sex techniques deliver gratification at several levels. They satisfy "performance needs" which are fundamental to the species. And when an act carries a role-implication of some kind it may balance or round out a person's picture of himself. Interpersonally, sex techniques provide both the strain and the contact which enable people to express a possessive affection for each other. Certainly these psychological achievements form a major part of all sexual interactions—actions that share quite a few other commonalities as well.

Every sex technique is shaped and biased by influences which stem from four broad sources: *physiology, social considerations,* particular *partners and situations,* and a *psychology* largely their own.

Physiology

The physical influences on sexual behavior stem from the evolutionary background of the human species and from the individual physiology a person inherits. Man's mammalian inheritance has determined the supply and distribution of nerve endings, and, accordingly, which areas of the body have a certain "starting advantage" in sensitivity. The mucous membranes of the mouth, anus and genitalia, certain parts of the head and neck as well as breasts (male and female) are especially sensitive and therefore easily become sexually relevant. Certainly this is the basis on which contacts of genital-to-genital, mouth-to-mouth, and mouth-to-genital have become particularly well established in sexual patterns.

But the human tendency to place restrictions around these directly sexual contacts has frequently made them the target of personal inhibitions and various social taboos. These inhibitions, coupled with man's ability to respond to symbolic cues, often result in far less sensitive areas of the body becoming super-charged with sexual meaning. To many people, a simple touch, a stroke, or a kiss on the shoulder is more exciting than a directly sexual stimulation. Interestingly, the erotic importance of rela-tively insensitive areas of the body may extend into fully activated sexual situations. Many individuals become geared to reach orgasm less on the basis of genital stimulation than of some last-minute seemingly peripheral occurrence, perhaps a tongue-in-ear contact, a moment of hair pulling, hearing or saying particu-lar words, or seeing a detail of one's partner's excitement.

Such cues sometimes gain their importance from various kinds of individualized conditioning, but more is involved. Even people who have little (conscious) interest in small or symbolic cues and who are especially interested in genital acts—acts which perhaps have always been exciting in fantasy—are often surprised to find that these are much less effective in practice. For instance, simultaneous mouth-genital contacts ("sixty-nine") are widely *thought of* as very exciting, and yet they seldom if ever work well in either heterosexual or homosexual relations. For men, this activity places the partner's tongue on the least sensitive side of the penis—and for anybody, it is highly distracting. To both give and receive the same kind of stimulation at the same time is confusing, much like trying to enjoy receiving a back-rub while giving one. Beyond these true but somewhat mechanical expla-nations lies a larger observation: that what works best in day-dreams and in masturbatory fantasies is seldom what is best in practice, and vice versa.

A disparity between fantasy and practice is apparent in the timing of orgasm, too. In fantasy, simultaneous orgasm may be an ideal achievement. But in practice it is so disappointing that experienced partners, especially if they are well matched, try to avoid it. A vicarious participation in a partner's reactions is part of the enjoyment of sex—and since a person's awareness of everything external is at a minimum during his own climax, simultaneous orgasm blinds both partners to each other at precisely the wrong moment. Their synchronization is much more effective when their timing is slightly out of phase—just far enough out for the person who "comes" first to have regained awareness (but not far enough out for his arousal to have plunged too far) by the time the partner reaches climax.

Sex techniques tend to be more varied in homosexual than in heterosexual relations for both physical and psychological reasons. Besides the fact that male-female relations have a highly effective genital-union stereotype to begin with, heterosexuality itself is more subject to convention—an influence which always works against variety. Then, too, clear-cut role-expectancies tend to regularize it. And of course, heterosexual stereotypes are backed further by being socially recommended—even demanded, since variations at any distance are widely regarded as "abnormal." By contrast, no forms of homosexuality have the head start of being approved, let alone demanded. No doubt the range of homosexual techniques is extended further by the fact that none of the choices has any notable anatomical advantage over the others, leaving the whole matter of selection even more to individual invention and preference.

Sometimes, certain physical aspects of sex techniques play a far larger role in determining their feasibility than is commonly supposed. Or to put it the other way around, the difficulties a person may encounter in a particular technique—difficulties which many people quickly ascribe to "psychological blocks"— are often, in fact, attributable to physical details. The man or woman who gags when trying to perform fellatio is not necessarily "rebelling against the act," but may simply not have discovered that a deep breath is required at the start. (Taking a deep breath raises the uvula in the throat, thereby neurologically blocking the gag-response.) Similarly, it is widely assumed in both heterosexual and homosexual relations that anal intercourse either works or doesn't work due to "size" considerations or to various psychological factors—when, in fact, its feasibility largely depends on whether or not at least one of the partners knows to push certain "neurological buttons."

The effectiveness of particular sex techniques is also determined by individual differences that stem from both the nature of the species and from a person's individual heredity. The "neurological hookup" of many men and most women is such that once a fairly high level of arousal has been achieved, any interruption or change of pace is disconcerting. Other people are just the opposite and feel cheated by a straight-line approach to climax. They are especially delighted by the delays and diversional activities that a partner may invite or introduce. The momentary delay entailed in a shift of body position, for instance, may be extended into a protracted period of embracing and stroking, giving the whole contact a more affectionate, more personal quality. A person who especially enjoys sexual surprises and delays is inclined to make the most of mood changes and off-beat body explorations. There may be elaborate techniques where a tongue is run over an eyelid, while hand and finger pressure are applied to the perineum and anus, and a toe is simultaneously pressed into the partner's instep. Just as unexpectedly, a clear-cut assertiveness may suddenly wilt into a submissive quiescence as the partner is invited to take over the initiative.

Most (but not all) of the sex techniques lesbians use may seem relatively bland by comparison. Their appearance of simplicity and plainness stems mainly from an emphasis on gentle, largely peripheral stimulations as opposed to the more definite, more focused, and more genital techniques of males. This difference in emphasis is attributable to fundamental differences between women and men rather than to anything unique in lesbian psychology. Far more than most men imagine, most women require—and most lesbians deliver—protracted amounts of subtle, continuous, tactile stimulation that is relevant to an emotional context and is focused more on the total person than on any specific genital contact. Thus, for women especially, heterosexual activity is a compromise between the requirements of men and women—while among lesbians, sex is geared toward a diversified emphasis on what nearly all women consider most important: a build-up starting with peripheral stimulations that eventually concentrates on genital actions last, if at all.

The initial build-up of sexual interest between two women usually involves a relatively protracted period of social and affectional responses—affectional exchanges which may look like nothing more than that long after they have actually become intensely erotic. Even after overtly sexual actions are begun, kissing and generalized body contacts of the sort used in heterosexual petting may remain primary. The build-up to orgasm may entail oral and manual stimulation of breasts, clitoris, and labia minora, but it sometimes involves only generalized body contacts and an intertwining of legs in which pressure and friction are delivered to the labia. Not that the sexually articulate lesbian is so indefinite; she knows how to deliver exceedingly high levels of stimulation by such techniques as exerting thumb pressure inside the lower side of the vaginal vestibule while simultaneously making a mouth-clitoral contact—techniques which in sheer efficiency probably exceed anything a man would know how to deliver. But even where sexual actions are so simple as to seem pale to people who have a phallic concept of sex (including numerous heterosexual women) lesbian techniques zero in on female responsiveness with great effectiveness by placing the stimulation precisely where the sensitivity is.

The sex techniques of homosexual males are quite effective, too. What they lose by not having vaginal intercourse appears to be fully compensated for by the efficiency of their own techniques. As a result of their common physiology, partners of the same sex know intuitively how particular actions feel and how these are likely to be interpreted by each other. Thus, male homosexuals, too, are often able to make simple techniques exceptionally effective.

Social Influences

Social attitudes affect sex techniques mainly through the pressures of particular expectations and taboos. Whether sexual activity will occur face to face, whether the mouth may be used, whether a person is permitted to fondle a partner's genitalia, and dozens of other rules and recommendations are specified by the mores. In a number of ways, sex techniques and the mores themselves are sharply affected by the basic values an entire culture (or a particular social level) lives by. For instance, the romantic idealization of a sex partner can occur only where there is the underlying hope of improving oneself by possessing and "orally incorporating" the desired qualities of a partner. These attitudes clearly underlie all the connections between kissing, admiration, and the use of the mouth in sex relations. And to some extent, every kind. of caressing, touching, and probing fulfills at least a momentary desire to possess what is seen and admired in the partner.

Viewed from this angle, the relatively simple, straightforward genital techniques used in most primitive tribes and among most people at lower social levels in our own society appear to be much more a matter of how sex is conceptualized than simply a result of taboos. Certainly whenever sex is thought of mainly as a release or as a means of conquest, it is likely to be faster and more directly genital than are the excursions taken by partners who want to savor and possess particular qualities of each other.

These differences in conceptualization and hence in motivation are the same in heterosexual and homosexual situations. In both, a lower social level background tends to abbreviate a person's sexual repertoire. But at higher social levels, the whole cultural emphasis upon affection, idealization, and reciprocity has the effect of expanding the repertoire of actions that are seen as sexually meaningful. And with this expanded range of response, the emphasis people place on any particular activity tends to be reduced, both by the greater variety of choices and by the shift toward psychological details: *What* is done is usually less important than *who* is doing it, *how* it is done, the spirit with which it is done, and the extent to which the partner enjoys it.

On broader levels, too, sexual priorities are shaped by a combination of moral edicts and personal conceptualizations. Certainly there is less homosexuality in our society than there would be if taboos against it did not exist. But the same kinds of taboos also dampen heterosexuality, often to the extent of making homosexual choices seem the least violational. Every particular sex technique is subject to much the same fate: It is conceptualized by a portion of the population as "bad" and therefore out of the question, by others as taboo but exciting, and by still others as entirely acceptable, even poetic. Because of such variations, many homosexuals enforce a personal ban on mouth-genital contacts, or on anal intercourse, or on kissing, or on all of these—but perhaps not on masturbation. For others, the sky is the limit—except that masturbatory techniques are utterly out. In fact, not a single sex activity fails to be taboo for particular individuals while being rated as especially valuable by other individuals, whether heterosexual or homosexual.

Often a person's attitude toward a particular sex activity and his freedom to use it depend on the context. Many people feel free to use techniques in their homosexual contacts that they would not feel free to use with members of the opposite sex—and vice versa. For instance, a man may confine any show of affection to his heterosexual contacts, either because affection between men embarrasses him or because it makes him see himself as more involved in homosexuality than he cares to admit.

But it is worth remembering that taboos and personally held restrictions do not always inhibit sex—that they may, in fact, enormously intensify it. Anatole France used to say that one of Christianity's greatest contributions to Western civilization was the impetus it gave to sex—by which he meant that Christianity's antisexuality reinforces the barriers behind which sexual contacts are made more thrilling. Certainly for people who are conditioned toward homosexuality, the high taboos against it not infrequently add a note of surreptitiousness and mystery that heightens its appeal—just as most people derive extra erotic arousal from violating taboos of one sort or another. The turning of a normally repugnant contact into something that is sexually exciting is commonplace. An everyday example is deep kissing, where the hurdling of hygienic concerns sparks additional arousal. Thus, it is precisely those persons who are most aware of sanitation—who would not consider using a public drinking cup or another person's toothbrush—who are most inclined to practice deep kissing.

More intense examples are mouth-anal contacts (rimming) and near or full-fledged sado-masochistic practices in which biting, pinching, skin sucking, abusive language, and moments of sharp pain are brought into sex. The enjoyment of sado-masochistic techniques is usually limited to persons who have had exceptionally strong social training in either the be-kind-to-others direction or the sex-is-sinful department, or both. But from the extremes of sado-masochism down to the mild infractions of deep kissing, the establishment of a firm taboo is required to transform the act of violating it into an erotic excitement. Thus, a taboo that successfully restrains the activity of many people acts as a special incitement for many others.

Partners and Situations

Particular partners and situations can profoundly affect what people do sexually—and the enthusiasm with which they do it. Sometimes these influences are obvious, as when a person is "turned on" by a partner who is especially attractive, or else recoils from a normally enjoyable activity when either the partner or the situation is not acceptable.

Some people enter into a sexual situation with strong preferences and with definite expectations of what the other person would like. A bias in favor of particular kinds of acts, perhaps mouth-genital and/or anal contacts, may be communicated by a person's shifting his own or his partner's position. Or he may simply say what he wants to do, or have his partner do. (In both heterosexual and homosexual situations, men frequently make specific requests and, by being verbalized, these may add to their excitement. But very few women find "sex talk" exciting—a difference between the sexes, incidentally, which is cross-cultural and thus more fundamental than mere social training.)

Much that is stimulating in a sexual situation may not appear until the interaction is well under way. Such things as the special desires of a greatly admired partner, an appealing way in which a request is made, or the unexpected discovery of a novel excitement can be so effective that people are surprised at the intensity of their own response: An activity that is low on a person's preference list, or even one which has previously been imagined with abhorrence, may suddenly become not only acceptable but preferred in a particular relationship.

Sometimes a person's arousal and enthusiasm are sharply increased by the discovery of something he especially appreciates—perhaps a great deal of return affection or what he sees as the perfect mixture of things gentle and harsh. Both partners may then elaborate their actions, a mutual feedback situation that can quickly extend sex techniques and reveal new levels of excitement and meaning. In short, a person's preferences can be sharply altered by the "chemistry" of a situation, especially when he makes the most of new opportunities he finds with a particular partner.

A novice may quickly have his whole sexual repertoire expanded by contact with a highly experienced, sexually articulate partner. But the partner gains something new, too. Revelations and sensations that are new and dramatic to someone else can be vicariously enjoyed as if for the first time. In fact, the capacity to derive enjoyment from other people's sexual reactions, and to relish one's own role in bringing them about, are virtually universal. An element of vicarious pleasure is apparent in such diverse situations as when a person responds to someone seen at a distance, when aroused by merely watching the sexual activity of others, or by projecting oneself into the action of a motion picture. And certainly a large part of the enjoyment most people gain from their own sex activity is derived from noticing the reactions and imagining the feelings of their partners. In fact, vicarious sexual gratifications are so important that many people are able to thoroughly enjoy a sexual contact in which only the partner reaches orgasm.

Sometimes what a person is ready to do sexually depends much more on the situation in which he finds himself than on anything else. A man who has always met his partners through ordinary social channels and who usually chooses them after carefully assessing their personal qualifications may find that in an orgy-situation he is quickly aroused and soon becomes a participant, sometimes without knowing anyone present. There are many other sexual situations in which a person, largely on the instigation of someone else, quickly finds himself ready to engage in unanticipated sex. He may be asleep in his bunk at camp, at the house of a friend, or even in an army barracks and suddenly awaken partially aroused by someone he cannot clearly identify. Or a sudden sexual liaison may be formed with a friend or business associate when they are in an unusual circumstance—perhaps on a hunting trip or at an out-of-town convention where they are together in a new context.

Even partners who have drifted away from each other in a long-standing relationship may be revitalized by a change in the context in which they see each other. Realizing this, they may have sex at unusual times and places, discuss their fantasies, or have sex in the presence of—or with—a third person. The basic psychology is the same as that of the heterosexual couple who are sexually refreshed by being away from home on vacation or visiting friends in the country.

Certainly novelty is invigorating. It gains part of its effect from the newness it offers and the rest from destroying the routine that has gradually crept into everyday life. The big-city homosexual—who, if he is promiscuous, may have more sexual opportunity and fewer social restrictions than the most resourceful heterosexual Casanova—may have even his high sex-rate increased by rearrangements in his daily life. If he does "street cruising" for a portion of his contacts, he may be stimulated to do more of it during a subway strike, a power failure, after a deep snow, or as a result of some other change in routine. It is as if every life situation offers certain sexual possibilities and blocks others, so that any circumstantial shift tends to open newly stimulating paths while closing off others that have become routine.

Of all the forms of sexual activity which are fueled by novelty, probably none arouses righteous indignation as much as the various forms of homosexual activity that occur between strangers in semi-public places. A combination of strong violations is involved. Ordinary homosexuality is taboo aplenty under the best conditions before it is jaded further by happening in a men's room or the shady recesses of a park. Most homosexuals themselves share the public's sentiments against on-the-spot sex; not even the homophile organizations have a kind word for it.

But what is it? Is it really what so many observers have interpreted it to be?—"pure sex" or sex-for-sex's-sake, with a bow to the fact that for some people its lure lies in the risks and dangers that feed the tensions of sexual excitement.

Probably there is such a thing as "pure sex," especially if one is referring to the kinds of immediate stimuli that can sometimes trigger a sexual response. And yet, when carefully examined, nearly all sexual arousal turns out to be replete with conceptual and symbolic connotations—at the very least, the kinds of associated values shown by the heterosexual male in his response to the shape of a breast or the curve of a hip, and by the homosexual male in his response to a masculine body-build or to the size of a penis. Sex with a stranger is often much more complex. It can contain elements of affection and of action that are motivated by the desire of one or both partners to relive an emotionally profound experience by a momentary repetition of fragments of it. Or a person who has only dreamt of having a rich relationship may want to try out part of the action he imagines it would contain. In either case, it is quite important that his present partner should be and remain a stranger, for he is only a catalyst—the mannequin on which the royal robes of a past enthrallment are draped.

The Psychology of Sex Techniques

The whole psychology of human sexuality to a large extent recapitulates on a mental level what has happened physically in sex for eons. Just as the physiology of sex involves a certain fit and stress between the partners, the psychology of sex involves a stressful personal interaction. Nearly all of the sexual motivations which have been mentioned thus far have emphasized the partners' attempt to exploit their accessibility to each other. But it is important to remember that the transgressing of barriers is itself a major element in promoting sexual arousal. In fact, sexual motivation is always advanced at least as much by factors that resist or retard a sexual impulse as by those which directly accelerate it.

It is easy to see that sexually-ready mates encounter many barriers in their access to each other, but it is harder to keep in mind that impediments of some kind (accidental or deliberate) are *necessary* precursors in the psychology of sexual arousal. Every human society places various restrictions on sex, but when mates finally satisfy or evade all the rules and regulations and are at last ready for intercourse, they must themselves find new resistances to focus on right up to the moment of orgasm. If they fail to do this, they risk a collapse of their sexual interest in each other.

Whatever the system is that combines strain, stress, and resistance with sexual satisfaction, it is evidently as old as sex itself. Certain single-cell animals (protozoa) which accomplish most of their reproduction by the presexual method of simply dividing in two (fission) must occasionally rejuvenate themselves by conjugation. Conjugation, a true sexual process, is accomplished as two cells come together, dissolve their body walls at the point of contact, and exchange a portion of their body fluids. This "refreshes" both individuals, each of which is then able to go through many generations by simple fission. But for conjugation to be truly effective, the mates must come from slightly different (resistant) strains. If protozoa that need to conjugate are exposed only to their closely related offspring and are therefore forced to accept partners too similar (too unresistant) to themselves, only a very small portion of their body fluids will be exchanged. As a result, their conjugation is then minimally refreshing, leaving both partners capable of only a few generations by fission before they must again conjugate.

Under laboratory conditions, protozoa can be forced into the reverse problem. Two individuals that are from strains ideally resistant to each other for a perfect mateship can be placed alone in separate drops of water until they are desperate for conjugation—and then suddenly given access to each other. The combination of their extreme craving and of each being faced with the ideal partner results in their overexchanging their body fluids. Each loses too much of itself, and they both die.

To the extent that this is a valid model of sex, it would seem that a degree of resistance or "stressful difference" is an integral part of all sexual attraction and that it plays several roles. As a complementary difference, it can supply the needed and refreshing elements in a sexual exchange. But beyond a certain point, resistant differences amount to an incompatibility, a clash of identities, that acts as a barrier to limit the extent of each individual's commitment to the partner. From this vantage point, it is possible to infer that from the protozoa to the psychology of man, mates are able to refresh themselves by importing and exporting elements of contrast up to the point of being refreshed, but must be able to resist excessive exchanges that would threaten their own integrity, their identity as individuals.

Although there is always a danger of arriving at false analogies when drawing parallels between lower and higher animals—and no doubt more danger in drawing parallels between single-cell animals and the psychology of man—there are also dangers in not doing so. One could easily overlook important phenomena which run through vast spans of evolution—processes which have culminated in, and partially explain, curious elements in human psychology.

Certainly if there is one condition which accompanies sex in all its forms it is that some degree of resistance between mates is always present—often to the point of violence among animals. Throughout biology, sexual interest is whetted by stress and by barriers that have to be surmounted. These may take the form of one mate's reluctance, or the pain they both may have to sustain, or outside interference to their easy access, or any combination of these. Sexual intercourse itself is often painful—dogs, for instance, have moments of excruciating discomfort in their genital union. The females of many species tend to become aroused and to ovulate only after being considerably mauled by a male. In other species, the male is impotent or sterile unless he faces a situation in which he is forced to fight his way through a crowd of competing males. Among most animals at every evolutionary level, the female is resistant in various ways even while she is being seductively teasing or even while actively presenting.

Sexual resistances of all these kinds are at least partially present in man; many are loudly evident. Any persuasion that has to be used or hurdles that have to be vaulted tend to make the mate more attractive, provided the resistance is not discouragingly high. And any moderate degree of hesitation shown by an otherwise responsive partner can easily constitute a barrier. Couples who have achieved a balance of interest in each other, or who have learned to become aroused together so that neither partner feels resisted by the other, tend to solve the problem of impending disinterest by inventing techniques that inject an element of resistance into their relationship. Each partner may surprise the other with a gesture, a statement, or an approach that has a certain shock value. They may approach each other at unusual times or places, or adopt a posture of playful abuse or mock independence in order to suggest strain or strangeness, or to produce a refreshing view of each other. As part of this effort, they sometimes invite an outsider to watch or to participate. These and dozens of other techniques have been used to arouse new sensations and bolster sagging resistances.

The heightening of sexual interest by combining resistance with an initial appeal is evident in situations where the main stimulation is openly sexual. Pin-up pictures of scantily clad girls are often more erotic than those of total nudes. And in burlesque, the nude fan-dancer arouses far more response by offering partial views and flashing glimpses than she would if she were constantly nude. Small barriers which one's imagination can easily hurdle and flash views interrupted by barriers that promise to disappear again for another eye-filling (but not appetite-satiating) view are extremely exciting—whether the flashes are those that come between the strokes of a moving fan, glimpses the Peeping Tom gets through a curtained window, or meaningful glances that pass between persons who are responding to each other across a crowded room.

Flirting involves much of the same psychology: It always involves stimulating attentions that are interrupted by momentary withdrawals. The meaningful wink is a cameo example. And in early courtship, the ardor of both mates is fanned by moments of obliviousness to each other interspersed within a superattentiveness. Such examples suggest that the growth of erotic arousal is more accurately described, not as a stream of interest, but as an alternating current of piquant contact broken by fleeting interruptions—interruptions that supply the moments of drabness against which each new spark of response is displayed.

Many people (especially those who have had numerous partners) are disappointed to find that the intense desire they feel while winning a new person quickly disappears when sexual contact becomes assured. In establishing an intimate relationship, new revelations and challenges are tantalizingly mixed with moments of incomplete communication. But once the barriers are down—particularly if they are entirely down—what is about to take place in the bedroom may seem all too familiar, all too predictable to be alluring.

Interestingly, the barriers which are sexually stimulating can be present anywhere in a situation—in a partner's partial standoff-ishness, in one's own fear and fascination with an attractive but "dangerous" person, or mixed in to the feelings of both partners as they move through the backing-and-filling maneuvers of exploring each other. Or resistance may appear in neither partner but in something that intrudes between them—an unavoidable delay or some other bittersweet separation. Some of the most poignant romantic situations involve the displacements of wartime or dealing with the interference of disapproving parents. Romeo and Juliet were incited by the distance of the balcony, the feuding of their families, and the impending marriage of Juliet to another man. Likewise, the appeal of a Lolita, the fascination for a virgin bride, and the erotic feelings that some experienced homosexuals have for inexperienced ones are all instances of particular kinds of social barriers that act as stimulators. And when partners are at last together they move on to a new challenge: the use of sexual intimacy to assault the bastions of each other's personal mystique.

The clash between social levels, between races, between partners who are dispositionally mismatched can all lead to arousing situations as easily, or more easily, than contacts between conventionally compatible partners. Little wonder that the very taboo on homosexuality often feeds the erotic intensity of it, much as various inhibitions of prudery can bring exhilaration to heterosexual relations. In fact, socially disapproved contacts of all kinds are especially capable of generating sexual arousal. But they are less commonly used than milder violations because the height of the barrier is critical: The higher it is, the higher the erotic crescendo, up to a point. Beyond that, exceedingly high barriers usually present enough resistance to dampen attraction or to squelch one's enthusiasm for overriding them.

In courtship and eventually in the bedroom, the whole sequence of events is determined by the tendency to keep a certain balance between the resistance and the "conquering range" of the sexual response. One result is that the "engagement point" of the resistance tends to travel, like the battle-line of an army that is taking over a land of unknown fortifications. When an attractive person is first seen, the resistance may be in the problem of starting a conversation, or even in getting close enough to try. When these barriers are overcome, other social impediments, including perhaps the partner's hesitancies, become the next line of battle. Making a physical contact may be the next. Any gesture or proposal that is viewed as sufficiently risky to constitute a resistance will produce a thrill as it is overcome. But each new level of intimacy quickly loses its challenge— and the "front" of resistance-engagement moves on.

The examples cited thus far have shown more of *how* than of *why* sexual arousal is stimulated by resistance. Though simply describing how resistance is used may be sufficient to clarify particular examples, it is necessary to raise more fundamental issues in human psychology if we are to understand why it functions as it does. Resistance is contradictory in a sense, for while it is always present in sexual arousal, it has the curious effect of drawing partners together when they are apart and of keeping them slightly apart when they are overly close. If we can unscramble this paradox further, we will be in a better position to understand exactly why resistance is an essential component in sexual arousal, in the techniques that are used, and in the broader investments that people feel ready to make in each other.

The Origins and Functions of Resistance

It is almost impossible for the human mind to remain indifferent to any impressive object, person, condition, or event. To be indifferent to something leaves one unprepared to deal with it— either to defend oneself against its possible dangers, or to reap the rewards that it may offer. Consequently, man tends to structure his environment, and his attitudes toward it, by erecting a system of values. These values may be derived from the edicts of some god, from his own experience, or from objective fact. His aim is to be able to rate and hold definitive attitudes toward every item of contrast—be it thunder, lightning, the phases of the moon, in fact, any unusual event—and certainly toward every emotion-evoking interaction with his fellow man. The more impressive the item, the more imperative structuring becomes. Emotion needs a channel, and when action is wanted, clear-cut attitudes point the direction. This need for clarity and for unequivocality no doubt plays a part in keeping man's moral systems as crude as they are: Black and white judgments of good and evil, right and wrong, natural and unnatural predominate—especially where intense emotions such as those raised by sex have to be dealt with.

But this raises a new problem. For while unequivocal attitudes permit the expression of strong opinions and emotions, one cannot long tolerate an excessive commitment in any single direction, even when it is fully sanctioned by some belief. Thus, primitive tribes that lavish affection on a totem animal and prescribe the death penalty for its accidental slaughter periodically turn the tables and actually or symbolically kill and eat that animal. The Christian communion in which the body and blood of Christ are ritually eaten is a ceremonial holdover from the totem feast. Here, as in close personal relationships, overexpenditures of love tend to exhaust affection and threaten a person's narcissistic integrity, his self-possession. It is as if a touch of resistance or opposition were necessary to save the giver from losing himself in the gift. (Shades of the protozoan that killed itself with an overattractive mate.) Likewise, extreme forms of hate are unstable, for besides cramping one's style, they tend to absorb too much attention as they build a fiendish fascination for precisely what is hated.

A person's full commitment seems always held in check by an opposing note—a touch of his own ambivalence, or its substitute in the form of an outside resistance of some kind. Certainly, there are situations in which a person feels totally *for* someone. High romance is an example. It is a situation that may be defined as one in which the partners are not yet aware of the negative side of their ambivalence toward each other. Are their feelings an illusion? No and yes. Their affection may be intense and pure, unclouded by any conscious hesitations, or by unconscious ones either, if they have yet to overcome all barriers to their contact. But the lovers' impression that the intensity of their feeling is something other than the fragile product of negative components having been temporarily hidden or displaced outside the romantic situation *is* an illusion—as is their impression that such intense emotion could exist more than moments after all barriers to it were removed.

Certainly the exorbitant emotional investments in each other that lovers feel ready to make are more than they would find tolerable if they were able to reach in practice the contact they imagine in fantasy. Often the full satisfaction of their olympian appetites for each other is blocked by the kinds of worldly intrusions and barriers mentioned before. Or the exaggerated readiness of one lover may be held in check less by outside difficulties than by the standoffishness of the other. In still other situations, lovers may be intensely affectionate and may have surmounted all external barriers besides—a truly *gung ho* situation that immediately invites self-contrived resistances, as the negative side of at least one partner's ambivalence rushes forward to preserve a semblance of balance. These internally bred resistances may take the form of doubts about the partner's sincerity, or fleeting moments of self-doubt, or jealous anticipations of losing one's partner to someone else.

It is traditional for people to think of the pleasure of sexual activity as a product of moments of maximal contact—and it is. But even here, gestures of withdrawal, resurrected barriers, and moments of pulling away from a partner are equally important. Fortunately, resistances can be expressed inside a close relationship without the slightest unpleasantness or any other penalty. A fairly loud example might be the excitedly submissive partner who is urgently saying, "No, no, no" near the point of orgasm, or who at any point is struggling as if to get away; the main focus of enjoyment appears to be on the resistance, but there is no penalty. These oppositions, like the barriers inherent in all sex techniques, have the advantage of stimulating arousal while satisfying the partners' need to resist each other in situations of maximal contact.

In other situations, much quieter resistances—the kinds preferred in softly affectionate situations—may be used: A person may suddenly withdraw from a directly sexual action, concentrating instead upon some peripheral stimulation, perhaps teasing or merely talking to the partner. That these diversions eventually pay off in renewed arousal does not alter the fact that they are delays which partially resist sexual expression. Whatever restrains gratification, of course, raises tension in one or both partners—but this is like water behind the dam that eventually contributes to the deluge.

Sado-masochistic sex expressions are extreme examples of tension-raising resistances being used, first to inhibit affectional contact, and then to express it. The homosexual priest or anyone else with much training against both aggression and sex, and consequently with a certain revulsion for anything brutal or sexual, may combine the two and weave into his sex performance enough actual or symbolic punishment to "pay" for it. His partner's genitals or his own, or any other parts of their bodies, may be subjected to insult if not overt abuse. It is as if the most conventionally puritanical objections to sex—that it is vile, outrageous, and utterly contemptible—were given credence and acted upon with all the vigor and harshness that a most moralistic authority might want. All this having been expressed and thus largely exhausted, and much tension having been generated, both partners attain a supercharged sexual release.

Evidently, then, resistance plays a variety of roles in sex. It is present all the way from the momentary withdrawal of eye contact in the seductive wink, through the intrusive violations of privacy and of hygienic taboos that are overcome in ordinary sex techniques, to the overt punishments of sado-masochistic abuse. Throughout all these variations, resistance may be seen as an expression of anticontact—an anticontact that is sometimes expressed so as to surface and thus purge negative feelings: At moderate levels of sexual intensity, where one person is attempting to arouse a partner who is not yet fully responding (as in flirting or courtship), resistance may be used to separate and polarize the components of the partner's original indifference.

An attitude of indifference amounts to a state in which potential assets are balanced out by potential liabilities. The person who flirts attempts to unbalance a partner's indifference either by seducing positive reactions from him, or by deliberately arousing negative ones in the hope of reversing them later. Here, as in most other forms of arousing a partner, moments of intrusive contact are interspersed with moments of sharp withdrawal. If these forward and backward movements were added together, undoubtedly they would level out to something approaching the indifference from which every attitude is originally precipitated. Thus, the resistances and barriers that partners use in their momentary separations from each other permit them to afford their excursions into moments of intense overcontact.

These same back-and-forth commitments are apparent in overt sex techniques at all levels. They are physically reiterated in bodily gyrations, and they are psychologically evident in the combination of frenzied contact and conservative, momentary withdrawals of attention. Where the partners in an overtly sexual situation are interacting at extremely high levels of arousal and therefore feel ready to make exceptionally close contact, exceptionally high resistances are searched for—larger and larger violations of privacy and of taboos are in order. These may involve elements of pushing and shoving, harsh language, or with sweet gentility merely the roaming invasion of finger or tongue into violational places.

Or the resistance-violations may be expressed on other, entirely different, levels. Most of the resistance may be displaced to points outside the contact itself—as when a couple suddenly turns to sex at a time when one or both partners are already late for an important appointment. In other instances, the resistance may be divided between the partners' inside and outside world: Where they view their contact as illicit in some sense (perhaps because it is a disapproved extramarital or homosexual event), the partners may be able to position their scruples into the very kinds of restrictions that most fan their ardor. Here, as everywhere else, the resistances involved in "outrageous acts" operate as substitutes, as stand-ins, for the negations born of taboos and felt inhibitions. In short, the resistances embody, and yet fence off, the forces of anticontact—the negations born of taboos—and thus realign those negations to feed the very flames they were originally designed to quench.

One begins to comprehend the magnitude of resistance phenomena when, in a single sweep, it is recognized that the barriers within a teasing come-on, the shock of an intimate invasion of privacy, and the lash in the hand of the sado-masochist are all made of the same stuff. Ordinarily, the height of the barrier is proportional to the height of the sexual pressure against it—i.e., proportional to the urgency of one's desire for contact. But since barriers also serve as reiterations of antisexual inhibitions, they reach excessive heights—in sado-masochism, seemingly more related to savagery than to sex—only where the reincarnations of prudery build them to the sky.

Male-Female Comparisons

In many ways, men and women are identical in the extent to which their interest in a partner may be sparked by resistances of various sorts. Consider, for instance, an adolescent girl with several boyfriends whom she holds in about equal favor. If her parents then harshly criticize one of them, perhaps forbid her seeing him, he is likely to become her favorite. With a boy, too, parental dictates are notoriously prone to sweeten forbidden fruit. It is as if one's enthusiasm for a partner is ordinarily held in check by the negative side of one's ambivalence—until a voicing or some other surfacing of it expresses and thus weakens it, leaving one's positive feelings purified and intensified. Much the same thing happens in a lovers' quarrel, where both members express and thus weaken the negative side of their ambivalence; the result is most often a revitalized affection. Men and women are alike in these respects, perhaps because they hold an equal stake in affectional matters.

But in areas where the sexes are usually unequal, as in sexual arousability, there are marked differences in the extent to which men and women are ready to use various forms of resistance. Men are generally more sexual, at least they are more "driven" by sex than are most women. They easily develop strong feelings for attractive partners they know little about. And since the use of resistance in sex is intimately related both to controlling commitment and to focusing sex into hot-points of intense interest, males are by far the main users of resistance. Thus, all forms of sex which employ extreme focus or extreme resistance—sado-masochism, fetishism, exhibitionism, and the paraphilias in general—belong almost exclusively to males. Heterosexual men who "go in for" extreme sex practices often entertain the hopeful fantasy that the women they inveigle into cooperating with them will enjoy these too, but this is seldom the case. The generally lower sex-drive of women, and particularly their peripheral rather than focal interests in sex, leave them quite unmoved by the more resistant forms of sex.

There is a connection between all this and the reputation homosexual males often have for being "compulsively" if not fiendishly obsessed with sex. Is it a reputation they deserve? No and yes. What people are ready to do sexually is highly dependent upon their individual conditioning, social and sexual. A great many people who are involved in homosexuality are very conservative in their sex attitudes. Others are not. Most are in-between. But when two men are excited and unrestrained in their sexual interaction, the fire that is fed from both sides often does whip up levels of eroticism that are rarely reached elsewhere. Particular partners may elaborate a single technique into a huge number of variations, or try out purely sensual experiments that are too seldom enjoyed by women to really work in heterosexual relations. (Much the same is true among lesbians, remember, except that their techniques are so lacking in focal resistances that their actions tend to seem bland even when they are very elaborate.)

There are local instances, of course, in which the "excessive" possibilities of homosexuality are combined with a particular individual's fascination for one of the especially high-resistance forms of sex. The homosexual man who also happens to have a sado-masochistic requirement and who manages to find a similar partner may, indeed, arrive at spectacular techniques. To hear him tell it, he finds his search for the "right" partner almost impossible. But in view of his requirements, he is lucky to be interested in males. For while he may have to do his choosing from a small fraction (perhaps one or two per cent) of the homosexual men who would otherwise be available to him, even this small fraction affords him an incomparably better chance of finding what he wants than he would have if he were searching for the "right" woman. Thus, what he finds rare is exceedingly rare everywhere else. Or to put it the other way around, the additive effect of two males together does sometimes facilitate high-resistance sex practices, making them *relatively* frequent in homosexuality—practices which are rare in heterosexuality and are virtually nonexistent among lesbians.

In the final analysis, what is to be said of all these various sex techniques? To assess them fairly is harder than one might suppose. For it is curious in a way—and in other ways transparent—that nearly all sexual practices of every kind tend to be judged derisively. A cool consideration of what other people do sexually invites contempt. Even recalling one's own practices out of context may cause a person to shun the thought, if not to bridle at it. Much larger issues are involved than mere prudery and social training. To some extent, all sexual interactions are threatening in that they dissolve the boundaries of self-containment—a disquieting prospect in the absence of an attractive partner. Nor is it always appealing to recall, while unaroused, the barriers one seeks out and hurdles with ease in moments of passion. Thus, it is easy to be a bit disdainful of one's own sex practices and ruthless in judging those of others.

Certainly a fair judgment of what other people do requires the utmost caution—all the more so since each and every sex technique is destined to seem ridiculous to those for whom it has no value. And since few people ever practice more than a small fraction of the techniques that make up the pool of possibilities, most of the choices of other people inevitably seem either too narrow or else odd and pointless, if not downright repugnant. But most of what appear to be major differences in technique turn out to be trivial variations in form. Broadly considered, what is most striking is not the difference between various actions but the essential similarity of people's motives. The one nearest to being universal is not without honor. It is the attempt to touch and to possess qualities that are admired, and to help one's partner do the same.

7

The Social Shapes of Homosexuality

Homosexuality occurs everywhere—in communities of every size, at every social level, in every profession, and among people in every walk of life. This wide dispersion, and people's understandable need to conceal the parts of their lives that could subject them to social disdain, are only two elements that make the total situation hard to grasp. The nonsexual expressions of homosexuality—the social shapes of it—are greatly affected by the extent to which people are drawn to it, by the kinds of social pressures they face, and by their very different ways of dealing with the personal conflicts that can arise from it. These and still other sources of variation complicate the task of bringing the picture into focus and into a perspective from which appropriate conclusions can be drawn.

Part of the difficulty in viewing homosexuality is that it is largely amorphous—a behavioral category of individuals who are about as diffusely allied with each other as the world's smokers or coffee drinkers, and who are defined more by social opinion than by any fundamental consistency among themselves. And since homosexuals differ at least as much from each other as they do from heterosexuals, it is not feasible to divide them into "types." Nor has an adequate understanding of their variations been gained by the attempts of various writers to describe "gay bars," particular groups, and scenes from the daily lives of a few individuals. The distortions implicit in any such approach are equal to those that would arise if one tried to glean basic knowledge of heterosexuality from visiting nightclubs, or from interviewing a few volunteers.

The enormous social variation between people who engage in homosexuality tends to gain what little uniformity it has from the kinds of pressures they may or may not have to contend with. Externally, this means that the social milieus found in various cities and towns can affect the styles of homosexual expression. And internally, a person's individual psychology and his way of defining himself can greatly affect what he does and how he does it. In an effort to reduce feelings of being at odds with the society in which they live, people have found many ways of avoiding the inner conflicts that are invited whenever their sexual requirements clash with the mores of the society around them.

Cities and Towns

There is a popular notion to the effect that men and women who are predominantly homosexual need and want the anonymity of city life and that they gravitate toward it and away from small towns. Since there are many more small than large towns, it would be conceivable that only a slight drift in this direction could enormously increase the homosexual density of cities while having little effect on small-town populations. But before even this speculation is carried too far, it should be remembered that sex studies have consistently shown that differences in the frequency of homosexuality from one community to the other are more apparent than real.[142] Certainly the quiet, conventional community has a far higher homosexual representation than a casual observer might suppose.

Moreover, an atmosphere of personal liberty and a freedom from the restraints of rigid conformity are not necessarily correlated with a town's size. There are large cities that are rigidly conformist in their social attitudes; and there are many small communities that are free and sophisticated in tone. In fact, there are quite a number of small towns in America—and not all of them are art colonies—where persons living discreet but undisguised homosexual lives (often in the form of fairly obvious ongoing relationships) make up a sizable portion of the population. They may participate in town councils and in other ways be thoroughly integrated into the community. And there are still other small towns where a more or less obviously homosexual segment of the population is small and keeps to itself, yet is free from social discriminations.

At first glance it might seem that this much personal freedom owes much to a general atmosphere of social sophistication. Certainly there are more small towns near New York or San Francisco than close to Podunk where a person's private life remains private and where fairly obvious homosexual populations comfortably fit in. Yet some of the most rigidly conformist communities in America are close to large cultural centers; and there are a few quite free towns near hotbeds of social conformity—especially within the Southern Bible Belt and in the largely provincial Midwest. It is clear that "sophistication" and social freedom are unreliably correlated, a sure sign that other variables are present. It will be useful to understand how homosexuality manages to become accepted in some places and not in others, particularly since the factors involved may affect all of the social shapes into which homosexuality is cast.

From tribal communities to modern cities the enforcement of particular codes of behavior tends to be proportional to the degree of social organization present. Where people of a tribe or town know each other and have close affiliations, they are able to watch and keep track of one another—a mutual surveillance that tends to set and enforce a single code of behavior, and to discourage deviations from it. In an environment of middle-class morals, homosexuality is relatively hazardous and tends to be practiced as furtively as any other form of nonmarital sex.*

---

*Interestingly enough, homosexuality is not necessarily furtively expressed, even in circumstances that would seem to demand the most caution. Particular individuals have found various ways of solving the seemingly un-

In small towns that have little social organization, there may be little conformity and no prevailing clique to sit in judgment. Such towns vary enormously in character and in the origins of their social leniency, but they do have one trait in common: All lack a dominant, controlling middle class—often because the most prominent citizens are well-educated people in the professions or the arts who have larger than local interests. They want their own privacy and tend to respect that of others. By their codes, it is a breach of etiquette to visit without phoning, or to call without having a specific purpose. To gossip is worse than trivial and bad manners; it carries the degrading stigma of provinciality. Friendships are not made by proximity but by specific personal interests or compatibilities. Homosexual liaisons are not big news, and when noticed at all, tend to be judged on their own merits. The closest of friendships may be between heterosexual and homosexual individuals and couples.

Other small towns achieve this same liberality and the luxury of individual privacy simply by having an essentially transient population. A town may be a summer or winter resort, perhaps famous for its climate, its music festivals, or otherwise be a lure to outside visitors. In this atmosphere, all sorts of new relationships (hetero-

----

solvable problem of living against the mainstream of a tightly organized social morality without becoming the victims of it. A person who is known to be homosexual may be so friendly and sociable, so impervious to criticism or simply so amusing to have around as to be fully accepted, sometimes becoming a social favorite, despite anything in his private life. Similarly, more or less obvious ongoing homosexual relationships can become accepted and respected as a unit in an environment that is otherwise quick to attack nonconformists. People who are seemingly vulnerable to criticism may move themselves off target by maintaining a certain friendly distance. Others may be especially sociable, yet parry every challenge with grace or charm (i.e., defeating the adversary arrangements that are a prerequisite for every continuing conflict). Still other individuals insulate themselves from conventional expectations by centering their lives around off-beat interests— perhaps running an experimental farm at the edge of town, or being an artist or writer. It is not just that being off-beat protects a person by confounding provincial judgments with exotic mysteries. Rather, it is a person's ability to be himself with tact and confidence that best guards him against the hazards of being out of step with an organized majority.

sexual and homosexual) are easier to make and to dissolve than elsewhere. The year-around portion of the population tends to adjust to these mores and, in any case, is outnumbered by the influx of visitors. There is little tendency for any one group to dominate the scene, to see its own values as preponderant, and thus expect conformity. Nor is·the busy social confusion of the place conducive to the leisurely pastimes of noting and commenting on other people's behavior. Here, people find it especially easy to live their own lives.

On the other hand, both of the extremes noted in small towns (much or little pressure from conventional mores) may coexist in a city of some size. A person who grows up in the highly organized middle-class milieu of Dallas or Denver, or even in Boston or Philadelphia, may find it hard to isolate himself from the watchful expectations of scores of social and business friends he has made over the years. For him, the place is a small town, and a conservative one at that. Yet even an exclusively homosexual newcomer to the same city may find it utterly liberal, may tap in to its cosmopolitan aspects and find it a playground of opportunity. Starting as a stranger, he can pick and choose his social and business contacts and with each he can more effectively regulate his desired closeness or distance than can the long-time resident whose deeper roots in the community increase the price of privacy.

Once a city has reached a population of several million, its organized, watchful, middle-class factions have all but disappeared; they have themselves become a minority and have lost their impact. For the most part, close neighbors and cordial friends at work are not integrated into each other's social lives. People with homosexual proclivities use this easy compartmentalization in very different ways. They may lead entirely homosexual private lives, or simultaneously belong to primarily heterosexual groups. It is not unusual for people in ordinary business and professional settings to maintain patently homosexual life situations, living with the same partner for years with little notice or complications arising from it.

Curiously, this big-city anonymity, and especially the social feasibility of two males living together, is quite strictly limited to the English-speaking world. In Paris, Berlin and Rome, there is a rigorous underlying conventional structure which allows both the business and social friends of a person to keep tabs on him. (The popular notion that European societies are relatively tolerant of sex in general and of homosexuality in particular stems from naïve observers who overemphasize a few liberal facets of foreign mores, and are unaware of the rest.) Not even the newcomer in these societies is out of sight, for there is the everpresent concierge, or the knowing desk clerk, and soon the butcher and baker who make it their business to know what's what, and to talk about it as well.

But even this surveillance pales in comparison to that found in Spanish-speaking countries. In Mexico City, for example, few local citizens would risk a visit to the one homosexual bar. Located in the center of town, it is mainly for tourists but is run with such decorum as to tax the talents of even sophisticated eyes. Yet along the side streets, where a knowing native can find his way with little chance of running into anyone he knows, there are over a hundred sexually oriented baths, more than in all the rest of North America combined.

The moral rigors within a Spanish society are seldom felt by the tourist; often they are strikingly reversed for his benefit. The visitor to Puerto Rico, for example, may find San Juan exceptionally free, with its bars, beaches, and nightclubs. The natives are genuinely friendly toward the foreign homosexual, and are disinclined to judge him (unless he happens to be patently effeminate). Every facility is offered, even more for the homosexual than the heterosexual visitor. The clubs, restaurants, and bars are usually owned by enterprising immigrants who are encouraged, protected, and given tax concessions by a sophisticated government. The aim is not merely financial. As in most Catholic countries, segregation (including a certain openeyed blindness) rather than suppression is considered the practical way of handling all extramural sexual behavior. (Recent newspaper talk and token action against homosexuality are just that.) The upper-middle class is greatly outnumbered by tourists on the one hand and by lower-class natives on the other. But this small, tight-knit middle class controls city policy—and within its own ranks, controls itself with extraordinary rigor. Homosexuality for any of "their own" is particularly taboo. For a young man to so much as drive slowly past a "known" guest house may incite jokes about him or raise eyebrows, though the neighbors who report the event can afford to be on entirely friendly sugar-borrowing, ice cube-lending terms with the residents.*

The same young man would endanger his reputation much more should he go alone to a gay club, even late at night and across town. The channels of communication in a Spanish-based middle class are probably nowhere outdone. It is less a fear than simply a social reality that the cop on the beat or some other observer has a sister who works in the office where a friend of her friend knows the brother of the young man's neighbor, each in the market for news of any sort and delighted to pass it along. Consequently, more than a few hometown citizens avoid all this by seeking their contacts with tourists in the daytime, perhaps on a beach or at the bar of a first-class hotel. Said one young man from San Juan's city hall, "I try to do everything in the sunlight because it blinds all my regular friends."

The conflict many people feel over homosexuality stems as much from their self-judgment as it does from social disapproval. A person might be able to hide what he does from others, but to avoid self-criticism he may need to find an emotional or logical basis for daring to follow his own desires. (Relatively few people, including heterosexuals, are able to simply do what they want without protective rationalizations. Nor are the rules and regulations of the mores themselves offered without excuses to justify them.) On the other hand, popular agreement bypasses conflict at source. Thus many homosexuals try to reduce the contrast between themselves and others either by making various changes

---

*Sharp differences in people's mores (especially when they see each other as foreigners) give them a chance to be compatible and lenient toward each other. It's as if their contrast removes any risk of infection. Thus a middle-class Spanish family may merely be curious about, and amused by, the homosexual activities of people who are clearly differentiated from themselves, while the same actions by one of their own would be cause for much alarm. For what appear to be similar reasons, societies which have the strongest taboos against homosexuality are often the ones that make it most available to visitors.

in their situation or by redefining themselves within it. Sexually, they may insist on taking certain actions and not others, or with inhibitions of a different sort they may relegate their homosexual activities to particular partners, or to particular times and places. Still other individuals redefine themselves as particular kinds of people, or they may reinterpret society's mores to provide a common footing for all sexual tastes. And certainly there are a few individuals from every sort of background who are able to accept sexual variations without having to find excuses for them. All these ways of viewing homosexuality greatly affect the social shapes into which it is cast.

Systems of Denial

There are four basic denial-umbrellas under which people can practice homosexuality without having to admit to themselves or to others that they are homosexual—though they may be exclusively so:

1. *The Gender-Role Umbrella:* Many men feel free to respond to other males when and if they can maintain a "masculine" role in their own eyes by avoiding emotional expressions that would imply an investment in the partner, and by otherwise seeing their actions as free of anything "feminine." They preserve their male image by being the dominant partner in anal intercourse, or by lying back to be fellated. That both acts are highly phallic, that neither is receptive (in the sense of being penetrated), and that both could occur with a heterosexual partner all support the rationalization that what they are doing is "not really homosexual." These notions seem to remain self-convincing even when such a person goes to great lengths to find exactly the right partner, to choose this or that one over others who are more easily available, and to unhesitatingly show jealousy when the partner's attentions are directed elsewhere. It is interesting that many law-enforcement officers and judges accept the whole rationalization, arresting and sentencing only the receptive partner, who may have been the least aroused and the least responsible for having arranged the contact.

The odd notion that same-sex contacts are homosexual only for the partner whose gender-role is inverted has a long tradition.

The idea is reflected in the popular notion that effeminate persons are homosexual, that homosexuals are effeminate, and that lesbians are tough and somewhat "phallic," if not Amazons. It is reflected in the King James version of the Bible, where homosexuals are called effeminates.[45] And it runs through centuries of erotic art, where homosexual scenes between males nearly always depict the receptive partner as weaker, smaller, lighter colored, and with smaller genitalia than the other. The phallically aggressive partner, by the way, is often further protected against any charge of being sexually inferior by being given especially large genitals, great strength, and other attributes of a supermasculinity.*

It is understandable that these naïve conceptualizations have gained a foothold in popular lore; and it is even more understandable that many men who want sexual contacts with other males seek a way of making these contacts without incurring the penalties of the label. But it is astonishing that so many observers have been taken in by these posturings, and are willing to believe that male homosexuality requires inversion, that it only applies to the submissive partner. Even a few social anthropologists have claimed that homosexuality is rare in particular tribes (and in particular areas of our own society) "because there are only a few males who submit to most of the others." With this rationalization a great many males in more than a few societies have been able to satisfy their homosexual requirements. with equanimity.

---

*The erotic art of Ancient Greece is a notable exception. By their acceptance of homosexuality and the affection that went with it, the Greeks gave both partners respectful treatment. When they depicted an age difference between the partners, they were careful to retain the younger man's virility; they especially did not want to imply any weak receptiveness since they strongly condemned effeminacy and were careful not to confuse it with homosexuality.

Erotic art from all over the world tends to depict sex between two women in ways that are devoid of any inversion. This accuracy and respect is undoubtedly due less to an understanding of lesbians than to the fact that, in the eyes of heterosexual males, women who are sexually responding to each other are demonstrating their arousability and their probable readiness to respond to the beholder if he were there.

The fact, of course, is that sexual contacts between males are patently homosexual for both partners. Both are usually extensively motivated, too (nobody responds easily to a partner who is seen as sexually meaningless).

2. *The Personal-Innocence Umbrella:* Unlike those men who insist on performing only the "male" role, many others who want their homosexuality while denying it are not "role conscious" at all. Indeed, they may feel especially free to be submissive, since this is entirely in line with their particular rationalization: that the whole motivation for sex comes from the partner. Often they are ready to be actively oral, too, *provided* the partner is clearly responsible for having started things. Sometimes these men become expert at seducing others into making advances. Or more accidentally, they may have the sort of personality that conveys an easy approachability which, in turn, results in homosexual advances. But whatever the source, a great many individuals feel guiltless and free to respond in homosexual situations that appear to be precipitated by others. The underlying assumption seems to be that to overtly move toward a partner is the essence of commitment and desire, while to react to a sexual opportunity is "only natural," especially if one is caught up in another person's desire.

If this whole posture seems transparent, it has nevertheless convinced quite a few people, including judges and, again, a few anthropologists. Margaret Mead has gone so far as to say that the word homosexual is misleading since it fails to distinguish between activities and preferences.[177]

And the other part of the rationalization—that guilt belongs to the one who starts things—has a long social tradition. Ancient theologians held women more responsible than men for sexual sin on the grounds that they were temptresses—initiators and premeditators capable of arousing innocent males. In civil law and throughout moral philosophy, premeditated acts of any sort carry more responsibility than impulsive and cooperative acts. Being an accessory to a crime does not necessarily imply full awareness of it, and in any event, the designation carries less penalty. Thus, the wife or husband caught in an extramarital affair is frequently viewed as less guilty than the "homebreaker" who supposedly set out to ensnare the sexually placid victim.

Many a man with homosexual desires knows how to look or to get himself ensnared.

The excuse for a homosexual contact often is that one was drunk or asleep at the time—again, lacking in premeditation. No doubt there are instances in which there is genuinely no fore-thought, not consciously at least, and yet a careful examination usually reveals that the initiator correctly senses encouragement in the situation, though this may not be immediately apparent on the surface: Two people may find themselves in close rapport, perhaps listening to music or merely talking, a situation that can suddenly become sexual when one of them takes the initiative. Men usually accomplish this transition from a social to a sexual context at a more or less clear-cut moment of thrust, perhaps a physical touch, or a direct verbal suggestion. Women usually accomplish this changeover in a much more gradual way. Tactile stimulation may slowly increase in a general ambience of affec-tion. Sharp thrusts and "sex talk" are out. As one lesbian put it, "You can [slowly] do almost anything, but if you say it you may get slapped."

In many other sexual situations, the same kind of umbrella is used. Men and women who are seldom if ever able to exercise their homosexual proclivities in one-to-one relationships may find it easy to do so in an orgy situation. Here again, the assumption is that one is only proceeding within a situation which has been defined and set up by others. Oddly enough, the very same psychology is sometimes evident in the prostitute where he or she, by being the partner who is chosen, feels free to do what would be guilt-provoking if done under the banner of one's own desire. Here, as in most of these examples, the other person's responsibility is crucial. The rigors of a personal morality can stand like a fiendish sentry over the choices one makes on his own. Said a lower-level Southern Negro prostitute to Dr. Kinsey after having given a personal history containing virtually every conceivable sex act, "But I is proud to say I ain't never done none of these here things with my husband, and neither is we never undressed afore each other."

3. *The Only-For-Now Umbrella:* Many people take the curse off their homosexual activity, at least in their own eyes, by

conceiving of it as merely temporary. They may think of it as a holdover from what they did when they were younger, or as a pleasurable activity that happens to be available now but which will lose its appeal when they settle down or "grow out of it." The person (of either sex) who uses this rationalization may even be having considerable heterosexual activity. Yet heterosexuality, like homosexuality, can lack erotic zest and emotional meaning when it fails to honor the demands of a personal value system. Many people who are more attracted to homosexual than to heterosexual contacts delay their open recognition of the fact by attributing their lesser heterosexual response to an inability to find the right partner. They are much like the cowboy who is wary of girls, kisses his horse instead, and tries to see his homosexual contacts as temporary while "waiting for the right girl to come along." It is a long wait. For although there are a few largely homosexual persons who are capable of switching to heterosexual partners when, indeed, just the right one comes along, a desperate attempt to explain away homosexuality is seldom conducive to giving it up.

For many people, the transitory nature of nearly any activity, or the mere thought of it as temporary, is enough to keep them from feeling guilty about it. This is evidenced in many nonsexual contexts, such as the ease and abandon with which people tell of the social violations they committed when they were drunk or high on drugs. And conversely, people are often overconcerned when they realize that some small personal quirk in their behavior is ongoing. In sexual matters, where the stakes of approval and disapproval are higher, many people find it important to attribute their criticizable behavior to outside influences—if not to the partner or to the situation in which one finds himself, then to a limited span of time.

The rationalization that a person's homosexuality is a temporary phase is so powerful that it can remain self-convincing in the total absence of heterosexuality. And if a person is engaged in heterosexual activity as well, then one's homosexuality can be even more readily explained away as incidental. With such protection, a person can even initiate homosexual contacts and feel free to be sexually receptive within them, often with an unparalleled guiltlessness.

4. *The Special-Friendship Umbrella:* Still other people ward off the implications of a homosexual involvement by interpreting it under a more acceptable label. A professor, for instance, may have what is actually a full-fledged homosexual relationship with a colleague or a student; both partners may see it more as a special friendship than as anything sexual, let alone homosexual. Their interpretation may be correct as far as it goes; they may, indeed, be placing much more emphasis on their intellectual and social interactions than on sex. Such special, often highly romanticized relationships gain their credence not only from the emotional intensity that may be present, but from the feeling that no other person of the same sex could possibly "turn them on" in this way. As in all romantic situations, the purely sexual elements may be utterly eclipsed by what is felt as an abounding affection. When such a relationship, including the sex that goes with it, is the first of its kind for a person, it may very easily seem unique and simply not be recognized as a classical homosexual experience.

Similarly, many young people who have an intense first homosexual experience may still not realize that it indicates anything about themselves. They conceive of homosexuality, if they think of it at all, as something utterly alien done by strange or effeminate people, certainly nothing that causes emotions to soar as theirs do.

But a special-friendship situation can also lift the curse off homosexuality for people who are fully aware of its implications. The person who restricts his activity to one or to only a few special partners is often able to continue these contacts for years without viewing himself as "a homosexual" or feeling particularly defensive. A man who is primarily heterosexual and settled into a comfortable marriage may continue his homosexual contacts with one particular friend. Or if he is late in discovering this side of himself, he may feel especially free to exercise it with an occasional partner here and there when conditions are right. The heterosexual equivalent is the man who feels free to have a mistress or to have only a few extramarital partners over the years, but who would feel like an immoral rake (or thinks he would) if he had the same number of sexual contacts scattered among many partners.

Since the whole special-friendship defense deals with uniquely powerful moral concerns, it is not surprising that it should occasionally present itself in an exactly opposite way: that extramarital or homosexual contacts are entirely permissible *provided* they are promiscuous, opportunistic, or otherwise unimbued with emotion, because then "they don't mean anything."

In looking over the several ways people have found to deny their homosexuality while practicing it, certain central themes stand out. Each rationalization avoids the dreaded moral or social implications of homosexuality. Each denies homosexuality as a preference (if not by denying it altogether, then by claiming it is in some sense opportunistic, or by relegating it to the narrow confines of a particular situation). Each carries at least the implicit claim that the person's heterosexuality is primary. Each is usually as self-deceiving as it is socially defensive. Each is geared for one-to-one relationships; homosexual social sets are out of the question. Thus in each of these systems of denial the person finds a way to engage in homosexuality while continuing to define himself as a regular member of society, one who in no essential way is set apart from it.

In the eyes of many observers, all of these denials show a profuse mixture of personal dishonesty and social deception. But the issues of honesty and of social appropriateness are not to be lightly settled. The distortions of fact carried in people's rationalizations are often hardly more than corrections for the errors that are contained in established thought itself. The connotations attached to homosexuality in the minds of a person's friends and neighbors could easily make their interpretation of the bald truth less accurate than is the twisted version of the truth that he offers them. Thus, a person who goes out of his way to hide his homosexuality from himself and others, though he deals in major distortions of reality, is nevertheless more correct in defining himself as a regular member of society than as an outsider.

Self-Acceptance and Encounter

It has been fairly easy to describe the ways people practice homosexuality while denying it. Each mode of denial restricts the people who use it to relatively few variations. But the life-styles of people who consciously accept their homosexuality vary far more. Self-acceptance opens the door to a great variety of possible arrangements. Some people opt for a more or less exclusively homosexual environment in which there may be closed or overlapping circles of friends. Others choose to live seemingly conventional lives in which they camouflage their homosexuality or pursue it in the clandestine ways popular opinion imagines. It would be a sizable task to adequately depict these two variations alone, for there are many different kinds of predominantly homosexual social sets, and people have found a great many ways of guarding their sex lives from critical view. But since most homosexuals manage to find life-styles by which they neither isolate themselves from the heterosexual world *nor* live surreptitiously under a cloud of caution, the problem of depicting their variations is formidable.

One reason most of the social shapes of homosexuality have never been described even fairly accurately is that none of the group-phenomena are representative. Reporters and more than a few serious students of homosexuality have fallen into the trap of reaching their conclusions from what they see at clubs, particular resorts, and other gatherings that obscure rather than elucidate the private lives of those present. A gathering place can be a pickup point, a social club, a place to take out-of-town visitors, or a place to act in ways that would not be appropriate elsewhere. Or it might be all of these things to a person on different nights and still not reflect the central trends in his life. Any effort to guess how people integrate homosexuality into their lives by noting their behavior in special groups is doomed from the start.

Several investigators have realized the impossibility of making valid generalizations about homosexuality from "social moments" in a person's life, and have turned, instead, to carefully analyzing a few life-styles. Evelyn Hooker's work has been particularly accurate. (In fact, she seems never to be wrong—a remarkable feat.) Yet even her excellent descriptions fit mainly the population she chose to study (males who live in a fairly tight-knit subculture of their own).[114,115] When attempts have been made to broaden the view by including people who live quite differently—for instance, those who are more integrated into a heterosexual milieu, and those who are less so—then an astonishing new difficulty comes into view: Every life-style fails to define a set of people because each one turns out to be used by very different individuals who have very different reasons for choosing it, and who may be well or poorly balanced.

This disconcerting variability is found even within extreme and rarely chosen life-styles that may seem thoroughly ominous from a distance, but which do not necessarily prove to be so. For instance, a person may conduct his homosexual life as a loner, making only fleeting contacts simply because he is too fearful or too hesitant to do otherwise. (Some of these individuals are fully as disturbed and miserable as they are widely reported to be.) Or with no neurotic inhibitions, a loner may be a man so thoroughly devoted to his career—or to his wife and family—that he much prefers to satisfy his homosexual needs with quick, transient contacts that do not divert him from the mainstream of his life. The ongoing homosexual relationship may similarly be used by the partners to escape even further from the rest of the world than they would be able to alone. Or it may richly endow the partners—who perhaps move to the suburbs, get to know the neighbors, and exchange visits with their friends in town.

The fact that particular life-styles can be entirely different for different individuals means that by themselves they are poor indicators of "adaptive efficiency." A broader view is needed, one that will show how people manage to practice homosexuality without having it become dangerous or inhibiting. In a sense, the problem of making the homosexual alternative feasible is much like making any other kind of unusual behavior socially acceptable. A person has to find ways to retain his spontaneity and yet avoid flagrant confrontations with people who do not agree with him.

The two popularly imagined choices of the homosexual—to hide his private life or to live in an isolated homosexual subculture—generally prove to be too limiting or too uncomfortable to maintain. Many homosexuals seem to sense this in advance and never seriously consider either of these choices. They are often able to do everything they want and still avoid trouble simply by making a quiet separation between their workday and their private involvements. For a surprisingly large number of people, not even this much adjustment is necessary. They may be self-employed or in one of the increasingly numerous occupations in which homosexuality carries no disadvantage, or where private lives are simply of no concern. And for the homosexual who is largely free of fear and self-doubt, there are often more social (and sexual) opportunities than he has time to exploit. Furthermore, there are many social circles (many of them primarily heterosexual and almost as many of them in small as in large towns) in which a person's acceptability depends much more on his social behavior, his brightness, and his view of life than on his sexual tastes—and where, in fact, if he is boring or narrowly conventional this much sooner disqualifies him.

But what about the person who, regardless of the success of his private life, lives and works in a conventional social setting that brings him into daily contact with many people who might quickly join any moral clamor against him? This is a situation which is almost universally imagined to be frightening to the homosexual and perilous to his position. But often it is neither.

A professor in a small-town college may be homosexual and even fairly actively so with little danger *provided* he is discreet in certain ways—ways that do not include an overguardedness that would signal his vulnerability and thus raise his risk. By the time he has been at his post several years, many of his colleagues and quite a few students may have at least a tacit understanding that he is homosexual. Yet as long as there is no scandal, and gossip is held within reasonable limits, he is surprisingly safe. In fact, he may have several protections in his situation. When he shows an open friendliness and is reasonably secure within himself, people are not prone to attack nor to gossip about him; any snide remarks seem to bounce off him (if, indeed, they are not squelched at source nowadays by a ready admission of his homosexual interests whenever the question arises). Or with no entourage of personal supporters, he may be a specialist, a scholar or an eccentric about whom the mention of anything entirely personal seems out of place—and his homosexuality perhaps the least of his peculiarities. Almost equally invulnerable to attack is the person in some middle position who, being neither especially friendly nor remote, is so bent upon his work and on keeping up with a busy schedule as to make his discreetly handled personal life irrelevant.

There are many other social contexts in which the homosexual finds safety, often without especially looking for it. A person who has reached any sort of power position—be he the dean of a school, vice-president of a corporation, head of a department, or who holds power behind any throne—is often too dangerous to attack with anything less than tangible evidence, and even then, at more risk to his attacker than to himself. And there are instances aplenty in which a person has the protection of neither power nor personability and who may be surrounded by dangerous gossip besides, but by refusing to recognize the danger, or acting as if it does not exist, he fails to supply that fragment of vulnerability or of fear that any denunciation seems to require.

But how does the socially integrated homosexual manage to avoid being as fearful, as defensive, and as nervously surreptitious as popular opinion imagines he would have to be? He can be casually and easily circumspect about his private life in several ways. When he has a guiltless acceptance of himself and an exact understanding of what triggers—and does not trigger—other people's objections, he is often able to effortlessly steer a course of social discretion that proves to be neither dangerous nor particularly hampering. (With years of experience and no feeling of being disloyal to anyone, his circumspection may be far easier and "cleaner" than that of many heterosexuals who are involved in extramarital affairs.) Or with none of these advantages—and up to fairly high levels of neurotic conflict besides—he is usually safer and far more comfortable than is generally supposed. Anyone's sex life, at least in its details, tends to be a private matter and it is, after all, only one of many life-involvements. The homosexual generally becomes accustomed to taking whatever precautions are necessary, just as the heterosexual automatically gears the amount of self-revelation to what seems appropriate as he moves from one social ambience to the next. But by and large, the homosexual annuls his "difference" problems by thinking of himself—and thus causing others to think of him—less in terms of any sexual classification than as a regular person who holds a particular position, be it teacher, scholar, banker or bricklayer.

Even in sexual matters the socially integrated homosexual is not especially guarded, much less frightened and furtive. His adaptations tend to become effortless and smooth within numerous possible life-styles that only occasionally require special caution. Ultimately, his protection seems to lie most in the respect shown him by his associates and in the rapport he maintains with them; a healthy relationship deters the gang-action of rejection. Yet it is hard to say whether his safety stems most from his social integration, from the respect he shows for other people's life-styles by not flaunting his own, or from the fact that his very unguardedness (his lack of self-condemnation) is itself the most disarming. There are instances in which all of these elements are equally evident, and others in which a person's whole style is based on only one or two of them. Suffice it to say that high-level modes of adaptation are really so effective that the homosexual requires only a few; he can generally afford to ignore or even to mishandle numerous of his possibilities without paying any great penalty.

But then what about the opposite observation: that people can have their lives ruined or at least lose their social position as a result of scandal, or even mere exposure? Such instances certainly do exist. (They exist even more in fantasy where, to many people, a possible disaster is viewed as a constant threat.) And perhaps the picture is made still worse by the realization that such calamities can happen to the best-adapted people, quite as the best of pilots sometimes crash. To this charge there is no very consoling answer. The world is, indeed, a dangerous place—and no doubt it is more so for the particular homosexual whose position happens to require the ongoing approval of, say, a school board or any other tightly organized group. But even in this context serious trouble is rare. Certainly there are millions of people who quietly and uneventfully pursue homosexual interests while remaining thoroughly integrated into conventional social settings.

What are not so rare are the brief occasions in which the homosexual, especially while he is still young, is confronted with direct questions or verbal insinuations that probe or slander his private life. Such challenges vary all the way from being playfully curious to pointedly hostile. How these moments are handled can greatly affect a person's view of himself and his image in the eyes of others. The price of failure—and many homosexuals do fail—can be quite high. A person may be so poor at handling personal challenges, and therefore so uncomfortable with them, as to back off into one of the "safer," more isolated life-styles. If his work does not permit this—perhaps because he is in an institutional setting—then he can stay where he is and learn to live with his increased vulnerability. His responses range all the way from very nervous to quite relaxed. His discomfort tends to be and to remain inversely proportional to his ability to handle challenges.

On the other hand, many homosexuals learn very well (by intuition or by trial and error) how to handle confrontations, and may relish any opportunity to do so. With no trace of insolence or defiance, no chip-on-the-shoulder substitute for self-confidence, such a person enjoys maintaining his social integration and his freedom to choose his close friends by criteria which cut across sexual boundaries. By having both respect for himself and an easy rapport with people (many of whom know about his private life), he sometimes lives with great safety on what might seem from a distance to be the brink of disaster.

A comparison between homosexuals who fail to handle themselves well under pressure and those who succeed in doing so presents interesting contrasts. In a conflict situation where a person needs to protect himself (hopefully without resorting to defensive measures) he greatly increases his danger if he fails to control either the challenger or himself. If he fails on both counts, he is in serious trouble. But curiously enough, neither a charge hurled at a person nor his answer to it carries much force by itself; the intended victim's poise and general demeanor count much more. For no charge can be completed unless the victim agrees to take it seriously, to honor its validity in some sense, and thus to cooperate with his attacker.

For instance, in leveling a charge that means "Your sex-life has been discovered and is a very serious matter" the challenger cannot continue without establishing a dialog. He needs a reaction of some sort to guide his next blow. Such guidance may take any of several forms. The victim may dissolve on the spot, try to escape, or rush forward with a denial. In fact, if the victim so much as hangs his head while being challenged, he validates the moral premise that underlies the charge against him.

The homosexual who is guilt-ridden and not very competent

socially can be crushed by blindly stepping into any of these pitfalls, or into many others that gape before him in the dark. He may have to sustain many defeats before he learns—or he may never learn—that in handling nearly all conflict-situations, it is he who most determines his fate. Often he allows himself to be drawn into an opponent's target area where virtually any move he makes can turn a merely threatening charge into one that is perilous. When serious trouble develops, he tends to choose *fight* or *flight*—alternatives that are poor for anybody and are likely to be disastrous for him. There are elements of rigidity in the picture too: The socially incompetent person, almost by definition, has great difficulty in modifying his behavior, even after he knows what is wrong with it. To try out different things, to make little changes here and there, and to "play around" with his *modus operandi* are not easy for him.

By contrast, the flexibility of the socially integrated homosexual is notable. According to the particular situation, to his personality, or to his mood at the moment, he may handle small challenges by answering them, ignoring them, fielding them, taking them seriously, fluffing them off, or simply responding with a bland or friendly smile. Sometimes he intuitively knows how to join a resistance and to wipe it out in one stroke—"I can see that you take such matters very seriously; exactly what would you like to know?" or "The trouble with gossip is that so much of it is true." Often he is free and easy in keeping the door open to almost any subject matter but he is prepared, if necessary, to rigorously control the level on which it is discussed.

In the face of sharper challenges too, he can take the initiative in a flash, often without seeming to, and he is careful not to be defensive, especially in clumsy ways such as lying, backing away, or explaining himself. When facing even the worst kinds of derogatory remarks he may move not an inch either forward or back but simply step aside, perhaps into a kind of observer's position—"You'll have to fix that charge a bit if you want it to stick"—"Man, you're really laying it on the poor bastard"—"Don't think I wouldn't spin your head with a good sharp answer if I had one." Or, he may move in to strike at the *manner* of his assailant (without so much as a nod to the rock in his hand)—

"Please don't do that"—"Say it again so I can see if it's that bad the second time"—"Them words is m-i-g-h-t-y unfriendly." His own words can be mighty unfriendly too—"Cut that out"—"Now don't shit me." Again, just *what* he says is not overly important; the power of his responses is in his equanimity, his refusal to knuckle under or to plead guilty in his demeanor (not even if his choice is to confirm the charge outright).

Certainly he does not always succeed. His modes of dealing with conflict require practice and the kinds of self-control which may be lost in moments of anger, or when he is suddenly taken aback by embarrassment or surprise. Nor is every situation itself perfectly solvable. There are a few challengers (especially if they are drunk or are personally disturbed by homosexuality) who will fire the same charge again and again. A few others throw their darts and walk on, closing the door to dialog. Still others dislike him from the start and work against him from positions of polite silence. Nevertheless, if he generally manages to stick to his guns without firing (thus forcing other people to do all the work of withdrawing) he will maintain a self-respect which sooner or later gently wins the respect of most people—regardless of whether they actually know anything about his sex-life or bother then to think of it even if they do.

When the kinds of examples which have been cited here are discussed with homosexuals and with the not very numerous clinicians who are aware of such matters, several objections are raised. It is often insisted that while such masterful social adaptations clearly exist, they are fairly rare. It is said that "clever answers" are offered up only by clever, highly verbal people who are probably well educated and thoroughly aware of what they are doing in their social interactions—an altogether rare breed. Perhaps so. But the very best modes of social adaptation require no such talents (except that "clever answers" require a good deal of cleverness to keep from being disastrous). A college teacher who was part of the present study and who grew up on a Texas ranch had a way of handling even the most complex confrontations by varying his inflection on a single phrase—"D'yuh reckon [what you think is true]?"—"D'yuh reckon [any of that makes any difference]?"—"D'yuh reckon [I'd be any better off if I did what you suggest]?" Other people are able to turn minor body gestures and no words at all into a silence that can strike any note from sheer imperturbability to a blistering retaliation—with or without including the message, "The charge is true but so what?"

In the broad picture, it is apparent that any degree of commitment to homosexuality increases a person's need for adaptive mechanisms, including special ways of protecting himself from rejection. But it is also apparent that there is no shortage of such adaptive means, and that very different people with very different personalities manage to find their own ways of blending into the structure of ordinary society. As might be expected, people vary in how well they blend in. There are those who land on the fringes of society as a result of not wanting or not being able to adapt. And there are those who "turn a profit" on their homosexual adaptations—individuals whose personal development and whose special abilities could not have evolved in a relaxed, conventional atmosphere. Both of these alternatives are clearly in the minority, leaving most people who are involved in homosexuality in the middle: By and large they are sufficiently integrated into the mainstream of everyday life to comfortably fit in—and in the process, they blur most of the social shapes of homosexuality into an indefinable formlessness.

In looking back over the socially integrated homosexual's basic assumptions and ways of responding, a few central features stand out. The best of these are worth noting in their own right (and possibly borrowing from, since nobody is exempt from threatening confrontations). He consistently defines himself as a regular member of society—refusing to see himself or to let others see him as set apart from it. In facing both small and serious charges that may arise from time to time, he knows better than to quail, to cower, to flee, or to strike back in anger. (He finds other ways to deal with an assault or to discipline an assailant.) No matter what happens, he refuses to drop dead after being shot. Thus he manages to adequately control himself, and ultimately the challenger as well. It's as if he has come to understand, and then to validate, a major sociological postulate: That every adversity feeds on the victim's collaboration, and that charges hurled at a person seldom stick unless he himself supplies the glue.

8

Brief Encounters and Ongoing Relationships

Every kind of relationship exists in homosexuality—a wide variety of promiscuous contacts, many brief encounters which do not quite qualify as promiscuous, relationships of longer duration, and still others which would be considered ongoing by any standard. Most people, including more than a few investigators, have not been fully aware of this wide range and have thought of male homosexuality, particularly, in terms of its promiscuous examples. The more personalized and more stable relationships have seldom been examined, let alone analyzed, though they are numerous.

Each kind of homosexual relationship has its special character, its own dominant motivations which are likely to be present but more clouded in all the other relationships. For instance, the man who makes a quick sexual contact with a stranger is forced in a sense to fragment his response. That is, from the whole range of sexual and emotional responses of which he is capable, he selects-out (and then usually exaggerates) only a few—sometimes as little as a single, specifically sexual activity. Although he may engage in the same actions when he is with a partner he loves, in this richer context each of his responses tends to be blended with so many others as to be virtually indistinguishable from them.

Thus promiscuity with all its fragmentations is a particularly useful source of information, a veritable cornucopia of sexual and emotional variations nicely sectioned-off for easy viewing. In fact, an analysis of homosexual promiscuity proves to be even more enlightening than its heterosexual twin since, besides all its other distillations, its male-male and female-female pairings demonstrate certain fundamental differences between the sexes—differences which are relevant to everybody's sexual orientation.

But what, exactly, is promiscuity? It is usually thought of as a person's readiness to have sex with a variety of partners, often on short acquaintance. In addition, it carries a number of highly pejorative implications which have made it hard to examine with objectivity—implications which do not always fit. It is usually assumed, for instance, that the partner-choices are made with little discrimination, more or less purely for sexual reasons, and with little affection. These assumptions are reinforced by particular instances which appear to bear them out, and by the fact that many men make a point of later describing all their brief encounters in these terms.

But whether these descriptions of indiscrimination, of pure sex, and of no emotion are true or not (they are seldom all true in a single instance), there are many other examples of promiscuity which reflect a different, often contradictory picture. Homosexual promiscuity, in particular, frequently entails a remarkable amount of discrimination. Even a person who never wants a second contact with any of his partners may spend much time carefully selecting each from dozens or even hundreds of possibilities. In fact, some of the most promiscuous individuals sustain considerable frustration not from any lack of opportunity but from being exceedingly selective. Nor is affection always minimal. Besides turning up in the most unexpected places, affection is often promiscuity's main motive or its salient result.

At the opposite extreme are many examples of an entirely impersonal promiscuity characterized by little discrimination and no affection. These are the kinds of contacts, prevalent the world over, in which more men than one might suppose respond to other males and find ways to signal their interest. Whether men check out the sexual readiness of strangers in a men's room, on a busy street, or wherever, they are often able to quickly arrange for an overt contact and may complete the whole experience without a word being spoken. The striking anonymity of these contacts is no accident; usually it is a deliberately maintained barrier, a carefully placed screen designed to let through particular aspects of the partner while blocking out the distracting details of who or what he actually is. It is not that a person does without such details, but rather that he fills them in from the controlled inventory of his own fantasy.

From these few examples, it is perhaps already clear that promiscuity has many faces, and is not a neatly defined entity. People vary considerably in how much personalization and socialization they want with their partners. One person's promiscuity may be expressed entirely as fleeting contacts with strangers while another person may have a series of short-range affairs. In fact, the ordinary notion of promiscuity includes virtually every kind of sexual encounter other than strict monogamy. Yet even by this too broad definition it has a certain unity: It always implies a desire and a successful search for something more than can be obtained from one partner. Thus the main questions are: What causes people to want to be promiscuous, or to not want to be, and sometimes to be promiscuous without wanting to?

The prevalence of homosexual promiscuity certainly has not gone unnoticed. Numerous investigators have verified what the Kinsey Research first found: That many homosexual men have hundreds or even thousands of partners before middle age—a variety of contacts seldom matched by the most active heterosexual. But of course, the homosexual male has his way cleared for him by dealing with partners who agree with him in their male attitudes toward sex and in their readiness to respond as quickly and on the same levels as he does.

On the other hand, promiscuity is certainly not universal; many homosexual men have no urge for it. Some have already "had that scene" and are tired of it. Others, due to various fears and preferences, and occasionally due to a low sex drive, never respond to any partner without first having substantial social interaction. Almost nobody (of any orientation) is at all drawn to other partners while having an intense affair. For other people, an ongoing relationship which is no longer intense may still be sufficiently satisfying to leave them almost invulnerable to the lure of new contacts. And promiscuity is often held down by conventional barriers—a person's moral inhibitions, or simply the realization that the social context of his life limits opportunity. More than a few people who would be open to a variety of contacts are simply unaware of the opportunities that exist.

Still, homosexual promiscuity is relatively prevalent. Indeed, the variety of sex the heterosexual male usually longs for in fantasy is frequently realized in practice by the homosexual. Clinicians have often attempted to read various neurotic insecurities into homosexual promiscuity (in fact, into any promiscuity), ascribing it to a person's need to compensate for felt deficiencies or to "prove" himself. Such motives sometimes do exist. But there is no indication that homosexual promiscuity is any greater than its heterosexual equivalent would be in the face of equal opportunity.

The promiscuity of most uninhibited males rests partly on biological traditions—a high sex-drive, an easily triggered responsiveness, and perhaps a kind of species-history of the sexual chase. This trend may have become exaggerated in the human male by his visual orientation to sex coupled with his capacity to imagine sexual possibilities (and to be aroused by them) before the fragments of a potentially sexual situation have materialized into anything approaching an actual opportunity. Thus as males go about their daily interactions they are, in effect, immersed in a pool of arousing sexual stimuli made up of actual and suggestive cues—cues which are easily assembled into active fantasies. Their situation is in sharp contrast to that of most women, who are neither so "driven" nor so visual, and who usually require a certain psychological preparation (later, even tactile stimulation) before attaining an equivalent arousal.*

---

*Since it has become fashionable to believe there is no essential difference between the sexuality of men and women—even that female responsiveness might be higher—a few guidelines are in order. Of the total female population, approximately a third have little sexual response, or none at all.[144,142,125] Another third respond, but slower and with less intensity than

It is not surprising, then, that a specific desire for promiscuous contacts is mainly the province of men and not women. The issue is somewhat clouded in heterosexuality, where males are restrained by a shortage of instantly ready partners—and where women sometimes concede to male demands for reasons other than sexual desire. But in homosexuality, the difference between the sexes is sharply drawn, not only by the ease of male-male contacts but by the near-total lack of promiscuity among lesbians. In fact, the most extreme forms of promiscuity, those in which the partner is and remains anonymous, simply do not exist among lesbians.

It is easy enough to see that promiscuity is supported by biological factors, but it is much harder to trace exactly what gives rise to it in practice. Besides satisfying a person's desire for sexual variety, promiscuity frequently gains part of its impetus from social motivations. By "playing the field" a man earns a certain status (the envy of his friends, for one thing); while if he holds back he runs the risk of looking prim and inhibited both to himself and to others. In addition, to take on many partners is sometimes the young homosexual's way of meeting people, of exploring the world, and of getting to know what different kinds of individuals are like—more a social than a sexual curiosity. Many homosexuals view their own promiscuity as a hopefully temporary transitional stage in which they more or less systematically search for the "right" partner with whom they can have a lasting relationship. Many observers have scoffed at this as rationalization, a mere excuse for promiscuity. But excuse or not, the search for a right partner and for a significant relationship often is indeed a major motivation in promiscuity.

---

males. Most of the remaining third have a sexual responsiveness which is equal (at least in amount) to that of males. The rest, approximately 3 to 4 per cent of women, have an arousability no male can match—as evidenced, for instance, by their ability to reach orgasm by fantasy alone, or while simply walking along with a desired partner. But not even this extraordinary capacity opens the door to the kinds of promiscuity many men display: the ability to respond to entirely anonymous partners, and frequently to prefer them.

Other people move from one partner to the next for quite the opposite reason: primarily to avoid entangling commitments. Sometimes a person justifies his promiscuity with the rationalization that he is only "trying everything out" and so "isn't really homosexual." In still other instances, a person's life-situation is simply more conducive to fast than to ongoing relationships. There is a broad class of very busy people who live in an endless whirl with twenty irons in the fire or their eyes on a single, burning ambition—people who have no time and no taste for more than moments of anything purely personal. (On the subject of serious affairs they often explain they "have had all that" and, indeed, they often have.) Also there are many married men who have a definite homosexual appetite but who do not want (and may not need) more than fleeting contacts to satisfy it.

Not that quick and easy partner-choices are always a matter of deliberate intent. A person who is not dispositionally inclined to initiate any contacts, often by this very quality comes across as all the more approachable. If he has an attractive personality or happens to be especially handsome, he may be deluged with propositions. He may back away from most offers, but the remainder (those in which he likes the person or finds that person's arousal contagious) can still add up to considerable experience. In other situations, too, the easy response of males and the often high availability of homosexual contacts can favor a casual, not quite deliberate promiscuity. Part of the reason many homosexual relationships do not survive the first serious quarrel is that one or both partners simply find it much easier to remarket themselves than to work out conflicts.

But deliberate or not, the motives for accepting or pursuing ever new partners rest on more than biology and social advantages. There are numerous ego-rewards to be gained. In fact, it is unlikely that even the most fleeting sex contacts are devoid of at least a few such rewards. These include the gratifications of making a conquest (or of being conquered), of having one's way with a partner, and of being accepted or appreciated. Sometimes the promiscuous male is charged with being vain and utterly superficial for wanting to sexually cash in on his affluence, his fame as a celebrity, or other status symbols. But the reverse is more often true: Many people derive a unique gratification specifically from being found attractive by partners who know nothing of their status or position in life and can have no other motive for choosing or yielding to them; it amounts to having one's market value affirmed on its own merits. Nor is it entirely valueless that, with a stranger, a person can cast himself in an off-beat role or attitude of the moment, one that may be too contradictory to other aspects of his personality to be believable to people who know him better.

Sometimes promiscuity includes surprising elements of affection. Even the fleeting contacts between males who meet in Turkish baths or other impersonal settings often contain elements of emotion that go beyond "pure sex." The actual contacts may be quite gentle and affectionate—particularly in those situations in which the partner is used as a kind of fantasy substitute for an ideal partner. But in less special circumstances, too, affection often develops as a by-product of sexual activity. It is not always welcome; thus many men later feel a need to deny the affection they felt during a brief encounter. Their denial may take the form of the heterosexual male's reference to the "broad" he "had" and whom he describes as having been "not bad," or references by homosexuals to their "numbers" or "tricks." Why these showy displays of emotional indifference toward partners who were previously warmly treated?

For one thing, affection carries a note of commitment, not only to the partner but to the action itself. People who in any way feel guilty about their sexual exploits seem particularly inclined to wipe out lasting vestiges of them. But even without regrets there are grounds for later denials. In a quickly made contact a person often exaggerates what he likes about a partner—an exaggeration which sometimes has its motive in seducing the partner, or in simply helping him ignore the partner's less attractive qualities. In any case, to overemphasize a positive emotion is to wind the pendulum for a swing in the opposite direction. Other people are simply embarrassed by affection. Many men see it as "soft," as a threat to their status as a free agent, or as raising the ogre of dependence. Any of these reactions makes denial imperative. The lower-social-level male may go much further, displaying an image of dashing braggadocio—especially if his audience (such as a group of other males) places a value on rakish noninvolvement.

A denial or reversal of affection, on the other hand, is by no means the inevitable aftermath of a brief encounter. There are many instances (seemingly more frequent in homosexual than in heterosexual relations) in which a single sexual contact, though never repeated, lends a certain warmth to what becomes an ordinary friendship or to the memory of a partner who is never seen again. In fact, the tendency for instant sex to carry a charge of affection can be considerably stronger than that. More than half of the ongoing relationships examined in the course of the present study began with contacts which started out to be nothing more than brief encounters.

Not that an element of affection is always present in sexual contacts, and is then either denied or allowed to blossom. Many people go out of their way to avoid affection by deliberately seeking partners who are, and who remain, entirely anonymous. But before even these examples are too hastily ascribed to "pure sex" (whatever that is) it must be understood that they contain emotion and a considerable ideology, the raw materials of affection. Even the man who in the dark fondles and is aroused by a partner he has never seen is responding to physical cues which symbolize qualities of maleness he greatly admires and has eroticized. The fact that his response has ideational underpinnings certainly does not mean that his actions are any more personalized than they appear, or that they are at all close to affectional expressions. But neither can such examples be correctly described as mechanistic, vacuous, or "compulsive." They are more than that. They manage to be personally meaningful without being interpersonally so. But this realization—that even the most fleeting and anonymous forms of promiscuity employ meaningful value-associations—only intensifies the original question: Why do people want and sometimes prefer the partialness and incompleteness of brief, impersonal encounters?

The answers range all the way from the most superficial considerations of convenience and propinquity to the most elaborate psychological motivations. Certainly a quick sexual contact is sometimes made because it is the only possibility which exists at the moment, a take-it-or-leave-it opportunity that seems better taken than missed. Frequently some detail, either in the circumstance itself or in the way a partner presents himself, strikes a person as intriguing. And something is to be said for sheer novelty, especially when opportunity occurs, as it often does, in the tension-raising atmosphere of risk. Thus many men are interested in impersonal sex only when it can be had in semipublic places—men's rooms or the sand dunes of a beach—or in outlandish situations, perhaps with a bus driver at the end of the line, or with a passenger or crewman during a plane flight.

Whether under odd or plain circumstances, the appeals of a brief encounter usually include an element of fantasy and projection. Something about the partner, perhaps his bearing or his facial expression, may stand for the qualities a person has especially wanted or enjoyed in the past. Precisely because fantasy projections of all sorts draw heavily upon a person's reservoir of past experience, the most promiscuous people are those who have previously had serious relationships. In fact, it is extremely unusual to find really high promiscuity in the history of anyone who has not been in love at least once.

Some of the most powerful motives for promiscuity stem from special, individualized meanings that each experience may offer. Constantly new contacts have an intense appeal for a person who is able to view each one as a telescoped version of an entire meeting-to-mating sequence, a kind of love affair in microcosm. Each contact may proceed so rapidly from meeting to parting as to look to the casual observer like a leaf in the wind. But to the participants, each experience may be intensely romantic. In other instances, an especially fast and impersonal contact may be entirely polarized around a sexual theme, and yet its very narrowness may be designed to round out an existing imbalance in a person's life. He may use just such a contact to re-experience something of the spice and challenge which has dwindled in an important ongoing relationship he presently maintains and wants to keep. A person's desire to preserve an emotional fidelity to a permanent partner is frequently his major motive in keeping any other partner at the arm's length of anonymity.

In looking back over these examples of promiscuity, one sees that no general system of classification will hold. Since even the most fleeting, impersonal contact may rank anywhere from being utterly superficial to being a richly motivated aspect of a person's life, its meaning and its value to him are impossible for anyone else to assess. (Even very astute observers can misjudge the importance of their own brief encounters; to accurately judge the personal significance of other people's contacts is beyond the pale of possibility.) Moreover, there is serious doubt, anyway, as to whether there is any intrinsic connection between the quality of a contact and its original motivation. The soon-felt impact of an experience, as well as the meaning it may come to have, are both latecomers to the scene—emotional spinouts which occur too late in the sequence of events to qualify as more than accessories to promiscuity's motivation.

In the final analysis, the most important observation (and the only safe one) is that males have an abounding capacity to quickly respond to new partners, a readiness which is activated primarily by their ability to read value-connotations into such fragmentary cues as the bodily features of the particular kinds of partners they have previously eroticized. The relatively high promiscuity of homosexual males is almost entirely attributable to a combination of circumstantial opportunity and the escalating effect of males dealing with males.

Ongoing Relationships

Every kind of relationship works. When people are attracted to each other—for whatever reason—they are capable of developing attachments which are rewarding and lasting. Thus heterosexual, homosexual, sado-masochistic, transvestitic, and dozens of other special relationships hold the potential of working well and of maintaining the symbiosis of ongoingness. Homosexual relationships are particularly feasible, largely because they overlap and duplicate so many of the interpersonal arrangements which have been stabilized in heterosexuality. In fact, the two are not very different in most of their basic aspects.

Certainly a few sharp differences do exist. The dominant-submissive arrangements of heterosexuality (including plenty of variations to suit individual tastes) are demonstrated on every side. In interacting with each other, men and women are guided by traditional social mores as to what to expect of each other in terms of the division of labor and of leadership. In homosexual relationships these particular arrangements have to be individually worked out. Then, too, the sharp contrast between the sexes gives heterosexuality a whole series of advantages and stumbling blocks which are largely replaced in homosexuality by a quite different set of problems. The fact that homosexual partners are alike in so many ways gives their relationships the mixed blessing of high rapport—a similarity of response and of outlook which affords certain advantages, but also conveys a host of disadvantages for which there is no set of social stereotypes to furnish guidelines.

But if ongoing homosexual relationships are workable, then why the almost universal impression that they are rare? Part of the answer is that they are far less conspicuous than are promiscuous examples. Nor are they easy to visualize at a distance. Almost anyone can imagine what might go on in a fleeting sexual contact but it is hard to picture what an ongoing homosexual relationship is like without ever having seen one. Thus an image of promiscuity tends to drown out the possibility of knowing that most homosexuals (including very promiscuous ones) sooner or later do establish ongoing relationships.

It has often been suggested that while homosexual relationships may not be rare, most are relatively unstable and short-lived. Both viewpoints are valid and yet either one taken alone can be misleading. In fact, the very cases cited to support one interpretation, on close examination, will often support the other. Consider, for instance, the man who has had perhaps a hundred brief encounters, a number of short-range affairs, and one profound relationship which lasts for years or for the rest of his life. This combination of experiences is not at all unusual and it lends itself to three correct statements about the man: that he is highly promiscuous, that most of his relationships do not last, and that he clearly can and does maintain an important and substantial ongoing relationship.

The seeming contradictions here—though they exist more in the observer's head than in reality—cannot be overcome by ascribing different kinds of experiences to different periods in a person's life; he may have them all more or less simultaneously. Nor is it appropriate to strike an "average" for experiences that differ widely in impact and duration. Since promiscuity by its very nature involves many contacts, and ongoing relationships only a few (perhaps only one), they must not be given equal weight. To do so would make it possible (but highly misleading) to say of nearly every sexually experienced person that "most of his relationships do not last."

But none of this quite gets to the nub of the matter. What must an ongoing homosexual relationship have in order to deserve the title—and by what measure is its stability to be judged? These are already difficult questions even in heterosexuality due to a lack of any general agreement on criteria. To the person who expects a lasting relationship to be permanent, it "fails" if the partners ever separate. A few people build monogamy into their expectations and thus tend to disqualify even permanent relationships if the partners have side-contacts. Still others grant little credence to matters of "fidelity" or to sheer lastingness, insisting instead that the only true measure of a relationship is the duration of affection. But sophisticated observers tend to reject all such criteria as either patently moralistic or as simply naïve. They point out that many relationships continue to exist (and continue to be rated by the partners as "good") long after affection has disappeared, even after antagonism has replaced it. (Couples may stay together as long as they find their relationship at all useful—a usefulness that may amount to as little as the avoidance of being alone or the holding of a close, not necessarily liked, partner with whom one can "be himself.") In other cases, an affectionate and well-balanced relationship may suddenly break apart due to a particular conflict neither partner knows how to resolve. (One partner may discover another's "infidelity," view it as an adulteration of the whole relationship, and walk out while the partner, lost for words, fails to refute the false case being made.) Thus, it must be realized that the durability of a relationship is only one indication, and not necessarily a very good indication, of the essential stuff of ongoingness.

Whether an observer would recognize a homosexual relationship as ongoing after it lasts a year, ten years, or a lifetime depends on the particular criteria he uses, just as it does in judging heterosexual ties. But one thing is certain: If any relationship is to outlast its original fascinations, the partners must be able to deal with most of their conflicts, to live with those that are not resolved, and to find enough appeal in being together to sustain the loss of quite a few of their initial attractions.

Virtually all that is unusual about homosexual relationships stems from the similarity of same-sex partners—that is, from the relatively little contrast between them. At first glance, this may seem self-evident, and yet it takes a fair amount of sophistication to realize that intimate expressions of sex and affection can even occur between partners who are alike in their gender and in their general behavior. Thus, when people who are not familiar with homosexual relationships try to picture one, they almost invariably resort to a heterosexual frame of reference, raising questions of which partner is "the man" and which "the woman." (Naïve homosexuals sometimes share this logic and, on first realizing their sexual proclivities, may judge themselves through conventional eyes; a few have their faith in their own "identity" shaken to the point of beginning to act like the opposite sex.)

But since neither partner in the great majority of homosexual relationships shifts gender-behavior, how do they manage to interact smoothly? From a distance, one might expect them to face formidable problems of dominance and submission, problems in the division of labor and of who is to lead or to follow. But these particular problems seldom arise. The division of leadership into neatly complementary spheres of action and decision-making often equals the very best meshings in heterosexuality. Such matters as who is to fix the screen door, or do the cooking, or feed the cat as well as which partner is to wield the most influence in social or in household decisions all seem to fall into place as if by prearrangement.

Incidentally, these role-relegations are notoriously unpredictable from the surface. The boy with the bulging biceps may fancy himself (often quite rightly) as a gourmet cook and spend all day in the kitchen, while the partner who arranges the flowers and greets the guests may have to rush in from heavy outdoor labor to do so. Or the talkative lesbian with the charm or the force to dominate social conversation may compliantly defer to her near-silent partner in matters of structure—when to buy a new car, which friendships to encourage, and when to go home from a party.

This is not to say that it is always easy for two people to successfully blend their various dominant-submissive attitudes, nor that the homosexual relationship itself is particularly conducive to tranquility. In fact, the evidence suggests that homosexuals are relatively intolerant of clash, and that they are not particularly good at either contending with it or reducing it. But they often are good at avoiding conflict by other means. The high priority they place on smooth relationships, coupled with their advantage of dealing with easier-to-understand same-sex partners, makes them quick to detect a mismatch at the time they are first choosing a partner. And since it is relatively easy for homosexual partners to backtrack from their mistakes in partner-selection simply by separating, the relationships which do last tend to be excellently balanced.

But while dominance problems are rare in homosexual couples, there are other consequences of partner-similarity which are decidedly troublesome. The very fact that the partners understand each other as well as they do can make their arguments and fights especially painful (each knows where to sink the knife). By comparison, heterosexual partners are relatively insulated from each other by their differences. Men and women do not even pretend to fully understand each other; when they quarrel, many of their verbal assaults land off-target. The woman who lambasts her husband as being an insensitive brute hurls a charge accidentally so loaded with he-man connotations, it may almost be a pleasure to hear. But an angry male partner knows exactly where a man's ego rests and how to zero in on it—just as an angry lesbian can be far more cutting to a woman's pride than a man can.

In the bedroom, too, the high rapport of same-sex partners can be a mixed blessing. Their similarity permits them an easy, quickly perfected intimacy—a super-contact that may allow them to touch the stars but which soon hurdles all the barriers on which sexual fascination depends. Of course, the newness and high voltage experienced in the early stages of any relationship are short-lived, but sexual interest between homosexual partners tends to decline more sharply than in heterosexuality. It is not unusual for a man and wife to retain a workable if not very intense sexual interest in each other for twenty years or longer, but such time-spans are rare in male relationships and exceedingly rare among lesbians. (Unless the partners take certain special precautions, the erotic side of the male relationship usually descends to critical levels within five to seven years; many lesbian couples largely give up overt sexual contacts within two or three years.)

The extraordinarily fast and deep decline in sexual interest between lesbian partners deserves a special note. Evidently it stems not only from the high rapport and high intimacy of the partners, but from the relatively low libido of many women. And yet the fast decline of sex can hardly be interpreted as a fundamental flaw in the lesbian relationship. On the contrary, the lesbian couple frequently achieves what virtually no relationship involving a young male ever can: It can continue smoothly and at a high level of intimacy and personal reward following the double event of a hot fire having quickly cooled. It is a remarkable achievement and one which is full of implications. It suggests that women have certain "nest building" proclivities which permit them to extract more nonsexual rewards from a close relationship than men can. And if it is fair to transpose the "lessons of lesbianism" over into heterosexuality, as it almost certainly is, then there is much to be said for the ancient idea that women generally supply much more of the glue and the constancy of ordinary marriages than men do.

On the other hand, the male-male relationship frequently has great lasting power, too. Where does it get its stability? It is well and good to say that any two people who are well matched build up a substantial affection and a spreading dependence upon each other which resist the forces of separation. And of course, a continuing relationship tends to elaborate itself into a network of shared experiences, mutual possessions, a growing similarity of tastes, and frequently a whole social structure—all of which support ongoingness. Still, the relatively short-lived sexual intensity between two males, coupled with their eventual appetite for the drama of new contacts, are formidable challenges. These have to be met if the relationship is to continue—and met with more effective means than moral intent and guarded abstinence.

The sophisticated homosexual couple (usually having gained that sophistication through previous relationships) tends to anticipate the problem and build a bulwark against it before their initial fascination with each other begins to subside. They may carefully avoid setting up a "fidelity contract" with each other and gear their expectations to include sexual contacts on the side, contacts in which an emotional investment in any new partner is deliberately avoided. Often more inventive arrangements are made. These may include threesomes in which one or both partners bring home a person who is shared in bed but who is not permitted to intrude on the basic relationship. There may be foursomes, or orgy dates, or conservative variations on the common heterosexual solutions such as the spoken or unspoken arrangement that any side-contact is to go unmentioned—or that almost any side-contact is all right if it is *always* mentioned. Not infrequently, partners who have been together for some time and who are secure in their affection go considerably further. Each may bring home partners who are not to be shared. Sometimes one or even both partners have hot, short-range romances which are discussed at home, often with amusement and a certain seasoned benevolence. While the possible arrangements vary considerably, most have several features in common. There tends to be an aboveboard recognition by both partners of the value of what is fleeting as well as of what is enduring, along with a realization that these appetites are far safer if not placed in competition.

The ongoingness of a relationship, however, depends on much more than the management of sexual problems. In both homosexual and heterosexual ties there are strong indications that people who come from particularly stable backgrounds are more able and more inclined to maintain stability in their own lives than are those whose parents and relatives easily resorted to divorce. And there is considerable evidence suggesting that an individual's personal tradition is itself influential. The teenager whose first affair lasted for years not infrequently shows a tendency to "stick with" any subsequent relationship as long as possible—sometimes to the point of being blind to the most obvious mismatch, or of steadfastly continuing a relationship far past its usefulness.

Finally, beyond all matters of sexual management and personal tradition, the ongoingness of a relationship may owe much to the kind of platform on which it began. If a person is especially turned on by a particular set of physical and psychological traits, and if he then manages to find these in a partner who returns his affection, he may find himself irretrievably bound to that partner almost regardless of how unbalanced the relationship may later become. It is as if the power of the original meshing forms a near-indestructible attachment which continues to sustain the relationship despite later disappointments and conflicts. It is noteworthy that the original formation of this platform of enthrallment does not necessarily require high admiration or other romantic elements. A person can be enthralled (the word itself means emotional enslavement) by a partner who hardly has more in his favor than the fact of his being first.

Of course the power and influence of *thralldom*, as the Victorians used to call it, is a classical observation. It repeatedly appears in the mores and folklore of most societies. It is reflected in the legend of the Sleeping Beauty who is (sexually) awakened and becomes permanently attached to the man who first kisses her. And the same idea is elaborated in various notions of the virgin bride: From primitive tribes to high civilizations one hears that a virgin makes the only true wife—that only this kind of woman can be captured and captivated forever by the firstness of her husband and is thus not inclined to respond to other men.

Despite all the exceptions and various logical objections which could be brought against this basic idea, there appears to be a note of truth in it. Certainly there are a variety of situations in which a first enthrallment proves to be especially tenacious. Perhaps this is because a person's first strong attachment frequently entails a naïve and uninhibited all-out commitment which he or she may never again quite match. In any case, the trend is highly apparent in homosexuality where some of the most durable—even fanatically indestructible—relationships are those in which at least one of the partners has had no previous experience.*

But of course, most lasting relationships develop between partners who have each had previous attachments to other people. *Their* affection for each other is based on less magical sources than enthrallment and tends to last to the extent, and only to the extent, that they retain their compatibility. Certainly the basic components of compatibility are the same in heterosexual and homosexual relationships. Both require sufficient rapport (a similarity of response and outlook) to support closeness and affection, along with sufficient resistance (distance and dissimilarity) to support complementation and sexual interest. But while the basic components of compatibility are universal, the problems encountered in balancing heterosexual and homosexual relationships are strikingly different. The heterosexual blend tends to be rich in stimulating contrasts and short on rapport—so much so that popular marriage-counseling literature incessantly hammers home the advice that couples should develop common interests and dissolve their conflicts by increasing their "communication." By comparison, homosexual relationships are overclose, fatigue-prone, and are often adjusted to such narrow, trigger-sensitive tolerances that a mere whisper of disrapport can jolt the partners into making repairs, or into conflict.

This relatively oversensitive attunement of many homosexual relationships has often been interpreted as one more indication of the homosexual's "neurotic instability." Sometimes it is. But in view of the fact that the individuals involved usually have a

---

*In discussions among sex researchers it is often suggested that a first relationship gains part of its tenacity and thralldom from the youthful dependence and impressionability of the younger partner. They have in mind the many instances in which an enduring homosexual relationship begins with an inexperienced adolescent falling in love with a much older partner. But in view of the many other instances in which the older partner is the inexperienced one and the one most desperately bound to the relationship, it is apparent that the kinds of impressionability and emotional dependence in question are less attributable to a person's age than they are to the newness and revelatory qualities of his first experience.

history of having "fine-tuned" only particular relationships (those in which their rapport with a partner was especially high) it is evident that an oversensitivity in two people's interaction stems more from their high rapport than from their having any unusual "personality traits."

In any case, the high rapport which characterizes many homosexual relationships can affect more than their compatibility. In particular instances it can greatly affect the kinds of complementation they offer each other. Pairs of lesbians or of males sometimes have an extraordinarily high similarity of tastes or outlook—a similarity which can cause them to greatly exaggerate whatever central tendency they share. Both partners may be gregarious and keep each other in a constant social whirl. Or if they are shy and retiring, together they may be able to live further from the social mainstream than either partner would have alone. When same-sex partners are equally committed to the same interest or attitude, be it running a business, raising horses on a farm, or of simply being alike in responding to the events of life, their match can have an almost fiendish unity, much as if it were made in heaven—or in hell.

At the other extreme,. the very ease with which same-sex partners are able to achieve rapport often permits workable relationships between persons who are separated by a far wider social gap than can ordinarily be comfortably bridged in heterosexuality. The basic contrasts between men and women are sufficiently great to virtually preclude ongoing heterosexual relationships between partners who differ sharply in age, race, background, or social level. (And of course, the whole social structure of heterosexuality works against the crossing of these barriers.) But it is not unusual to find homosexual relationships in which such chasms are bridged with ease. Sometimes the contrast between partners is enormous: the man of letters and a stevedore, a newscaster and a Japanese chef, the professional man and a construction worker, a biochemist and a truck driver. It is as if a fundamental rapport between same-sex partners not only permits them to hurdle huge social distances but often to be especially stimulated by them.

All of these extreme examples are, of course, potentially misleading. For while very high and very low contrasts between partners are much more frequent in homosexual than in heterosexual relationships, they remain more the exception than the rule. Certainly the great majority of homosexual men and women choose partners from backgrounds very like their own—rushing, as it were, toward all the advantages and disadvantages of same-sex similarities. The meshing and the degree of accord between two lesbians, for instance, quite generally exceed anything the heterosexual wife can reasonably hope for. Similarly, the accord and the ease with which two men may shift back and forth between following and leading as they engage in a task together often reflect a brand of congeniality seldom seen in any heterosexual context. And yet the local contrasts between homosexual partners await their chance to stand out in sharper detail (nearer to clash) than one sees in equivalent heterosexual relationships. It is as if heterosexual partners, swamped by their fundamental contrasts on every side, become inured to the shock of their minor differences as they struggle (perhaps in "a period of adjustment") to save what is enthralling. By comparison, homosexual partners bask in the warmth of an immediate accord which both hastens fatigue and leaves them relatively unprepared for the shock of discord.

The difference between the two kinds of relationships is perhaps most apparent to marriage counselors. In their arbitration of heterosexual conflicts they almost routinely see major collisions between the whole outlook and style of two people—a finding that leads, at worst, to the realization that a particular match is a mistake. But homosexual conflicts tend to have a fine-grained quality, frequently boiling up from items of such small substance as to suggest that the partners simply "want to fight"—or that the whole homosexual alternative lacks feasibility.

Counselors who mainly see effective relationships tend to gain a quite different impression: that homosexual and heterosexual bonds share a host of commonalities—as, of course, they do. In particular, the settled-in qualities of the homosexual couple tend to be precisely those which characterize the stable heterosexual relationship. The similarities evidenced in daily life are especially noticeable. The way the partners interact as they engage in conversation, the way casual affection is expressed and minor irritations are dealt with, as well as how visitors are treated, or dinner is served, and myriad other details of everyday life are all more or less indistinguishable. Viewed from this angle, there are clearly more differences between individuals and individual couples than there are between kinds of couples.

Finally, it is worth realizing that homosexual and heterosexual relationships are alike in a far larger way: They both drive toward the same set of ultimate gratifications. And certainly the "basic compatibility" aimed at by attracted partners is always about the same. What differ are the paths taken, and the kinds of problems that are encountered en route.

9

The Psychology of Effeminacy

Effeminacy is any style of male behavior that resembles the gestures, movements, or mannerisms usually associated with women. Although it is more frequent among homosexual than heterosexual males, effeminacy is relatively rare even in homosexuality and would not require as much attention as it does if it were not that, in the minds of many people, it characterizes the whole group.

In a few societies an even more extreme view is held, as evidenced by the fact that in several languages every word for homosexuality is a synonym for woman-like. More than sheer ignorance seems to be involved. The higher the taboo on homosexuality, the higher the illusion of heterosexual universality and the more incomprehensible homosexuality becomes as anything other than some sort of impaired masculinity. But when a high amount of homosexuality is expected (as in societies which encourage or at least do not ban it) there is little or no tendency to assume that homosexuality implies effeminacy, or that effeminacy necessarily indicates homosexuality.

Broadly speaking, effeminacy is always taboo, even where

homosexuality is not. But there are notable exceptions: In several American Indian tribes it has been interpreted as a positive trait earning special privileges or even a godlike status.[30] In other instances, the effeminate male—apparently because he is so easy to criticize that it simply becomes more interesting to react to him in some other wa —is lauded for his uniqueness. Even in our society there are a few odd situations in which a male's effeminacy brings him a position of high rank or a protected status. He may be seen as so far "out" that he is back "in"—for instance, when he is adopted by a group of ruffians as their mascot, anyone who abuses him becoming the target of the whole group.

Effeminacy is seldom a consistent style of behavior; it varies enormously both between and within individuals. Some people are effeminate in only a few areas of their behavior—perhaps in their body movements but not in their speech, or vice versa—and even then, only under special conditions such as when they are amused, angry, surprised, or drunk. Other people are effeminate only in particular gestures which remain unchanged through every mood and circumstance. More often than not, effeminacy is related to particular attitudes toward life and toward confronting other people. But there are individuals who from their earliest years show such a consistently high animation, or such delicacy in every movement they make, every word they speak, and every attitude they hold as to suggest some sort of decisive, even hereditary, predetermination. Unquestionably, effeminacy varies not only in intensity and in the parts of the personality that are involved, but in its origins as well. Clearly, there are great variations in the kinds of problems for which effeminacy is a solution.

In some people, effeminacy is reduced by the very circumstances that intensify it in others. There are men who are quite effeminate in everyday life but who lose these mannerisms when they are under pressure, when they need to accomplish something in a hurry, or when they are swept forward by strong emotion. It is as if whatever is curvaceous, fragile, or devious in their behavior is hardened and straightened by pressure from the outside or from their own emotions. But these same pressures drive other males into effeminacy, males who may have smoothly conventional ways of dealing with situations in everyday life.

Effeminacy is sometimes related to the social aspects of homosexuality. There are males who are quite effeminate until they "come out"—after which, a clear recognition of who they are and what they want evidently bolsters their self-assurance and the directness with which they deal with problems and handle personal encounters. Other males, on the other hand, show no effeminacy until after recognizing their homosexuality. They seem to have accepted not only the sexual alternative but the whole conventional idea that their sexual choice means a lowered masculinity, or that a potential for effeminacy has somehow been given sanction by the homosexual choice.

Actually, there is a clear consistency in the opposite reactions of both men after accepting their homosexuality. In each, there is a tendency for effeminacy to exist only on the hesitant side of "coming out" (i.e., before or after the event). For one man, this self-recognition is frightening, cuts his confidence and self-reliance, thus increasing his effeminacy. For the other, self-recognition is so clarifying that it increases both his confidence and his aggressive self-reliance, thus wiping out his effeminacy. Or to restate the matter a different way: It is approximately correct to say that the opposite of a soft effeminacy is an aggressive unequivocalness—an unequivocalness which some homosexuals gain by finding themselves, and others lose by the self-interpretations they make after fastening an outgroup label on themselves.

The popular notion which equates effeminacy with femininity is far from accurate. Or rather, it is accurate in a few respects and totally incorrect in others. But before straightening out these matters, it is useful to have a clear picture of "male" and "female" motion.

Masculine Motion

Body movements which match the stereotype of what is expected of males in our society display certain characteristics that are easiest to see in exaggerated examples. A masculine walk—such as that perfected in military training—is straightforward, energetic, and contains large, sharp-edged movements as opposed to small, hesitant, or soft motions. A man's long steps and straight-line approach, coupled with the relatively rigid muscular control he maintains over his body and joints, tend to give his gait a ready-for-action quality. Many of these features are apparent even when his walk is a casual stroll.

Masculine hand movements show this same self-control, often to the point of stiffness. There is relatively little wrist motion and few occasions on which the joints of the hands and fingers are articulated beyond the practical needs of comfort and expression. No muscular determinants are relevant; strength and muscular development are not correlated with the way a person moves. Atlas and Hercules might well have been effeminate.

When the ordinary man faces no challenge and is simply moving against gravity, as when casually sauntering across the street, he usually moves whole sections of his body together rather than articulating the parts. Elements of flexibility and animation are not in keeping with masculine self-concepts. Even a quiet stubbornness, repose, and a casual security require an immobility that relatively small amounts of animation would destroy. A tautness and lack of flexibility pervades not only muscular and joint activity but a man's psychological postures as well (his readiness to confront others, take risks, etc.), indicating that staunchness and a relative lack of animation are decidedly attitudinal in origin. Certainly aggressive attitudes increase a person's readiness to engage conflict—meaning a tendency to meet force with force, or at least not to flee and, wherever possible, to see that most of the motion that results from an engagement should occur *in* and *to* objects in the outer world and not within himself. Clearly the guiding principle in maintaining a masculine image is that a man should remain steadfast.

The masculine stereotype also imposes this same movement code in verbal and conceptual areas. A man of few words, the "strong silent type," implies great strength as he communicates the stolid qualities of utter masculinity. In meeting bad news he cannot panic, fall apart, or show any sign of hysteria without considerable penalty to his image. In speaking, only moderate and slow animations build his image; anything approaching the voice animations a woman might use are out of the question. And in reporting dramatic events from afar, he gains special credits of masculine maturity if he can imply that *others* were hysterical and nervous while he was coolly observant—or, in the telling, to arouse more reaction in the listener than he himself shows. Here, as usual, the masculine posture is one of composure while most of the motion and emotion take place outside himself.

Feminine Motion

The stereotype of feminine body movement is the "opposite" of what is expected of males. A woman's walk, for instance, is most feminine when not straightforward, forceful, or goal-directed. On the contrary, here, as in all her gestures, there are curvaceous movements and a fluid limberness of the joints, permitting various parts of the body to be moved relatively independently of each other. Smooth, willowy articulations are commonplace. Plentiful small and not too forceful animations of the body, voice, and general demeanor remain the ultimate expressions of femininity.

All this motion within the body implies little readiness to be aggressive or resistant; it communicates approachability and submissiveness. When the body motions of a woman's walk are extended to the point of being stopped by the limits of the pelvic joints, the hips and torso pick up additional movement, implying still less readiness to resist. At extremes, the result can be a Mae West-type hip-swinging seductiveness. (This flagrant brand of seductiveness plays especially well to lower-social-level males who find much appeal in a clearly shown readiness to submit. Heterosexual males who laugh at such obvious seductiveness are attracted instead by more subtle forms of feminine animation that are a better match for their particular aggressive-submissive expectations of what a mateship should involve.)

At its conventional best, the whole feminine bearing suggests that a woman is sensitive, highly responsive to every intrusion from the outside and every emotion from within—in a sense, a bit like the princess on the pea. Thus the central difference between male and female stereotypes is that males are staunch and rigid, ready to resist any intrusion (with anything from courage to bullheadedness), be it a challenge from the outside or an impulse from within—and that females, flexible and animated, do not resist but bend with the wind, responding to pressures both from the outside and from their own whims by animating themselves with a pliancy that extends from graceful gestures to hysterical scatter.

These conventional differences between men and women are also reflected in their attitudes toward events and situations—and occur with far-reaching implications in their speech mannerisms. Women animate their voices with many more inflections than men use, varying the emphasis placed on particular words. Men tend to be relatively straightforward in their speech, stacking the emphasis on words that have an external reference. A man might say, "It's so *hot* in here" or "It's so *damned hot* in here"—the more his emphasis the more heat is implied and the sharper his complaint. Slight variations in inflection may suggest that the listener is to blame, or that the speaker is ready to take action against the condition or against whoever is responsible for it. A woman is more inclined to change that emphasis and say, "It's *so* hot in here" or "*Oh,* it's *so* hot in here." Her focus has shifted from the outer condition to her own reaction and to how much she is affected by the heat. Thus the action is mainly internal and suggests there is little chance she will personally (much less, aggressively) do anything about the situation.

Effeminacy and Femininity

Effeminacy and femininity are by no means synonymous, yet their similarities and differences have often led to serious misinterpretations. It has always been tempting to think of a man's effeminacy as his tendency to use the movements and gestures of women, and then to conclude that effeminate behavior lies somewhere between the differing mannerisms of the sexes. But there are few—very few—examples of effeminacy that will fit anywhere between masculine and feminine stereotypes. (It is true that these stereotypes are at opposite ends of a single spectrum and, consequently, that much ordinary behavior fits between them. People of both sexes often do say such things as, "*Oh,* it's so *hot* in here," thus mixing strong internal movement with an external emphasis. But this halfway-house between personal reaction and aggressive complaint is almost never effeminate, as it surely would be if effeminacy were anything in-between masculine and feminine stereotypes.) For reasons which will be examined later, effeminate mannerisms either overlap those of women or else, as is generally the case, they turn out to be considerably "more feminine" than anything women use.

Effeminacy can look so much like an exaggerated version of female behavior that early observers thought it must be a take-off on femininity, a caricature designed to ridicule women. But this is not at all the case. In fact, effeminacy is only rarely used with the control and standoffishness that caricature requires. And when an effeminate man does resort to caricature, it is never directed against a group and is rarely if ever hostile, though it may be used to make fun of a particular person or attitude—often an oversensitivity in himself, the effeminacy of another male, or the peculiarity of a particular woman. But by and large, the effeminate male is naturally so and is quite unaware of exactly what is effeminate in his own behavior. Even when he knows he is effeminate (usually by having had people mention it, rather than through self-observation) careful questioning generally shows he has only a slight or even a totally wrong idea of exactly which parts of his behavior give this impression. (People are very poor at seeing themselves as others see them, particularly where their behavior is the product of fundamental attitudes.) In any event, the effeminate male, far from being hostile toward feminine modes of dealing with the environment, quite obviously finds nearby mannerisms comfortable and useful.

Four basic kinds of effeminacy need to be distinguished: Nelly, Swish, Blasé, and Camp. These can occur as pure types (as they will be described here) or they may be mixed in a person who shifts from one to the other or who combines them simultaneously. But whether pure or mixed, they denote very distinct styles of behavior that accomplish somewhat different tasks in adaptation.

Nelly

Nelly, used as an adjective to describe effeminate males, implies that their predominant mannerisms, often including their whole behavioral style, are quite purely feminine. Gestures that are nelly have a soft, round, graceful quality that is genuinely feminine. This constitutes a unique effeminacy since all other kinds entail a speed, an intensity, or a forcefulness of movement that sets them apart from anything found in women. Describing a man as nelly ("He's a bit nelly") is always a critical description, never a neutral or friendly one; it implies that at least part of his demeanor is entirely girlish.

At the present time, nelly as a descriptive term is seldom used outside homosexual circles, as are the labels for other kinds of effeminacy. The reason is not entirely clear. Perhaps it is because this form of effeminacy is especially rare, or because examples of it are lumped together under broader labels. Incidentally, homosexuals themselves are none too careful in their use of terms for effeminacy, often loosely intermixing them. On the other hand, a few descriptive boundaries are strictly drawn. For instance, camp is not misused. Nor would any male in "drag" (dressed as a woman) ever be called nelly, for whether he is seen as funny, crazy, or outrageous, his efforts are deliberate and carefully thought out. Nelly implies a spontaneous, casual femininity, one having a certain bone-marrow authenticity. Part of its insulting connotation is that it is so much in a person's nature that he is neither able nor inclined to control it.

To encounter a nelly male or even to find a few of these qualities in a man is disconcerting to most homosexuals—more so, in fact, than to ordinary observers, and more so than are other forms of effeminacy. For while other effeminacies (especially if they are prominent) are also disliked by most homosexuals, they are nevertheless seen as having a few redeeming qualities. They can be amusing, carry a dramatic comment, or amount to interesting self-expressions. But nelly, the presentation of a genuine femininity in the incongruous body and garb of a man, is confusing and a shock. And to the homosexual viewer, it is more than a little fraught with the contagion of stereotype associations.

From the heterosexual's point of view, on the other hand, nelly is one of the least disturbing forms of effeminacy. It is notably lacking in hostility, in bitchy qualities, or any flamboyance and consequently has the remarkable characteristic of being obvious without being loud. Nelly males tend to be unusually gentle; they seem never to be intrusive or sharp-tongued. And while their friendly, quietly sissy ways of dealing with people certainly do not guarantee acceptance, their lack of guile, obvious vulnerability to criticism, and often a kind of open self-confidence do not make them rewarding targets of attack. In fact, some of the most remarkable comradeships (occasionally even mateships) seen in recent years have involved nelly males. These have included a rough-and-tumble football team with a protective loyalty toward a nelly cheerleader; a group of ordinarily strongly antihomosexual men who have time and again argued among themselves over which one of them "Tommy likes the most"; and an extremely effeminate man of letters who has repeatedly demonstrated an ability to quickly transform almost any jeering critic into an admirer.

Most such examples have not involved anything overtly sexual—though some have. Among the most astonishing scenes witnessed in the course of this investigation were a few in which a rough-and-ready Puerto Rican male, in full view of his comrades and with no threat to his image of total maleness, was able to openly carry on an affectionate courtship of a nelly male, sometimes with much holding and kissing. In the eyes of certain lower-social-level men in particular, it is as if a male's effeminacy at the extremes of nellyness is simply a legitimate femininity—so much so that one's own actions, if kept dominant enough, are still seen as completely heterosexual.

The origins of nelly behavior are probably more varied and are certainly more obscure than those of any other form of effeminacy. Nellyness appears to be fashioned more from internal processes and a major elaboration of inversion than, like the other effeminacies, produced on the spot from a moment-to-moment avoidance of stress and conflict. Not that this should be taken to mean that nelly behavior is lacking in a certain defensiveness, or that it holds any patent on inversion. Probably nothing is more conflict-avoidant than the standard use of inversion. Throughout eons of mammalian experience, it has been a classical means of disarming adversaries and thus avoiding conflict—i.e., by a male's changing his behavior away from confrontation and toward a submissive compliance, he duplicates certain behavioral styles of females, styles which greatly discourage hostile assault.

But the nelly male's inversion is so well worked out (and is by and large so consistent) that it goes far beyond mere defensiveness; it obviously provides a wide range of positive rewards. His duplication of ladylike mannerisms can be virtually perfect, especially when he is playing out his role with an aggressive partner. But seen in context this flawless femininity is all the more baffling, for while every gesture is perfectly on target, certain fundamentally masculine components are operating at full tilt: The sex-drive is high, erections are vigorous, visual sex responses are in full operation and in moments of anger a savage directness can emerge. Usually this kind of effeminacy has a dyed-in-the-wool permanence—and yet sometimes, after years of consistent nelly-ness, a man can step out of it as if by throwing a switch.

Swish

A hand movement which may be gracefully soft when done by a woman can gain so much energy and speed when done by a man that it becomes swish—the very word denotes the rush of air around a high-speed motion. The exaggerations of swishy effeminacy—the same ones that can make it look like caricature by somehow being more feminine than femininity itself—are the result of rounded, highly animated motions being transposed into the more muscular and aggressive repertoire of a male.

Swish is such a loud violation of what is expected of males that it usually generates a considerable degree of irritation or shock in observers. Although there are local situations in which swishy movements and flighty, hysterical reactions in males are amusing (in comedy and in "nervous Nellie" movie characterizations), these styles of behavior more often arouse antipathy or even revulsion. The noneffeminate homosexual is often especially allergic to the swishy male's violations of masculinity. These reactions are important because they impose a certain social isolation on the swishy male, further increasing some of the social pressures that swishiness itself is sometimes designed to avoid.

There are instances in which an all-pervasive swishiness dominates nearly every movement and mannerism of a person who has been an outgoing sissy since earliest childhood. Swishiness may become evident in some boys only after puberty has put real force behind their actions and attitudes (a clear illustration of the drive and high energy-consumption of swish). In still other instances, a loud, swishy effeminacy seems to be actually cultivated by persons who, like the general public, associate their homosexuality with a lack of manliness and who then use a flamboyant effeminacy as a kind of homosexual badge—a way of being triumphantly out of step with the social mainstream, perhaps defiantly outgoing after years of feeling squelched.

But no matter what motivates swishy behavior, it always implies particular ways of dealing with external challenges and internal stress. Externally, it means that the individual is especially interested in avoiding direct confrontation with anyone or anything in his environment. He animates himself rather than the outside world. He may register complaints with flippant hand movements, disapproving glances, grimaces, or other nonverbal gestures. But his repertoire does not include simple straightforward statements of fact or opinion—much less firm commitments that imply some steadfast belief or a readiness for combat. In expressing joy or surprise he gesticulates, moving parts of his body around through a variety of animated emotions.

Internally, the swishy person is not only able to tolerate this fluid, hysterical display of emotion; he enjoys it as a style of expression through which he can spend considerable energy without having it brush against inner controls or outer confrontations. Tension is released immediately as he avoids the pain of sustaining stress and the frustrations of delaying his reactions to stimuli—the price which every other male pays for self-control and poise. It is as if he would rather be stampeded in any direction by every pinprick of life than suffer the amount of self-restraint and containment that steadfastness requires.

In accomplishing work, the swishy male's behavioral policy of dealing with inner hysteria and outer threat by dancing around every challenge and presenting a moving target to every adversary usually impairs his ability to be practical. On the other hand, it is an affirmation of the many-sidedness of the human mind and personality that the swishy male, for all his floundering, is sometimes, somehow able to organize this scatter into orderly achievement, even genius in some field. This, of course, is the exception and not the rule; but it is astounding that the precision required for directional accomplishment can ever spring from a fountainhead of lighthearted chaos. Evidently at some deeper level of the personality—remote to the point of being invisible at the surface—there can be discipline directed by an iron hand.

Blasé (The Queenly Gestures)

Many males with effeminate tendencies are uncomfortable with swishy gestures and attitudes, quite aside from the social hazards of being that obvious. To overreact to inner impulses and external stimuli can be exhausting—due both to the nervous energy it requires and to the scattered, unsettled feeling that results from such an extravagant expenditure of attention and energy. Although every effeminate person is somewhat hypersensitive—that is, overattentive to what goes on in his environment—there are other solutions to this problem. One is to adopt a posture of studied indifference—to rise above seductions to his attention, act as if he is oblivious, thus becoming blasé in his attitudes, his physical postures, or both.

Sometimes the blasé attitude looks like a hold-your-head-high-and-be-unmoved kind of posture. Or, it may have a quiet elegance—sometimes quite plain and genuine-looking, or overdone to the point of a regal standoffishness. Calling such a person a "queen" is the homosexual vernacular for this regalness, a seemingly haughty overcontrol and imperturbability that is reminiscent of real queens. The whole posture is clearly what psychologists call a reaction-formation, an exaggerated correction away from an original tendency—in this case, away from overreacting to everything and overanimating oneself.

A blasé attitude is also one of the classical postures of heterosexual females—who use it to arrive at a pose of elegance, a smooth casualness, or even some forms of suave charm. The main feature of blasé is the holding back or restraint of animation, both in terms of body movement and the expenditure of attention. Thus the central message behind high-fashion advertising of all sorts is the suggestion that some piece of clothing, some perfume, or some cosmetic will help a woman get more attention from people than she spends on them—affording her the luxury and security of standing back and looking oblivious to most of her environment (i.e., to imagined hoards of admirers), instead of being overreactive to them and overdependent upon them.

Blasé males share these same psychological problems and use the same behavioral techniques. And yet, only in a few very submissive males does blasé behavior come anywhere near duplicating what one sees in women. Ordinarily, due to the extra drive and energy of males, the conserving gestures they employ to control their animation are more pronounced and, consequently, are less smooth than those of women. A man's blasé body movements are more forceful and his control over them more stringent, with the result that elegance becomes overelegance and smooth casualness becomes a studied casualness. With the addition of more forcefulness, blasé easily becomes haughty and imperious. When blasé attitudes affect walking, peripheral movements are usually eliminated, resulting in a fast, straight-line, tight-hip glide; the gait may take on a mincing quality when a man's implicitly powerful steps are suddenly pulled back just short of their full stride.

In a man's speech, the blasé attitude often results in a kind of screaming understatement. He cannot be blasé and say, "It's so hot in here," for no matter where he puts the emphasis he runs the risk of either too much complaint for comfort or too much show of emotion. He can solve this problem in several different ways. He can say nothing at all and act as if it isn't hot—the very essence of blasé. Or he can dampen down "hot" by changing it to "warm"; get rid of "so," for that is too committal; then get rid of the declarative form by changing the whole thing to a question, so that it becomes, "Don't you think it's a bit warm in here?" If it now threatens to sound too prissy-polite (a constant risk in blasé), he can correct for this by emphasizing a word that has restraint built into its meaning, in this case "warm," so that it becomes, "Don't you think it's a bit *warm* in here?" If his speech is precise, as it often is in blasé, it may then have a British twang, which to American ears certainly doesn't reduce the effeminacy any, but it does take part of the curse off it.

Not that the restraints and overcontrols implicit in blasé attitudes are consciously thought out or used with much deliberation. On the contrary, whether a person's blasé restraints are exhibited most in his body movements, his social manners, or his speech patterns, they are spontaneously devised and put where they are because they "feel right" to him—and they feel right because of the work they do: They transform his various impulses to overrespond (to stimuli) into a pattern of underresponse, an underresponse which is conservative, safe, and usually somewhat elegant—if not overelegant.

In the eyes and ears of the outside world, blasé expressions generally succeed in doing exactly what they are supposed to do: They cover up the fragility, the vulnerability, and the animation of the user enough to give his behavior a smooth surface, a tone of quiet imperturbability. But the mask—like all corrections for original tendencies—is overdone in some places and fails to hide the animation in others, so that the acute observer, especially when motivated by anger or sexual interest, sees through it like a plate of glass.

Much the same can be said for the heterosexual equivalent in the aloof, quietly impervious female exuding an aura of seemingly self-satisfied independence. Her denial of vulnerability and her seeming self-assurance convinces many males, puts off a few others, and stirs everything from anger to envy in members of both sexes. But the interested male see through the façade. His appetite is whetted and he is stirred to conquest by the animation and responsiveness he intuitively knows is just below the surface, if he can but scratch it.

Camp

"Camp" generally means to cluster or gather together, thus to stack up or concentrate something. An army camp, a nudist camp, a summer camp, or even a political camp are all concentrations of people, actions, or attitudes.

Camp, used as a descriptive word for certain kinds of behavior, has a meaning not far from this—one which probably arose from the fact that in New York during the depression of the early 1930's, young homosexuals (especially those aspiring to the theater) often lived in groups, saving rent by sharing a single large apartment. These groups were called camps. Later, by association, the kind of behavior often seen there—highly animated reactions involving an overemotional stacking of emphasis—came itself to be called camp.

Until a few years ago, camp, used as a noun or adjective for certain kinds of emotional posturing (Susan Sontag has called it a "sensibility"[247]), was limited almost exclusively to the language of homosexuals. But it has proved so descriptive that it is now widely used outside homosexual circles. For instance, a drama critic may call an actor's portrayal "pure camp" or "campy," by which he means the actor (too expert to be called "ham") puts too much affected emphasis or play-acting emotion into his role. In fact, the critic is likely to be implying that the actor's performance contains several other kinds of exaggerations and pretenses that some of his readers will understand, and that can be understood here as soon as the meaning and mechanisms of camp are clear.

Camp usually displays an obvious effeminacy (in body movement it always does), but clearly effeminate or not, it invariably contains or implies a duplicity. (While *duplicity* ordinarily implies a dishonesty of some sort, its only meaning as used in this analysis of camp is a twoness, a polarity between opposite gestures, movements, or intents.) A campy gesture may couple a loose, oversensitive animation with an aggressive, pointed emphasis of some kind. Remember that in swish there was high animation coupled with a masculine forcefulness; camp extends this contrast much further. Loose, rounded body movements that at first may only be swishy (by being faster and more driven than anything found in femininity) are transformed into camp when the motion is momentarily or abruptly stopped, perhaps by a sharply bent wrist at the end of a sweeping arm movement.

This stoppage and sharp angularity causes a stacking (camping) of emphasis at the halting point. The duplicity may be in juxtaposing a soft, fluid movement with a harsh note at the end; or it may be in the separate directions of the arm and hand motions, or both. In speech, the swishy male's "It's so hot in here" in camp becomes "It's s-o-o-o hot in here"—both the affectedness and the vigor of the response are increased, but to the point that the listener no longer believes the reaction (or suspects, probably correctly, that the complaint has nothing to do with heat), thus the duplicity. Mae West's walk with its overanimated hip movement that is abruptly stopped at the limits of the pelvic joints is camp. (Practically everything Mae West did was camp.) The duplicity is in the display of a softly animated, submissive femininity put forth with an aggressive seductiveness in which all motion is momentarily stopped dead still.

But pure exaggeration, however extreme it may be, is not enough to produce camp. Thus cartoons and serious dramatic themes are seldom campy—although melodrama is, because its overseriousness, coupled with dubiousness, can easily give the major themes duplicity. Camp is an exaggeration that has been caught in isolation; it is usually a stacking up of emphasis made incredible by being outlandishly unnecessary or contrived. Oscar Wilde used a simple but intense form of camp when, on being asked how he spent the day, said, "I was working on the proof of one of my poems all morning, and took out a comma. In the afternoon, I put it back again." Another time, while staying at a country house, he came to breakfast one morning looking worn and tired. Asked if he was ill, he replied, "No, not ill, but very very weary. The fact is that I picked a primrose in the wood yesterday, and it was so ill that I've been sitting up with it all night." This camping of emphasis on one's own delicacy, carried to the point of being ridiculous and unbelievable, has the effect of throwing in doubt at least some of the effeminacy from which it springs.

Wilde also had the ability (not unusual among experts at camp) to overstate some personal sensitivity while using it to violently attack an idea, or even shatter a conversation, all without engaging the slightest resentment. Once when he was at an elegant dinner party, a highly analytic discussion developed as to whether or not the peculiar gait of Henry Irving added or detracted from his skill as an actor. In the midst of this, Wilde said, "Both Irving's legs are delicately intellectual, but his left leg is a poem." No serious discussion on this topic could continue.[210]

Camp can also be vigorously assaultive, as in the duplicity of exaggerating one's own frailty (stacking it up, so to speak) while highhandedly ridiculing an opponent's position at the same time. When a now well-known concert pianist was drafted into the U.S. Army and assigned to play in the band, he soon found the work very abrasive, so he decided to declare his homosexuality and get discharged. The short interview went like this: Psychiatrist: "Why do you want to get out of the service?" Pianist: "Well, you can't take a tree out of the tropics, plant it at the North Pole and expect it to blossom." Psychiatrist: "Are you a tree?" Pianist (while raising both arms straight up with his hands sharply bent out at the wrists): "Yes, and now I'm going to raise my leafy arms and pray." Such answers may infuriate an adversary, and invite him to give a moral lecture (as they did in this case), but they leave little room for effective counterattack.

Not all forms of camp are meant to be humorous, nor intended to be anything other than deadly serious. Something can become "a camp" in the eyes of the viewer whenever exaggeration and some duplicity are seen together. The image of a widow in mourning after the death of her husband is entirely believable, even if she overdoes it a bit. But it quickly becomes camp if she plays the role of brokenheartedness beyond believable limits, or buys Paris gowns in black to look her best in mourning. In fact, her sincerity matters not in the latter case, for as long as she combines a black withdrawal from people with a fashionable reaching out for their favorable attention, the duplicity is still camp.

It is interesting that some exaggerated stackings of emphasis that are eventually seen as camp are largely the product of historical changes in our own frame of reference. Thus many events of the past which seemed serious and reasonable at the time become camp when they are viewed against a backdrop of present-day standards. The image of a man decked out in a leather suit, scarf, and heavy goggles preparing for the hazards of a ten-mile-an-hour ride in some early automobile is camp—as are many of the extremes of rococo and Victorian ornamentation. Yet hoopskirts, fancy wigs, lace cuffs for men, and a thousand other excesses of some previous era are not camp—either because their context is preserved along with them, or because they cannot be ascribed to anyone's personal whim (a favorite platform for one side of a duplicity).

Moreover, the duplicity that is so central to camp usually cannot be seen in either an action or an object that is ascribed to more than one person. Thus if the early "automobiler" with goggles appeared in a group of similarly dressed persons, the image would not be camp, but merely strange costuming from the past. But when he is caught in a picture alone, and the viewer does not imagine that many other persons of his time dressed equally outlandishly, then his costume is likely to look like his personal attempt to be brave and overprotected at the same time—a duplicity that instantly makes its stacking of emphasis a camp. Similarly, it is possible to see a row of Victorian houses overdone with fancy ornament without finding any one of them a camp—for although each may be different, they are merely the style of a past era. But if one of the houses has curlicues and flourishes that reflect someone's attempt to be especially elaborate while conventionally stylistic, then it becomes camp.

The duplicity in camp can occur in any two parts of a scene and still have its effects. It may be entirely within the person, like the bravery and fear of the man with goggles, or the bitter-sweet exaggerations of some histrionic lover who is obsessed all too wrenchingly with both sides of his own involvement; "parting is such sweet sorrow." Or, the duplicity can be between a person's inside and outside posture. This is particularly apparent in camp that permits a person to pretend casual unconcern in a situation that has been carefully stage-managed: calling an expensive piece of jewelry "something I just picked up this afternoon"; lighting a cigar with a five-dollar bill; Nero looking bored while a few Christians are being eaten by lions before his eyes—or the opposite: someone going into raptures over a rusty nail presented as a serious piece of modern art.

"High camp" is that which presents several different duplicities at a time, especially when they operate on different levels. These double-entendres become especially high camp when they are syncopated into a unified whole, or are put at the service of some still larger duplicity. Oscar Wilde was so talented at this that he could turn the smallest incident into high camp. On his American tour he stopped at Washington, D.C., where he was to receive a correspondent who represented eleven different publications. As he put it, "I was slightly flurried, as you may suppose. I said, 'Now here is a man who moulds the thoughts of the West.

I must be on my best behavior.' In walked a boy of sixteen. 'Have you been to school much?' I asked. 'Oh yes.' 'Have you learned French?' 'No.' 'If you wish to be a journalist, you should study French.' Then I gave him a big orange and dismissed him. What he did with the orange I don't know; he seemed pleased to get it."

Here, there are all sorts of complex interrelated duplicities—of being light and serious at the same time, and of reversing the roles of who is interviewing whom (while keeping the vertical distances constant). There is the posture of caring what the West would think of him, coupled with the magniloquent stance that any journalist would need a language of culture to understand men like him. He implies that the interview was undercut by the unschooled youthfulness of the interviewer—or was it the unschooled youth of frontier America that awaited having *its* thoughts moulded? The situation is such that the interviewer had started out to get something from a big "fruit," so when a big orange was substituted, naturally "he seemed pleased to get it."

Both forms of camp—the first, where the stacking of emphasis and the duplicities are deliberately combined by the speaker, and the other, where one reacts to other people's stackings—have rapidly been entering everyday language and awareness. Camp certainly has great psychological utility. Not only does it allow its user to express his own emotional reactions and excesses but, much to the benefit of his listener as well, it easily detects and describes all sorts of excesses and duplicities in other people's ploys. Camp can amusingly blast what is square, challenge the Establishment, and otherwise highlight so many different kinds of human folly that it becomes a powerful cathartic. The campy complaint can get away with hurling daggers, even prescriptions for murder, because it suggests more the speaker's agony than any real danger to the victim.

In 1966–67, when the tide of public opinion turned against President Johnson for talking one way and acting another, a bumper-sticker lament asked, "Where is Lee Harvey Oswald now that we need him?" And against Nixon in the 1972 elections there were large posters showing a disheveled, disgruntled, very pregnant Negro woman morosely staring out at the viewer (already a camp) with the caption, "Nixon's the One." The speaker's display of his own pain and "helpless" fury (along with the victim's total invulnerability to the particular attack suggested) so tend to put the listener on the speaker's side that even a President's supporters can afford to smile. Nevertheless, any victim is in great danger from camp's assault, for while he is safe enough from the surface charge that may be totally outlandish—"Ronald Reagan is a lesbian"—camp is coming through a side door for the kill, just accidentally on purpose suggesting the *victim's* duplicity, and in this case, spotlighting precisely what is ersatz in him.

In order to see exactly what the various types of effeminacy have in common with each other and what they share with other styles of behavior, it is necessary to look behind the scenes at the kinds of human problems which every style of behavior must solve. So far, it is still possible to make the mistake of thinking of masculinity, femininity and now even effeminacy as fundamental adjustments, instead of seeing each of them as derivative. But derivative from what? From the basic human problems of controlling hysteria, managing aggression, and regulating emotional expressions. Each and every style of behavior amounts to a separate set of solutions to problems that everyone faces in dealing with himself and in coping with the environment.

Hysteria and Aggression

The human animal can be seen as fundamentally hysterical in a sense. His immediate ancestors are primates—monkeys and apes that have always depended upon a great many defensive adaptations to their environment. These have included agile flight, vocal threats, and the use of many nervous body animations capable of draining off tension and anxiety. Humans have retained much of this easily frightened, basically defensive orientation to life. They show a nervous temperament given to high animation along with a physical vulnerability guarded by a quick fearfulness, vocal challenges, and many joint-articulations near the outer extremes of the body—equipment left over from tree-living and which is somewhat more adapted to escape than assault.

Although man's larger brain has given rise to language, organized thought, intellectual systems, and other tools that can be much more useful for defense than are jungle screams, he remains as nervous and as wary of possible threats as were his forebears. His imagination, so protective in a few of its anticipations, has also brought fantasy—a major source of tension and fear found nowhere else in nature. And when he acts defensively (as by running away from danger) he is able to see himself doing so, a kind of "feedback" that confirms his vulnerability in his own eyes, and may insult his ego as well. As a counterthrust against all this fear of enemies and the unknown, man learned to use both his systematized (obsessive-compulsive) thought and his planfulness. And from these he has often conjured up a deliberate aggressiveness. It is as if he early realized that to flee too quickly, or even to recoil, is to have one's self-confidence undermined— thus the birth of still other aggressive compensations such as concepts of bravery and the heroic ideal, the launching platforms for most masculine stereotypes.

These are the kinds of compensations that are carried over into the attitudes and bodily expressions of males in our society. By example and by expectation young males learn to greatly restrict their fluid body movements, to harden themselves in attitude and stance, and to stiffen their composure to the point of virtually eliminating self-animations as feasible tension-reducers. (The light and lively, often lithe and facile body movements displayed by native tribesmen the world over are stamped out of our adult males.) Conversely, our model for female movement tends to call for somewhat overanimated verbal and bodily expressions, sometimes carried to the point of a childlike helpless frailty. But easy comparisons of these male and female models, particularly those that emphasize a tone of hardness and straightness in the male image, have been seriously misleading. They have suggested, almost as if it were self-evident, that the movements and postures of men spring from and epitomize their aggressiveness while the ways of women denote their lack of it—a trap made all the more tempting by the morsels of truth these notions contain.

There is, indeed, a certain aggressive-submissive balance between the sexes. And certainly the many straight-line movements of males and various other elements of their directness represent an aggressive readiness to engage or to penetrate the environment. Conversely, the softer, more curvaceous movements of women "hit the outside world" less forcefully, less aggressively. And yet a moment's reflection will quickly show that aggressiveness by itself is not the key. Many timid or tranquil males are nowhere near as forceful as more assertive men, but neither are they any more curvilinear in their body movements. And many women with curvaceous ways and gentle gestures show courage and "guts" in facing the world. These disparities between a person's surface behavior and his or her actual substantiality can be much more extreme in homosexuality, especially in the effeminate minority and its lesbian counterpart. Lesbians of the rare lady-truck-driver sort can be astonishingly direct and "masculine" in their whole manner and bearing. (Their posture is no mere pose either; when crossed they can be fierce and dangerous to deal with.) Yet in other respects these women are notoriously timid and unsure of themselves, often right when one might least expect them to be. Similarly, the sissy male with limp wrists whose willowy ways respond to every breeze often demonstrates an audacity, sometimes an ironclad will, that can not only withstand hurricanes of abuse and adversity but which frequently give him the gumption to be extraordinarily forthright in other ways.

Modern psychology cannot claim to fully understand such examples, every one of which is fairly loaded with unsolved if not unsolvable problems. Even to adequately describe what is known of human aggression in these contexts is a formidable undertaking—one which yields hardly more than a handful of tenuous formulations. But perhaps even these will be useful.

It is probably true that forthrightness in any form, a kind of conflict-readiness, always requires elements of aggression. But if aggression is to amount to more than bluff and bluster, a mere flash-in-the-pan, it must have substance and tenacity behind it. When these qualities occur in a person's surface behavior (i.e., at the "engagement front" with which he or she contacts the environment), they invariably add strength and straightness to body movements, cutting down on their animation and broadening their sweep; small gestures which happen to comprise curves and curlicues of motion then tend to be coarsened if not eradicated altogether. The total effect is a clear "masculinization" of body movement.

From this vantage point, it is tempting to believe that the ordinary timid male and the strong woman have simply accepted and copied the socially recommended patterns of surface behavior. Perhaps they have. But it can easily be shown that in order for a conventional surface behavior to "work," a person must both agree with its implications and be able to comfortably keep the various components of aggression in balance. If that woman becomes bored with the surface diversions and "passivity" of her role, or even if she continues to like it very much but develops a bit more ambition than is compatible with it, her newly energized courage is likely to show up at her "engagement front" in the form of directness and straightened out body movements. And if the timid male is to keep his timidity, he had better keep his low energy and low ambition as well, for if these were to increase in intensity without an equal increase in his conflict-readiness, they would instantly begin to "throw his body-parts around" into the conflict-avoidant curves of swish or of camp.

Admittedly, any such sudden changes are unusual, especially after adolescence. Ordinarily, the final structure of any personality gradually takes shape by or before then. The particular kind of hardening which a boy achieves is usually balanced out to satisfy both social expectations and the management of his own aggressive components—an adjustment which tends to suppress self-animations, increase his conflict-readiness, and reduce any apparent hysterical excitability. There is, of course, a good deal of leeway in how these adjustments are made, but not as much as one might suppose. Body animations of the curved and nervous variety are so well established in the whole history of man that only by relatively tough attitudes can they be suppressed down to the level our society defines as superbly male. There are risks in the opposite direction, too. At extreme levels, toughness and rigidity tend to reduce a person's resiliency—so much so that under conditions of very high stress the "tough" male is inclined to crack into open hysteria (sobbing, panic, or dazed shock) sooner than does a person of less brittle composure. Perhaps this is one reason the Ancient Greeks, while devoted to militaristic and heroic pursuits, held an androgynous concept of ideal manhood: great strength along with a supple, agile, and lithe body movement (an ideal, by the way, that is always more than a little conducive to homosexual modes of complementation).

In any event, the balance between rigidity and flexibility—between what amount to conflict-engaging and conflict-avoidant attitudes as expressed in a person's movement—greatly affects the behavioral techniques a person uses to reduce hysterical fears, to cope with his environment, and to feel comfortable in it. And as any behavioral style evolves, it begins to affect the whole economy of a person's psychic life, including how attention is spent and the consequences of spending it in different ways.

Paying Attention: The Cathectic Expenditure

The common phrase *to pay attention* contains an unsuspected accuracy. It denotes the fact that giving one's attention to something amounts to more than merely being receptive; it involves spending "quantums" of psychological energy on the object that one pays attention to. Freud called these units of investment "cathexes" (from the Greek *kathexis*, meaning *to hold*). Thus a cathected object is one that holds or receives an emotional payout.

Probably the paying of any kind of attention is exhausting in some sense. But when an emotional charge accompanies attention, the "outgoing cathexes" tend to drain or deplete the ego, making one feel less independent, less self-possessed than before. Conversely, the refusal to expend cathexes is a way of maintaining feelings of self-worth, even pride or conceit. Thus people are often able to achieve a "rich inner feeling" by various forms of stoic solitude, religious retreats, and Yoga-like withdrawals from the social scene. But to attain feelings of personal magnitude by simply clamping down on cathectic expenditures is frustrating—and it is risky, too, since it robs one of data about the environment, leading to wrong self-judgments and inappropriate social behavior.

Although the problem of controlling (partially inhibiting) cathectic expenditures is universal, "masculine" behavior contains a built-in solution. Any aggressive (conflict-ready) attitude toward the environment causes one to erect a certain wall against external objects, a readiness to butt against them, so to speak. It is as if targets of attention are seen in a context of confrontation, a "barrier formation" that effectively restricts any undue investment, particularly the large losses of cathexes that would be entailed in any affectionate or overfriendly attitude. Thus a man's relatively "tough" posture toward the outside world, or even his maintaining a quiet cohesiveness, amounts to presenting a solid front that lowers his animation and restricts his emotional investments.

"Feminine" solutions to the problem of cathexes control tend to be more elaborate. Relatively soft, conflict-avoidant attitudes do not permit the use of external (confrontational) barriers to resist the flow of cathexes; internal barriers must be set up instead. By stepping back from forthrightness, various coy and other nonassertive postures that evolve tend to restrain a person's cathectic investments at source. In situations where more action is necessary, a person can use curved body movements or animate one body part against the next, thus generating a twisting motion that affords a soft resistance against the outflow of cathexes. The relatively low "libidinal pressure" of very passive women can sometimes turn the resistance inherent in self-animations into a fairly effective barrier to cathexes. Ordinarily, however, the net result is not quite effective enough for comfort. Thus most people who use "feminine" modes of operating tend to overspend attention and "run a loss" in their cathectic economy, causing them to institute additional restrictive measures.

These measures vary. A few individuals use a kind of bland emotional flatness, squelching their expenditures from the outset. Others use an emotional standoffishness, a kind of narcissistic "selfishness," or merely a stubborn standpatism. More frequently and more pleasantly, many women choose to go ahead and engage in an exorbitantly expensive outpouring of animated attentiveness (be it flirtatious or friendly), designed to please both themselves and others, but also designed to "seduce back" enough attention and return-affection to replenish their losses.

But in this system, replenishments still tend to lag behind expenditures, with the result that a hunger for affectionate attention stays especially high—"A woman needs to be loved." Hence, beauty aids and other cosmetic attempts to gain attention and to generate admiration have been used by women throughout recorded history.

The inventory of feminine techniques designed to balance the cathectic budget includes, then, three basic alternatives which can be mixed or used separately: 1) A person can recoil into a passivity in which emotional expenditures are suppressed at source, or 2) The cathexes can be filtered through a maze of self-animations that partially block and reabsorb them on the way out, or 3) By various means of "extraversion" a person can generate enough admiration and/or attention from others to compensate for losses. These techniques may seem somewhat artificial, and in a sense they are, especially where cosmetics and elaborate modes of self-presentation are used to dazzle onlookers. And yet, a conflict-avoidant and therefore highly self-animated adaptation to the environment is so well established as a basic style of behavior, both for man and all his nervous relatives right back to life in the trees, that the top prize for a work of fiction probably should go to the male posture of imperturbability.

The effeminate male, like everyone else, must come to terms with the hysterical trends that are fundamental to humans—only more so, because he is more so. His conflict-avoidant attitudes pull him back from the alternative of aggressively confronting situations in his environment, leaving him all the more defensive and overattentive in orientation. Such an overattentiveness and overresponsiveness to people and to events entails very high cathectic expenditures—expenditures which are brought under partial control by erecting barriers within himself. These barriers may take the form of body animations that by their curves and angles impede the outward flow of cathexes. Or, instead, the outward flow may be impeded by placing one part of the body in opposition to an adjacent part—as by the sharply bent wrist, or by moving the whole upper torso out of line with the hips, or vice versa. In short, the effeminate male is driven to reinvent the basic techniques used by women—but with a vengeance, for his high "libidinal pressure" cannot be contained by the graceful angles and the gentle gyrations of femininity.

But how does a person's high animation succeed in conserving his cathectic expenditures? The simple answer is the same as before: By merely inserting angles and curves into movements which to the casual observer may seem to be little more than random gestures and scattered motions. In a sense, they *are* scattered since their main job is to allow a person to be expressive in a situation while at the same time permitting him to circumvent any direct engagement of an outside person or task. In other words, the outward impetus of a movement can be broken by an angle or slowed by being deflected into a sharply rounded line; sometimes most of its energy is spent in a maze of serpentine curves.

To visualize exactly how these body movements accomplish their aims, one can imagine a microscopic picture of the difference between straight and curved motions. If a straight-line movement is thought of as an almost infinite number of motion segments all pointed in the same direction, then a curved movement can be seen as the result of slightly changing the direction of each of these segments as they occur. Increasingly sharp curves are produced as adjacent segments are put at sharper and sharper angles to each other. And as the sharpness of the curves increases, more and more resistance is offered to the flow of cathexes, the force of which now begins to "push around" the body parts—as seen in a fast-moving hand, arm, shoulder, wrist, or whatever—increasing their speed perhaps to the level of swish.

But swish is not necessarily the result. Blasé or camp will be produced if a person tightens his "inner structure" against all this limberness. He may reduce the number of curves and small animations yet manage to keep the same amount of resistance to the cathexes simply by dividing the movements he does make into fewer segments that are more sharply angled to each other— perhaps a single sharp bend of the wrist, held for a moment at the end of an outward-moving arm motion. Where a considerable amount of force is involved, the placing of body parts at sharp angles can cause the cathexes to pile up at the curves, so to speak, or to be stacked up into camp at the end of the last motion.

It is interesting that this same angularity (a kind of going toward the environment and away from it at the same time) does not need "body parts" in order to be expressed. It is fully apparent in entirely verbal examples ("It's *so* hot in here") where the subject-content of a sentence points to an external fact, while the speaker's emphasis is on his own internal reaction, thus pointing the cathectic flow back to himself. Or the cathectic outflow can be resisted (and thus conserved) simply by squeezing down on its free expression. For instance, in the sibilant sounds of a lisping speech—"*Ssso* I *sss*aid to him, *sss*ee here . . .*"—one hears a kind of high-pressure leakage of air past an overanimated structure which is momentarily being held rigid.

In blasé, there is usually a preference for dividing the movement into only two or three parts that are placed at such sharp angles to each other as to utterly dampen both the apparent animation and the cathectic outflow. A typical choice is to point the body in one direction and the head in another, while the actual target of concern is the viewer, yet with little loss of cathexes through any of these channels. Blasé gestures, with their turning aside from any direct expression of attention, quite often produce an air of poise. But the tone of blasé is determined by a holding in check of whatever threatens the poise. Turning one's head away from someone to avoid spending cathexes on that person easily gives blasé a haughty look. But essentially the same movement may make a person seem suavely tranquil when the aim is less to turn away from somebody than to suppress his own animation—as seen, perhaps, in a static posture with head held high, pointed a bit up and to one side, as if modeling a stylish coat. Still other tones result when fast extensions into the environment are suddenly pulled back, as in the mincing walk or the quick, wordless head-turnings that some people use in expressing annoyance.

A person's momentary or ongoing preference for camp usually means that he feels a desire for forceful action and that he would be uncomfortable with either the ineffectuality of blasé or the overfluid animation of swish. The high energy of camp tends to make it robust, often pithy. And although camp usually presents both sides of a double-entendre, its central action is a stacking of emphasis which can sometimes attain duplicity with a single powerful thrust that causes the listener or viewer to supply the other half, usually a counterthrust of disbelief ("Yes, [I am a tree] and now I'm going to raise my leafy arms and pray"). In examples of this sort, camp demonstrates a startling efficiency. By lavishly overinvesting cathexes in the target-idea, the whole notion is made ridiculous and is therefore rejected, leaving the cathexes unspent and thus conserved.

From this vantage point, it is perhaps clear how the basic constellation of camp can sometimes unintentionally occur in various situations of emotional excess, where it nevertheless wreaks its havoc and seeks its dire economy. For instance, the overdone sweetness of art nouveau (a camp from the outset) so exceeds the limits of plausibility as to quickly deteriorate into mere decoration. Much the same can happen in life situations and in the theatre. The actor who stacks too much emotional emphasis on a scene makes his performance or the scene itself unbelievable—much as love or any other emotion stacked to its unbridled limits raises the ghost of its antithesis.

While it would be correct, then, to say that the salient features of effeminacy are its conflict-avoidance and its limber animations—features which certainly give the effeminate male his fast movements and an inordinate tendency to stack his emphasis in peculiar ways—the psychological problem which effeminacy faces and solves is not at all unique. Everyone faces, and must come to terms with, a superabundance of hysteria (though it is usually the first order of business to see that the solution rather than the problem should show). More urgently still, there is the problem of managing the flow of cathexes. Evidently the development of man's higher mental processes has turned what might be called his attention-matrix into a broad new parameter on which symbols of giving and of withholding are played out. The coin of cathectic expenditure has become a medium of real value, the stuff of which is capable of making one's ego feel anything from rich to utterly impoverished. Suffice it to say that in the management of cathexes the business of establishing reasonable exchange rates can enormously affect the way a person deals with his environment—and moves in it.

But in the final analysis, what is the meaning of effeminacy itself? Is it a "sickness" of some sort? Is it that the effeminate male, in the course of growing up, somehow fails to get hardened into tougher stuff due to some lack in his childhood, as has often been suggested? Hardly, if ever, will such explanations hold up—nor would they be of any particular value if they did. Worth remembering is that effeminacy is no mere lack of masculine attributes. Through all its variations it is a distinct style of behavior with a definite program of aims and accomplishments. Like every other brand of movement, it is adaptive in regulating a person's flow of energy within a framework of how inner and outer stress is perceived.

Objectively viewed, effeminacy might best be judged according to how well it serves a person's spontaneity, and thus his efficiency. But it is so rare and so contrary to the goals and styles of most people, it seems destined to retain its image of being bizarre. On the other hand, effeminacy looks very different in different individuals, largely depending upon what other qualities of personality are combined with it. It can come across as anywhere from tasteless and silly to something smoothly natural. In certain combinations it can give a person a radiant ebullience, or embody the very spirit of an effervescent wit.

But probably most of the differences in the way effeminacy is seen stem from subjective biases in the observer—mainly whether his own behavioral adaptations are momentarily helped or threatened by seeing a particular kind of effeminacy. The effeminate male's oversensitivity to a huge variety of minor irritations and his ready articulation of these in his body movements and in verbal exclamations can be full of humor, and make seeing the world through his eyes a wonderfully articulate experience. But those same gestures and exaggerations may be painfully obnoxious to someone else who sees them as making mountains out of molehills that were not bothersome in the first place. To watch any bit of effeminacy is to momentarily identify with it, to see and feel its conflict-avoidance in action and, willingly or not, to be whirled around by its ballet of self-animations. Thus, an effeminacy that may be hilarious and a joy to one observer may be excruciating and revolting to the next.

Still, most examples of effeminacy, when not imbued with wit or some other element of special appeal, are experienced as decidedly unpleasant, especially by males. The ordinary man (heterosexual or homosexual) has not developed his poise and a more aggressive straightforwardness for nothing. Over the years he has largely succeeded in freeing himself from the hysterical animations that dominated his boyhood and which, in ever new forms of fear and uncertainty, hover near much of his adult life. For him to now encounter effeminacy is to re-experience a nervous conflict-avoidance that screamingly violates the very compensations he has come to value most.

And no doubt part of the pain many people experience in viewing effeminacy stems from seeing how it deals with the cathexes. One of the ways the ordinary man maintains his self-esteem is to guard his cathectic expenditures by holding a posture of being unmoved, of being impervious to most bids for his emotional attention. Thus the whole economy of his psychic life is based on conserving most of his cathexes behind a hard front, a wall of regulations, letting go toward only a few objects he deems worthy of concern or of affection. From the moment he sees and thus vicariously "tries on" effeminacy with its animations, its indirectness, and its internal barrier-formations, he feels it foolish and full of artificial restraints. But then, other people's restraints always tend to seem ridiculous, especially when one already has a different set of his own.

10

The Politics of Homosexuality

There are several ways in which homosexuality can come to be politically significant. When highlighted as an issue of social danger or moral concern it can transform public apathy into a cry for action that can be very useful to the obscure and ambitious politician. Well-established political factions, too, often build moral platforms on homosexual scandals within the ranks of their adversaries. Within government agencies, homosexuality may have a quieter significance. Not infrequently, it must be carefully dealt with as a politically dangerous presence in the private lives of prominent figures. In still other instances, the talents of particular homosexuals are knowingly sought out, or unknowingly put to use. Of special significance are the ways in which the emotions aroused over homosexuality sponsor political maneuvers far afield from government—maneuvers that quite often circumvent the obligations of law, of science, and of scholarship. All these involvements are worth being understood, for they contain much that is relevant to the consequences of homosexuality, and to its social and sexual psychology.

In their desire to gain and hold public support, even politicians who would not ordinarily resort to sensationalism sometimes yield to temptation and climb aboard a bandwagon of moral reform. Less reputable politicians often deliberately whip up concern over everpresent sexual issues. A mayor, police chief, or district attorney may seek the political rewards of publicity, a dynamic image, or the special favor of his constituents by cracking down on "vice." The homosexual makes an alluring target— especially in the early stages of a "cleanup" campaign before certain· hazards of pursuing him have become apparent.

In fact, sweeping campaigns against homosexuality are fraught with political perils. Raids on particular nightclubs, for instance, can net the friends or relatives of prominent people, if not such persons themselves. Even the collection of preparatory information can lead to complications. It is easy enough to keep a safe-to-chase hustler under surveillance but this may lead straight to the son of a judge, or to the judge himself. A sex raid in Manhattan once swept up a crown prince who, by the time he was correctly identified, was so deeply entangled in routine police procedures that merely extracting him from the clutches of the law was a noisy event within the department. The cooperation of the press had to be obtained and an international incident was narrowly avoided. Lesser examples of this sort are common enough to make the selection of politically neutral targets risky and difficult.

Local moral campaigns aimed at the homosexual sometimes do initially benefit their sponsors. Preliminary plans may be worked out at City Hall, including news releases to stir up public indignation. But then hazards tend to arise on every side. For one thing, any broadly organized police campaign soon develops a target problem. A sizable number of chargeable offenses is required to sustain such a program—a difficult matter since homosexuals are not inclined to be disorderly. Charges of "disturbing the peace" are rarely possible without falsifying the circumstances of arrest. Charges of "loitering" or "congregating" net too few offenses to be useful—and anyway, they lack the credibility, the legal substance, and the necessary drama to satisfy any newly aroused public appetite for police results.

Officials caught, then, in the embarrassing position of having mobilized an army without a feasible adversary frequently seek to rack up the needed offenses by various methods of entrapment. These generally entail the use of carefully chosen police decoys to incite arrestable offenses, but such measures tend to jeopardize legal processes quite as much as they do the intended victims. The net result is usually a series of arrests that will not hold up in an honest court. The courts can often be "fixed" of course, which is not unusual, but this has the awkward feature of involving still other echelons of officials subject to graft and bribery at every level.

Intentionally or unintentionally, the public is sometimes actively brought into campaigns against the homosexual, and the greater this involvement the more dangerous it becomes—to everybody. The case of Boise, Idaho, stands as a classic example—one which took place back in 1955–56 but which was still replete with open wounds and lively political concerns when John Gerassi began investigating it in 1965, a full decade later.*

Judged from the surface, the whole Boise affair seemed logical enough at the start. It appeared to begin with the discovery and arrest of three men who were said to have seduced two young boys (actually the boys were rough, physically mature male hustlers aged fifteen and seventeen, but the public was not told this). The *Idaho Daily Statesman* sounded the alarm with reports of "lewd and lascivious conduct" and "infamous crimes against nature" followed by inflammatory editorials with such titles as "Crush the Monster" and "This Mess [of homosexual crime in our midst] Must Be Removed"—backed up by police department announcements that a thorough investigation was under way and that further arrests were imminent. In the meantime, the prose-

---

*Gerassi was an editor of *Newsweek* in 1965 but had quietly taken a leave of absence to check into the seemingly ancient Boise affair. He had hardly set foot in the place when word came—his first note of alarm—that the governor of Idaho was exerting pressure on *Newsweek* to stop his investigation. From other quarters, he was harassed with strong-arm methods and anonymous threats against his life. Nevertheless, he persisted; his final report, *The Boys of Boise*, was published by Macmillan in 1966.

All details, events, and summations cited in the present account of the Boise affair are from Gerassi's careful report.

cuting attorney and the courts were moving with inordinate speed. One of the first three men who had been arrested on a Monday night was promised leniency if he would plead guilty, which he did. And yet by Wednesday of the following week he had been sentenced to life imprisonment.

Four days after the first three arrests, a prominent banker was arrested as a member of a now widely assumed "homosexual ring." It would have looked less like a "ring" if the public had been told that the banker had never met the other three men, and that the only "ravaged children" involved were the same two rough, grownup kids. But these facts were carefully withheld both by the police and the district attorney. The big news on the surface was that the banker (a family man with a well-brought-up son of his own) admitted his homosexual interests and that he had had contact with the boys—although when the time came to get the boys' sworn statements, these were extensively "doctored" by the authorities, undoubtedly to make them read more convincingly in court.*

The police continued their search for "the others" and actually did manage to arrest a dozen people, but only by spreading their

---

*As so often happens in politically motivated scandals, the authorities themselves quickly became entangled in extraordinary cover-up procedures. The first coverup involved only the fact that the "innocent children" were really mature hustlers. But as evidence against the banker accumulated and formal statements were required, it then became necessary to cover up the original deception by hiding the fact that the older boy (Baker) was now in the U.S. Army, and that he had been well known to Boise police all along. (Baker had been arrested the previous year on a burglary charge and the police had agreed not to prosecute him if he would join the Army, which he did.) Now that a statement was needed from Baker (in order to prosecute the banker) a courier had to be quietly sent to Ft. Carson, Colorado, to get it. Unfortunately, Baker's statement (as he must have actually given it) sounded nothing at all like that of some innocent kid who had at first objected to being sexually "played around with" but who was finally seduced, so someone made numerous changes in it to reflect this scene, changes which also included a complete rewrite of the sex act itself. Just how the Boise courier managed to succeed in getting the U.S. Army's criminal investigator at Ft. Carson to witness and sign this remarkable document is not known—but succeed he did.

net to include relations between consenting adults—a fact nobody seemed to notice amid all the talk of lewd and lascivious conduct with "our youth." And to make matters worse—much worse—*Time* reported that the city has "sheltered a widespread homosexual underworld that involved some of Boise's most prominent men and has preyed on hundreds of teen-age boys for the past decade," that in recent investigations the "police talked with 125 youths who had been involved," and even that "the usual fees given to the boys were $5 and $10 per assignation."[259]

The people of Boise (50,000+), having been primed by their own press and now reading all this in a national magazine, were brought to a state of near-hysteria. Never before had people "known" that so many were involved, and that neither men nor boys were to be trusted. The police instituted a curfew on all youths below the age of 17. Men were embarrassed to meet in pairs, or to attend their clubs without their wives. Friday night poker games were discontinued (until somebody thought of arranging for at least one woman to be present), and inattentive husbands were viewed in this light. It became out of the question for a man to pause to watch football practice for fear of looking as if he were "interested in" the boys.

With the men's growing embarrassment at their own embarrassment, the hubbub subsided after about a year. Somewhat before then, the more intelligent among them correctly had the feeling they had somehow "been had." But many people continued to believe in the substance of the scandal—so much so that as late as 1965, Gerassi was assured that at the height of the goings-on, "Millionaires from all over America, indeed from all over the world, were flying into Boise because only there could they select fresh young boys for their favors . . . and, in fact, that there was so much homosexual traffic into Boise that United Airlines had to put special flights into operation during the busy season—the summer."

The truth of the matter was hardly less fantastic than that, and much less amusing. The whole scandal turned out to have been planned, financed and stage-managed by members of Idaho's ultra-conservative power-elite, a faction Senator Glen Taylor once characterized as "The Boise Gang—a small group of willful, well-heeled corporate politicians" who run the state. As is not infrequently the case, a homosexual scandal seemed ideally suited to the attainment of several side benefits and one central goal. Besides being a newsworthy shocker (the editor of the *Statesman* belonged to the conservative clique) and something to shake up City Hall with—making particular careers and breaking others—it was intended to "get at" the power of a man insiders knew to be homosexual but who had such wealth and influence it was felt he was untouchable in any other way.

These higher-ups demonstrated a remarkable flexibility in midstream, too. At one point they came to dislike a particular city councilman for "hollering too loud" and decided to punish him. (He was actually "hollering" for more and faster action, but undue haste is dangerous to a properly managed scandal.) Without saying a word to the councilman, the powers-that-be quietly arranged for the sheriff to fly to West Point and bring the man's son back to Boise, where it was shown that the boy had had homosexual relations years before when he was fourteen years old. As a result of these revelations, the boy was expelled from West Point, leaving his father humiliated and heartbroken.

The only part of the plan that went awry was the trap set for the rich, powerful mystery-man. The police were told of him immediately and "had a talk" with him all right, but he was indeed too hot to handle. He either bought off the police or, much more likely, simply brandished his clout to frighten them into total silence. He never had his name mentioned, let alone the bother of being charged with anything.

While the whole Boise affair was no doubt exceptional in its sweep and scope, none of its main details was unique or even very unusual. Certainly the political ramifications tend to be extensive in any affiliation of naïve, well-meaning laymen with sophisticated and much less well-meaning power factions. For regardless of whether a citizenry has more or less spontaneously become aroused over a particular issue (an alleged corruption of its teenagers is a favorite) or whether it has been systematically stirred up by stories designed to spark public reaction, the result is the same: the forging of a powerful political tool. In the hands of a political party, the "accidental" discovery of an instance of homosexuality within the ranks of the opposition can be very useful in casting the kinds of aspersions that shift votes. Exactly this ploy was used by the Republican party against the Johnson Administration a few weeks before the 1964 elections—the Jenkins case. And while in this example there was the substantiality of an actual homosexual event, the resourcefulness involved in its use pales in comparison with what certain Nixon Republicans did in using homosexual slander during the 1972 elections—and what still other Nixon Republicans evidently planned to do after that.*

With more frequency if less scope, the pungent blend of sexual sin and public clamor finds its most enticing uses in what it is able to do for or against a particular individual. To the ambitious but obscure political figure, nothing is more useful than a flag-waving "cleanup" drive. Thus such campaigns have usually been headed by one man who was not well known before. Armed with the ensuing publicity, he gains instant recognition as an energetic, courageous reformer. One is reminded again of Richard Nixon, who first rode to prominence on the Hiss-Chambers investigation, where homosexuality was a loud side issue. Ordinarily, however, where homosexuality can be cited at all, it is an up-front issue for reasons which are, indeed, perfectly clear. It cuts across every social level, it can be charged with existing in "high places," and because the public tends to think of it as infectious, it can often be described as "growing" and as a danger to young people. At least the charge that it exists in high places is true, and it can be an especially relevant fact. Whole campaigns against homosexuality have quite often originated as attempts to "get at" the power and influence of a single individual—as was the case in Boise.

---

*While the particular acts for which Donald Segretti went to prison involved the circulation of false homosexual rumors against a prominent Democrat, this was only the tip of the iceberg. Homosexual matters of more consequence were dealt with at the very highest levels of Watergate: Sexual and homosexual allegations against a number of political opponents were prepared in and for the White House (from unsubstantiated reports in FBI dossiers). Under a claim of executive privilege, these allegations along with suggestions for their possible use (spelled out in the unreleased "enemy lists") escaped the spotlight of known Watergate offenses by a hair's breadth.

But the power of publicity and public opinion extends far beyond politics in the usual sense. The vote of the public is crucial, not only in elections but at the counters of commerce as well. A few years ago CBS Television decided to produce a major documentary on homosexuality which would go beyond the usual points (that "experts" do not agree, that the life of the homosexual is a sad and sordid lot, and that the public is solidly against it). Thanks to various social changes and a genuine increase in public frankness in the early 1960's, it had seemed possible by 1965 (when the CBS project was first proposed) and even more possible in 1967 (the year the documentary was produced) to turn out a candid, interesting program on the subject. Young, talented producers were assigned to the task, and at other levels, too, the whole project was well motivated.

In an effort to give an inside view, five homosexual men were interviewed on camera with questions designed to show how their lives looked to them. The producers chose individuals with differing slants. Two were quite disturbed people who would provide drab reports, a third man would present a mixed picture, and two others would reflect a certain healthy cheerfulness. The blend was supposed to give the report balance, but this was not quite how it worked out. In preliminary editings, the two drab cases tended to come across merely as disturbed individuals, while for some reason the "happy" examples seemed to greatly outweigh them. A new balance was struck by editing the mixed case in such a way as to make it decidedly "unhappy." (This man later threatened to sue the network for misrepresenting him but did not actually do so.)

There were other "unhappy" notes, too. Included in the program materials were several short interviews with professionals, none of whom said anything very favorable, and the two psychiatrists among them (Irving Bieber and Charles Socarides) gave quite dire reports. With all this in mind, the producers wanted to leave the other two interviews with "happy" subjects alone. They especially appreciated the handsome, all-American-boy freshness of one young man—among themselves they called him Jack Armstrong—and they liked the note of relief he gave to what otherwise now threatened to be a too-dreary picture of the homosexual.[263]

But when the documentary was first completed and came up for executive preview, it was decided that this segment was still too supportive. It was not that anybody thought the ratio of "happy" material was too high. It was just that this particular man happened to have such a strong, clean exuberance that his whole bearing seemed (in the eyes of some) to "recommend" his style of life. This would be dangerous. It might bring charges that the documentary was "for" homosexuality, or at least be disquieting to advertisers and possibly draw letters of complaint from the public. Yet to cut out the segment would bias the program in an already strongly stated negative direction. What the producers finally did to "fix" the interview was remarkable. At crucial points they cut the sound track into separate words and phrases, and by rearranging these they managed to change the man's sentences and the gist of what he was saying.

The program was broadcast only once, for when "Jack Armstrong" saw what they had done to him—and heard himself say up-tight, completely unfamiliar things—he entered a formal complaint against CBS, citing fraud, withdrawing his release, and thus freezing all re-runs.[265]

Although this example is no doubt very unusual in the extent to which deliberate misrepresentations were used, it is typical in other respects. The news media and the advertisers who support them are both subject to the retribution of an angered public which can switch channels or buy someone else's product. Unbiased views are hard to arrive at in the first place, and are virtually impossible to express with safety when they are out of line with prevailing social attitudes.

Homosexuals who come to be aware of certain hand-in-glove relationships which spring up between journalists, policemen, lawyers, and judges (sometimes with the aid of psychiatrists and clergymen as well) have often felt there is some sort of conspiracy against them. But they are mistaken. An intermeshing cooperation does not require collusion. Authoritative actions of various kinds are unified by a set of shared moral assumptions—all the more so when matters of power and influence are at stake. When caught up in any of these contexts, homosexuality is merely a convenient issue; the public at large is the target of concern and the ultimate victim.

Paradoxically, some of the policies and campaigns most damaging to the homosexual have been engineered by homosexuals themselves. Sometimes the stage is set by hardly more than accidents of circumstance. A politician or policeman who happens to be homosexual may be nominated as chairman of an influential committee, or become the police chief of a town, a state, or the federal government. Up to that point, he might never have had occasion to take a stand on sexual issues, or to cast an influential vote relevant to homosexuality; his private life simply may not have intersected his career. But in his new position a local movement against "vice" or merely the tenor of the times may demand action. He has several alternatives. He may sit back and merely go along with programs that are activated by his subordinates. Or with special fervor he may prosecute particular forms of homosexuality toward which he happens to hold conventional views. Armed with an intimate knowledge of the subject, he sometimes organizes programs that zero in on particular targets with exceptional efficiency. The one choice he generally cannot make with personal safety is to be energetically liberal. This is a choice usually reserved for the heterosexual politician who, with no personal risk, is free to be as liberal as he likes. *He* can even afford the hazards of labeling a witch-hunt as such, or of calling for law reform.

The psychology of a high-ranking homosexual's antihomosexuality can be quite complex. Although he sometimes seems motivated by a simple desire to protect his own position, he more often exercises a complicated morality in which he justifies his own preferences by publicly attacking nearby variations as outrageous. He can do this with a certain honesty in his own eyes. The priest who has long maintained a single ongoing homosexual relationship may join a mayor's committee for the prosecution of promiscuous forms of homosexuality. Or a district attorney who is only attracted to older men may vigorously prosecute homosexuals who "contribute to the delinquency of minors." These are still simplistic examples, cited to show the kinds of motives that are part of more complex instances.

A Wisconsin Senator with a rigid Roman Catholic background—the one whose name became a label for the early 1950's and who was responsible for instigating a vigorous antihomosexual program within the federal government—was primarily homosexual himself. (One of his biographers ranked this as unfounded gossip but he was mistaken[231]; part of the gossip was squarely on target.) Though the Senator turned out to be notoriously wrong in his claim of having found Communist subversives in government and was equally inaccurate in his charge that homosexuals in the State Department were security risks, he undoubtedly felt both right and righteous. For quite beyond the political opportunism of his capitalizing on the public's fears of communism and homosexuality, these entities—so unrelated to each other—were both matters of personal concern. As a religious and political conservative, he had two philosophical reasons for being violently rightist. And while there is nothing politically leftist about homosexuality, in the eyes of conservatives it can spell a *sexual* liberalism, equally cursed. There also may have been an element of vindictive denial behind the Senator's righteous indignation—much as in the anti-Semitism of certain Jews. No doubt there was gratification, too, in loudly spotlighting the secret lives of "enemy others" precisely in an area in which he wished to remain anonymous himself.

Although there is no way to accurately rank the importance of this man's several motivations, there is something quite familiar in the whole picture—shades of the priest and the district attorney mentioned before, here greatly elaborated. It would seem that when a fervent crusader operates from two morality systems at once—one in which he believes wholeheartedly, and the other in which he is vulnerable himself (and thus wants to look conventional)—an aura of pious purity pervades the mix. All this is part of the psychology of the demagogue whose fervor can make his issues seem important, but it is enough to give us all pause.

If we now turn the whole problem around and look at it from the other side—the psychology of public opinion—it is apparent that certain social elements have to be present for any fear tactic to work. Certainly the issue of the "danger" of homosexuals in government could not have been stirred up to this extent without the presence of certain preconditions. The early 1950's supplied these. It was a time of seeming perils and pumpkin papers in which the loyalties of many Americans were being questioned. And in retrospect, it appears to have been a time when the last gasp of a particular brand of prudish morality was being heard. Sex in any form was big news and the very word homosexual was largely taboo. (It could not be used on radio and television, for instance, which of course made it considerably better copy than it is today.) The really odd part is that the whole question of homosexuals in government was, and is, full of a more than slightly curious set of ironies.

The notion that homosexuals ought to be ferreted out of government—particularly out of sensitive posts—was (and is) based mainly on one assumption: that their need to hide their private lives makes them security risks due to a supposed vulnerability to blackmail. While it is understandable that this reasonable-sounding concern has broad appeal (no doubt this is why it is so confidently cited) it is out of line with the facts on several different levels. In the first place, blackmail is not a problem at any level of government. With the single possible, though very doubtful, exception of Austria's Alfred Redl (who handed over entirely false military information to Russia in 1912), there is no case on record of any person in any government ever having been blackmailed into disloyalty or into anything else, though unquestionably there have always been homosexuals in sensitive government posts, and no doubt always will be.

One can be sure that if blackmail would work, it would have been tried successfully. Why won't it work? Of course, the question is a bit academic; there are few places in science and none in the humanities where there is any obligation to say precisely why something *does not* happen. Still, in the case at hand, there appear to be numerous reasons, depending on the situation and sometimes on the special requirements of blackmail itself. Certainly in serious espionage work (and in other of the secret services) any attempt at blackmail by an amateur outsider would be tantamount to suicide; he would stand a good chance of simply being killed immediately. On the other hand, to persons handling confidential information, a blackmail threat (the more subtle the better) from a foreign agent would qualify as fortunate indeed. It would be (and sometimes has been) an open invitation to a double-agent situation—i.e., a muchly prized chance to feed wrong information to an agent who thinks he has the upper hand when, in fact, he is himself being duped.

But what about the run-of-the-mill homosexual in government? Is he not subject to being blackmailed? At first glance, one might think he could be. The main reasons he is *not* (beyond the little value of what he could possibly supply) seem to rest on the peculiar requirements of blackmail itself. A blackmailer generally needs a clear-cut, preferably exclusively held bit of evidence against his mark—evidence which he can hand over or destroy and, by so doing, offer a measure of protection to the victim. Thus the homosexual sometimes has money extorted from him by a policeman who has the choice of being able to arrest him on some charge, or not to. But the idea of a foreign agent having any such "drop" on a homosexual is out of the question. The agent's inability to turn his evidence on and off, and therefore his inability to convincingly control the "protection" he offers, is one of the limitations involved. And there are still other reasons which apparently make it very hard to sell a person "protection" against the revelation of ongoing sexual events, particularly when they are already known to a variety of other people.

In any case, whether the blackmailing of homosexuals in government is made unfeasible more by the special requirements of blackmail itself or by the many other difficulties that are inherent in any attempt to use sexual information against a person, the actual danger is patently unreal. Not only are there no such cases on record, the shoe is on the other foot. For most of this century, in Britain as well as in the United States, the very highest levels of governmental confidentiality (particularly diplomatic and espionage services) have been in the hands, and often under the leadership, of homosexuals.

Attitudes toward the homosexual within a given department are often more the product of the level of government than anything else. At the upper echelons of diplomacy, the private lives of most of the individuals are certainly known by those whose business it is to know such things. The information is usually considered irrelevant, although there are instances in which a particular assignment can clearly turn homosexuality into an advantage. It is the lower-ranking agent or diplomatic courier whose career is abbreviated by the leakage of such a fact—and then because of the leakage and not because of the fact. And at still lower levels, where a person's sex life would matter least if it mattered at all, dangers to the homosexual's employment progressively increase. The head of a minor department may be summarily dismissed for homosexuality, particularly if some outside investigator uncovers it. At the level of clerk, the unlucky victim is harshly fired and given a moral lecture to the effect that working for the government is a privilege to which he is not entitled.

The truth, of course, is that the privilege is the other way around. Effective personnel are always in such short supply that not even a competent file clerk, let alone higher talents, are comfortably written off. Department heads are aware of this and wherever possible are usually happy to avoid questioning a person's private life—until some incident breaks the image of surface conformity and forces them to put moral issues ahead of common sense.

The almost casual tolerance of homosexuality at the upper echelons of governmental and diplomatic service appears to rest on several factors. Men and women at these levels tend to have more independence, more sophistication about people, and are often more pragmatic in their approach to the tasks at hand. What counts is a talent for getting things done and a levelheaded mastery of swarms of information, often untold and untellable. If an aide happens to be homosexual, so what? There are even instances in which a person's homosexuality gives his superiors a comfortable feeling—"With his private life, he wouldn't dare step out of line."

In fact, homosexuality has occasionally been so easily accepted at the upper echelons of government that not just quiet private lives but overt misbehavior has sometimes been tolerated against staggering odds: An important diplomatic appointee of Franklin Roosevelt—a man who was a presidential courier during World War II and who held many important posts, including acting head of the State Department—was so flagrant in his homosexual conduct (as in approaching bellhops) that it was often necessary for his aides to cover his tracks, squelch complaints, and see to it that no mention of such things appeared in the press. At one point, Roosevelt had to personally intercede to keep him out of the news. He must have been an exceptionally talented man, for he held the confidence of more than one President—and they held his.

Part of the equanimity with which high-ranking political figures accept homosexuality lies in their personal safety in doing so. A scandal involving sex (unlike matters of graft) can hardly reflect on them, even when they are close to it. Thus when a President's aide or an ambassador he may have appointed becomes involved in a compromising sexual situation of such obviousness (or of such usefulness to the political opposition) that it can no longer be safely contained, the man's "resignation" is simply accepted and life goes on.

Furthermore, there are various forces which ordinarily protect persons of high station against certain invasions of privacy. Not only a President or Prime Minister, but authorities at several echelons below can receive visitors, arrange rendezvous, and sometimes have sexual affairs that are totally off the record—off even the most private of records. (Insiders in Washington, London, or Montreal may know of some of them, but the public and most historians never will.) At these levels, communications and arrangements of all sorts can be totally private. By pressing a button a phone call goes through unregistered. (Such calls are not even tabulated by the telephone company for purposes of billing.) And should a reporter ask an improper question in any such personal area, let alone suggest the answer to one, he is finished. It is as if the press and all others concerned agree that the ship-of-state should not be rocked by waves from the private lives of those in command. Well agreed upon, too, is the idea that a man capable of shouldering great burdens of office should be left alone near his bedroom, and certainly protected against narrow moral complaints.

In those branches of government (usually quite removed from politics) where the collecting, mastering, and guarding of secret information is carried on, there is a kind of unspoken international tradition for accepting and using homosexual personnel. It is not that anybody necessarily plans it that way, or especially wants it to be so. It's just that the Eskimo finds his way into the ice house. Yet it is not clear whether homosexual diplomats, intelligence chiefs, and espionage agents actually have a higher-than-average representation in these fields, or whether dramatic events and locally high concentrations of such personnel only make it seem so. At any rate, the management of *sub rosa* information is a type of work for which the homosexual is often particularly well suited. Perhaps this is due in part to certain natural proclivities he may have for handling confidential material, or to a life-style that easily adapts to various kinds of social independence. But even where there are no such dispositional assets, and overt liabilities besides, there are places where the homosexual's services are of special value—just as there are specific uses for a person's heterosexuality. It is the very nature of intelligence work that no stone can be safely left unturned.

Some of the programs which have been specifically designed to utilize homosexuality would make the exploits of a Mata Hari look like child's play. During World War II, the Federal Bureau of Investigation set up a house of male prostitution (on MacDougal Street in Greenwich Village) and staffed it with homosexual agents for the explicit and, as it turned out, highly successful purpose of extracting shipping information from foreign sailors.[141,265] The decision to undertake this venture is perhaps less surprising than the Bureau's ability to effectively deal with the numerous quite subtle problems that are entailed in running such an establishment—not to mention the problems involved in coming up with a sizable group of young, handsome, multilingual, adequately trained homosexual agents who were willing and able to carry out their missions.

There are many smaller examples, too, in which one-to-one homosexual contacts are useful. These may or may not involve overt sex activity, but in either case they have to do with the freedom of an agent to circulate in particular groups and to smoothly fit in. Thus when any country orders the elimination of all homosexuals from government service and means it, as ours does not, it inevitably closes off certain channels of information and leaves itself vulnerable at other points. Hitler did this and his decision has been privately regarded as an intelligence disaster—

on much the same pattern if not the same scale as banishing Jewish scientists, first losing their services and then having a few of them wind up making atom bombs for other people.

Among diplomats, too, a man's private life can have a distinct relevance to his assignments. Often the connection is indirect, mainly affecting the ease and enthusiasm with which he mixes in ambient social groups. This whole principle is hardly more than an extension of the observation, common in diplomacy, that a man adapts better to a foreign land and is more effective there if he finds the people—meaning the women, or the men—especially attractive. In fact, an erotic interest can play a role even where there is not the slightest intention of any overt sex activity. In more than half the societies of the world, males run and dominate a community much more exclusively than they do in ours. Often the conferences and social gatherings a foreign representative attends are composed entirely of men. Protracted contacts with these all-male groups much sooner wear down—even begin to anesthetize—the heterosexual than the homosexual delegate—who, stripped to the waist like his hosts, may have to sit for hours through one tribal powwow after the other, or be unendingly ingratiating while dressed-to-the-nines in Cairo.

In the secret services, sexual biases are sometimes brought to a kind of ultimate perfection. Just as there are many places where a heterosexual interest improves social rapport, there are a few others where a homosexual slant helps an agent fit his assignment. In his pursuit of information, the ordinary agent (unlike those in spy-thriller novels and plays) may have to be a bartender or stevedore for months, merely tapping the flow of events and being capable of enjoying the social company of males enough to maintain a tone of warmth and interest in his contacts. Here, the homosexual responsiveness of an agent can be distinctly useful, both in giving him a high tolerance for overdoses of male company and in improving his ability to impart a certain genuineness as he leans forward to be friendly and sympatico. And when an overtly sexual contact is possible, as is not infrequently the case, a whole new realm of intimacy and confidentiality is opened up.

Certainly each of these utilizations of sex—whether merely occasional or central to a particular assignment—has a place in the repertoires of diplomacy and espionage. But to what extent are these applications planned or deliberate in some sense, or merely accidental? That depends. Agencies devoted to the collection of private information are often run by sophisticated professionals whose tenure extends for years through a variety of political administrations. With this much personal and departmental autonomy, and with the privacy of their undertakings assured, the leadership is free to use whatever it knows of human psychology. And it knows plenty, at least in certain quarters, for a most intimate understanding of sexual realities is required to make a success of such projects as the house on MacDougal Street and the infiltration of radical groups through their bedrooms.

In diplomacy the picture is quite different. It is probably fair to say that there are no local assignments where a delegate's homosexual tastes are consciously recognized as useful, let alone any that are specifically designed to tap these talents, though tapped they often are. Here, there is no upper echelon of directors who are impervious to prevailing political pressures and to the hazards of being in the public eye. On the contrary, the powers-that-be hold an *official* antihomosexual posture and immediately purge from their ranks any individuals who are so clumsy, so unlucky, or so unwise as to fail a routine security clearance. With more stringency, they could damage their departments considerably.

From the other side, one might think homosexuals would want to avoid the hazards and ingratitudes of government service by staying away from it. Undoubtedly many do. But of course, the better adjusted individuals tend to think of themselves not as homosexuals but as people, and to see their lives in a context of ordinary, sometimes extraordinary, hopes and aspirations. Can one imagine a Dag Hammarskjold, who eventually became Secretary General of the United Nations, refusing to enter diplomacy for fear of puritanical complaints? Not that there are many Dag Hammarskjolds, but there are a good many people who are motivated to some extent by the kinds of social interests that motivated him. Those among them who are partly or entirely homosexual often achieve personal safety, not by suppressing their sex lives nor by living furtively but, when on the job, by pouring themselves into their work and otherwise attaining a level of integrity that is not easily challenged. Not even a security team, let alone a departmental boss, finds it easy (nor for themselves, comfortable) to challenge a man who is not on the run with bits and pieces of circumstantial evidence. Often the homosexual intuitively realizes this, or simply gambles on no problem arising. As viewed from the inside, the possibility of being challenged on personal matters often seems remarkably remote, irrelevant, or at least quite differently poised than one might suppose.

Here are some of the comments elicited by questioning or simply by listening to a variety of people who are or were affiliated with the federal government—comments which reflect quite a variation in attitudes toward the relevance of homosexuality. (To preserve confidentiality, the names of places, fields, languages, and institutions have been changed to their approximate equivalents where necessary.)

• Sex is no problem. I wanted to see the world and I have. My [work] sends me all over the place.

• In my field, you either work for the government or teach in a university that pays you less.

• IBM assigned me to Washington as a technician on the budget computers. I like the [job] atmosphere here and decided to stay.

• I knew there *might* be trouble. So I applied first off for the foreign service. This made them hit me with top security clearance procedures at the outset, so then I was set. Have to be a little careful who I pick up, but then I would be anyway.

• I'm a specialist in Mongolese dialects; they came to me. I'd have been happy to stay at Yale.

• Hell, I was in the Service four years before I knew who I was and I soon became aware of who a lot of other people are.

• The government is just like everywhere else. Your strength is in friends and in public; what's private is private.

• I grew up in the American embassy in Peking; this is the whole way of life for me. Those security guys are no problem, and even if they were I'd slough it off. If that didn't work, I'd say I was drunk. What people don't know about homosexuality makes it dangerous, but also makes it safe, you know.

•Nobody in my family ever amounted to much, just business thieves; I wanted to do something for people, and have!

• When I was a child I wanted to be an Egyptologist. But it wasn't till I was there a couple of months that I began to understand how perfectly suited I am to that whole Arabic scene. If you mix with the people as I do, I think Security is more worried about your being too all-fired heterosexual and losing rapport.

•Just happened to apply to Civil Service first and they took me.

•I hate groups of queer guys, and being alone is no fun either; that's why I joined the Nigerian thing. I was pleased to find a lot of other people like myself. I'd say about half the outfit is homosexual, the better half too, but there's not a faggot among them. You can tell the straight ones in about a month; they get bored with all that male company and you can really tell it. They're less idealistic too, but that may be prejudice on my part. If Central knew what was going on here, I mean the kinds of ties the staff builds with the natives, they'd be shocked, but if they knew everything about it they'd be proud of themselves for having put such a staff together. There's nothing dirty about it; it's just that cultural exchanges work best when there are close personal ties, the closer the better.

•I never have sex with anybody close to my work. If what I do at a distance ever gets me into trouble, to hell with it; I'll quit and work somewhere else.

•Nobody can ever convince me that Security is any problem. I'm certain they already know pretty much everything about a person. Beyond your political ideas, those they really are very serious about, all they want to know is whether or not you know how to handle yourself.

•I knew the secret MPs were on my tail right after I got back from Viet Nam. They were closing in and had made their first move. Then I suddenly got that Presidential Citation and it really saved my ass. Those guys forgot I ever existed.

In America, government pressures against homosexuality vary all the way from indifference to a deliberate, paranoid-like seeking out and elimination of anyone who shows the slightest tendency in this direction. Superimposed on this variability are the attitudes of local department heads, attitudes that sometimes cause a relatively loose policy to be enforced with the energy appropriate to a dangerous crime. Or a department can be "tough" on homosexuals simply by its own traditions, even when headed by a man who is widely known to be homosexual himself. It's as if the boss is granted a special waiver. In other instances, the whole atmosphere may be entirely relaxed with so much concentration on the tasks at hand that private-life considerations extend, at most, to obtaining routine security clearances.

These differences in policy exist not only between individual branches of government that are under Civil Service, but in others as well—including our military complexes. The Army, Navy, and Air Force have strict regulations to keep out homosexuals, or to discharge them if they are already enlisted. To understand certain present-day oddities, these rules have to be seen in perspective. They were established decades ago when the military first depended on volunteers, and thus when every effort was being made to give the services an aura of wholesome respectability. Parents needed the assurance that their young sons would not be thrown in with rabble if they joined, nor subjected to immoral influences. The increased discipline of the armed services and the parade-ground image they attained by the 1930's was sufficient to give them a certain gloss and respectability. No special emphasis had to be placed on sex, and none was—except for the Navy.

The Navy had a special problem. According to popular legend and a variety of ribald jokes, there was the long-standing notion that men isolated on ships and bounced around by the waves were sexually aroused at sea and prone to make approaches to each other.* Extreme as the idea now seems, it was and still is

---

*There seem to be several sources for the traditional connection between men of the sea and homosexuality. Sea voyages frequently used to last a year or more, and a crew's freedom in distant ports was highly restricted. This led to the popular idea that men were thus more or less forced toward homosexual practices. But modern data from prison populations indicate that even where homosexuality is very high (71 per cent of long-term inmates) it is "new" for only 4 per cent of the participants; the rest had it in their

embarrassing to Navy officials. Consequently, all sorts of special regulations were instituted and are still in force: Men are not assigned to work alone in pairs except in emergency situations. When transporting personnel by train, never more than one man has been permitted in the lower berths of Pullmans (at what was once a sizable extra expense to taxpayers). An internal police establishment is maintained to search for anyone having, or having had, homosexual contacts—and when one is found, it is not unusual for him to be treated as a real criminal and dealt with in shabby and illegal ways. He is routinely urged (in exchange for a promise of slightly better treatment) to incriminate friends and acquaintances, each of whom is separately investigated. (In its search for information, Navy Intelligence will venture quite far into civilian circles, though here it is instructed to beat a hasty retreat when it encounters resistance to its off-limits inquiries.)

Unlike the other armed services, which demand strong evidence before bothering with a homosexual charge, the Navy does not hesitate to act on gossip alone. Even an officer of fairly high rank against whom there is not a shred of tangible evidence may be given the choice of either quietly resigning (incidentally, signing away his severance pay and other benefits) or be put through court-martialing procedures which, he is reminded, "are sure to raise questions about you even if you win."

Despite these strenuous efforts, there is not the slightest indication that homosexuality is any less prevalent in the Navy than anywhere else. In fact, the Navy still has a reputation for having more than its share, for its policies highlight the issue and keep it alive. Thus the connection between homosexuality and the Navy persists as the legend of the sea and the jokes continue, repeatedly backed by new evidence of the extreme measures the Navy

---

histories before becoming isolated.[125] Thus there is some indication that many men who chose a life at sea did not mind isolation from women. Furthermore, lost in the censored pages of history is a long tradition of homosexuality at sea. The Spanish galleons, for instance, had a spelled-out code of *matelotage* which specified the amount of sexual freedom and fidelity expected of all men who "belonged" to each other during a voyage; it was an attempt to control fierce jealousies and maintain better order aboard ship.[134]

"has to take to control the situation." Even the gods have been cruel to the mighty beast. For while none of the other armed services has ever had an incident approaching a homosexual scandal, the Navy has been fairly plagued by them.

Some years ago, Navy Intelligence raided a house of male prostitution (on Pacific Street, in Brooklyn), discovering to their chagrin that one of the place's regular clients was one of the Navy's own top officials. A few years later, another senior officer jumped to his death from the twenty-second floor of the Bethesda Naval Hospital, but not before his homosexual involvements had been considerably aired. And in a less public way, at least two admirals have been involved in ongoing homosexual liaisons— one almost flagrantly while aboard an aircraft carrier during World War II. Sometimes when Navy Intelligence has tried to investigate such events it has been brashly told to desist—and in the latter case, ordered off the ship and told to go to hell. From inside the ranks, nothing short of a Presidential order can rock the upper brass.

The case involving the Brooklyn house of male prostitution is now sufficiently in the past to be examined in detail. (It is worth considering, too, because the matter contains much that is not at all "dated" and is typical of the kinds of maneuvers which still occur.) During World War II, Navy Intelligence closed in on the male bordello near the Brooklyn Navy Yard. There were two reasons for raiding the place: It specialized in supplying its clients with service men, especially sailors; and some of its visitors were foreign agents who served much liquor and asked questions about shipping[191]—the house on MacDougal Street, in reverse. The place was run by one Gustave Beekman, who was assured both by the federal investigatory agencies (the FBI and Navy Intelligence) and by the eccentric judge who later tried his case that he could save himself by turning over a list of his clients and otherwise cooperating in the follow-up investigations.[194]*

---

*Beekman did everything he was asked to do and his evidence led to the arrest and conviction of three foreign agents, including a hard-to-track-down, self-appointed German spy (William Elberfeld), who was arrested in his Manhattan rooming house from which he allegedly but did not actually

His revelations were sensational—"the story of the year" as it was called in Washington cloakrooms—for, as luck would have it, the very first name on Beekman's list of regular clients was none other than the chairman of the Senate Naval Affairs Committee.[191] Navy Intelligence was thunderstruck, not only by this but by additional bits of information that kept cropping up, each of which seemed to make matters worse. For instance, the corroborating witnesses, most of whom were strangers to each other, all emphasized that the Senator always preferred sailors and went out of his way to have his contacts only with them. (At first it was thought that perhaps the wrong man was being identified, but this idea was dropped and the subject quickly changed when one young sailor named Zuber put the matter straight by proceeding to describe exactly where the Senator had "ripples of fat" and where he didn't.[191,193])

Both for the purpose of an orderly investigation and to allow time for certain political decisions to be made, the Senator's name was withheld for fifty-two days, not only from the press but from Congress as well. This, however, led to unimaginable complications. Although congressmen could not find out exactly who was involved, they did know it was one of themselves and that a homosexual charge was involved. And by cloakroom hearsay they knew—or thought they knew—who among them might want to visit a male bordello. Thus they began to fill in the blank with the names of various senators who were not involved in this particular case.

In self-defense, a number of congressmen pleaded with the investigatory agencies to hurry up and identify the right man.[192] But Navy Intelligence had reason to be slow in this, for there were still loose ends, one of which was a bit threatening to themselves.

---

operate a shortwave transmitter. As his reward, Beekman was double-crossed both by the federal agents and the judge. At the end of his testimony, he was arraigned on a common sodomy charge and received the maximum sentence of twenty years in prison.[196] He entered Sing Sing on October 5, 1942 and was finally released from the clutches of the law on April 1, 1963, at the age of 78.

For six weeks before their raid, they had maintained a full-time surveillance of the Pacific Street house (from a room in a hospital across the street), checking out every visitor who arrived—many of whom were public figures, but none of whom was the first man on Beekman's list: David I. Walsh, prominent Democrat from Massachusetts, chairman of Naval Affairs, privy to much confidential military information, and what was almost worse, privy as well to what Navy Intelligence itself was up to. His visits to Pacific Street had suddenly stopped the day before Navy Intelligence had rented that hospital room. How had Walsh known to stop his visits just then, and to continue staying away?

Probably nobody ever found out, for once again Walsh began to act as if he knew what was about to happen (and again he probably did know). He simply denied the whole affair, offhandedly called it a "diabolical lie," and mentioned it no further (though the newspapers continued to banner the whole investigation). He went about his daily business with an astounding aplomb, calling one press conference after the other to announce pleasant naval matters—that particular officers had done so well they deserved a raise in rank; that the sinking of the *Normandie* was not the fault of the officer in charge; that there was a new and promising way to handle the U-boat threat, etc. Meanwhile, from the very highest levels of government a firm decision was handed down, almost certainly by President Roosevelt himself: Save Senator Walsh.

This was what necessitated throwing Beekman to the lions. It also required acting as if the dozens of other witnesses did not exist, extending the coverup by still other means, and somehow pulling Walsh out of the flames. Fortunately for this difficult undertaking, there had been foreign agents in the picture, none of whom Walsh had ever met. Here was the "out": Increase the charge to a point at which it could be truthfully denied by high official spokesmen. The terminal summation was made by J. Edgar Hoover, and on May 20, 1942, it was formally restated before the assembled Congress by majority leader Alben Barkley: "The Federal Bureau of Investigation has reported that there is not the slightest foundation for the charge that Senator Walsh visited a 'house of degradation' in Brooklyn and was seen talking to Nazi agents there."[195] To this charge he was certainly innocent. The case was closed.

One of the central observations to be made here—besides the fact that in politics all things are possible—has to do with the nature of moral pressure. It is tempting to believe that Walsh's fate was greatly affected by his personal character. He was an unusually energetic, talented and well-liked legislator with a large following of admirers, many of whom had known all along about his private life. Certainly his popularity helped him when the chips were down. But what helps a person when the chips are *not* down is less clear. There are, for instance, many people in the public eye today whose partial or entirely homosexual private lives are widely known. Some are not particularly "sympathetic" figures and thus might suddenly find a whole claque ready to enjoy their troubles and throw stones should they become involved in a scandal. But in the meantime, stones are not thrown, and on the contrary, a full quota of respect is paid to them, according to their accomplishments. Evidently there is a certain mob psychology that enters as a late guest to public executions. It is a psychology that is powerful at the time, and quite seductive of public support. But it is ultimately dangerous to its organizers whose own motivations eventually come up for analysis.

Interestingly, the Navy never admits the real source of its embarrassment over homosexuality, nor does it follow the lead of the other services and simply stay quiet. Down through the ranks filter stories of its cloak-and-dagger methods and of its high-handed invasions of privacy, causing a certain mistrust and resentment. In an effort to counteract this, Navy spokesmen continually try to account for the "necessity" of their investigational methods. There is hardly a sailor who has not had the matter explained to him. And every officer, usually while being cleared with pointed questions about himself, hears of the "dangers" of homosexuality to Naval security. The whole policy illustrates how an emotionally laden issue, especially when deviously handled, can be spun into a paranoid delusion of major proportions. There is some sort of moral in it too, for the legend of the sea grows more robust with every attempt to drown it.

In the final analysis, certain curious consequences of homosexuality begin to emerge. There is at least a thread of connection between every one of the examples cited here. In each, the decision to use the homosexual issue as a target of concern has sprung from an ulterior motive—usually a search for some advantage in the eyes of the public. But this, after all, is true of all moral campaigns. What in homosexuality makes it so hard to handle, so prone to burn the hand that meddles with it? Only part of the answer can be found in its own peculiarities—for instance, that its distribution very often leads an attacker where he least intended going, and much too close to home for comfort. The rest of the answer, really the major part of it, involves the kinds of investments people have in heterosexuality, in the beliefs they hold, and thus in the Establishment as they see it.

Take the case of the television documentary. The producers began with an honest effort to tell the truth. As they learned more about their subject they were even prepared to deal with a "positive" aspect of it—that homosexuality works quite well for some people—and they thought this fact, if shown in a single clear example, would make their presentation balanced and interesting. It would have, too, but for the fact that for reasons they probably never understood, it put them on a collision course with disaster. Were the producers right in thinking (as one of them did) that they ran into trouble merely because of the prudery of a handful of executives? Absolutely not. The issue is much bigger than that and involves fierce battles that ensue whenever the media—which, in a sense, are the guardians of society—find themselves failing to protect it against certain kinds of threatening information.

At first glance, it may seem that these battles belong to the past, that censorship has died—when, in fact, it has mainly changed its form, becoming in some ways more insidious than it was before. At least in "the old days" the censor knew he was being a censor, and the public knew that information was being withheld. Not any more.* A brand of censorship is now widely imposed by

---

*That is, not any more in the public media. But in other quarters, the oldest, most rigorous form of outright censorship is still in force. To this day, the U.S. Army keeps under lock and key the second largest statistical

persons and institutions which often do not realize they are imposing it, nor does the public realize it is being imposed. On the contrary, the casual observer has the impression that he can expect to find virtually anything in print, and hear both heterosexual and homosexual matters discussed openly in documentaries and on talk-shows. Indeed, what he sees and hears has become notably explicit, and sometimes includes quite favorable views of assorted extramural sexual activities. Nevertheless, a considerable control is still being exerted over the flow of sexual information, a control which in certain ways is fully as suppressive as outright prudery once was. It strongly tends to protect and to justify the centerline mores, not by denying variations or by necessarily condemning them, but by setting them apart in such a way as to maintain a protective, comfortable distance between special "others" and the rest of us who are pictured as making up the social mainstream.

This new "system" has all sorts of interesting manifestations. It has repeatedly meant that television networks which have not the slightest hesitation in carrying homosexual news items (including "Gay-Lib" propaganda that turns up in the news) nevertheless seriously edit, or else veto altogether, homosexual documentaries on which they may have spent considerable time and money. Is this because "news is news" while a documentary comes across as the network's own voice? That may be part of it, but a documentary is edgy for other reasons, too. By its very nature it is an intimate medium, one that tends to thrust the viewer into close contact with the subject matter. And while this increased contact

---

study of human sexual behavior ever conducted—refusing to share any part of it with the numerous professionals who have requested it and pronounced it pertinent to their own work. This huge study examines the effect of military service and confinement upon the sexual behavior of males. It was originally designed and largely completed during World War II by a group of psychiatrists and sociologists who expected the results to serve both civilian and military interests. It would have, too (and still would), but for the fact that a group of chaplains promptly insisted that it be sequestered. Whether or not there would any longer be serious religious objections to its release is not clear, but Pentagon officials continue to view its release (even to professionals) as less than politic.[138,217]

with sexual variations can be novel and engrossing up to a point, many people quickly begin to find it uncomfortable if not overtly annoying.

In other media, too, similar reactions continue to plague editors and ultimately succeed in suppressing the kinds of information on homosexuality which are actually required for understanding it. Not that this partial suppression is an editorial aim or is always even consciously realized, nor does it involve any garden variety of prudery. The main considerations are strictly practical: that the reader should not be strained with ideas too far afield from prevailing notions, and that he should not be made uncomfortable by being brought too close to the subject, particularly not by the kinds of information that might intrude upon his own heterosexual assumptions. Thus a few years ago, well after *The New York Times* began to carry articles on homosexuality, it assigned a topnotch investigative reporter to look into it. He chose a difficult topic, lesbianism, and to his considerable credit he managed to win the respect both of the professionals and the individual subjects with whom he worked. Yet his findings were never published—almost certainly for "comfort" reasons—though the *Times* has continued to carry numerous quite ordinary articles on homosexuality.

Of course, these are the kinds of editorial decisions any publication has a "right" to make. And in addition, the editors may be quite correct in their assessment of what will or will not be palatable to readers—and of what is politic to publish. But then, neither is it surprising that the total picture throughout the media continues to reflect what sex researchers see as a paltry and conventionalized version of sexual realities. In fact, in one sense the picture is worse than that. For despite the wide dissemination of popularized sexual information, the disparity between what professional observers know, and what the public knows, has certainly never been greater than it is at present.

It is widely believed—to some extent correctly—that book publishers have less to worry about in terms of audience reaction than do the communications media. But here, too, there is always the problem of staying on good terms with the public, and of catering to its comfort. The situation is such that regardless of whether authors and publishers of anything sexual choose to reach for the sensational or to conform to conformity, there is little loyalty to basic sexual information. The publishers of textbooks and of the classics, as well as most of the timid if erudite scholars who prepare them, are good examples. In the politics of getting their volumes chosen by schools and colleges, they have shown a remarkable readiness to actually distort their texts. Of the numerous translations of Plato into English, all have been censored of much if not most of their homosexual content. And since the Greeks wove personal and sexual relations into the very fabric of government, these expurgations have altered the political and philosophical views of Plato very considerably. His poetic and ethical works have been distorted still further. In the prestigious Jowett translation, for example, both the *Symposium* and *Lysis* have been garbled almost beyond recognition:

Where Plato actually said:	*The Jowett translation says:*
There is dishonor in sexually gratifying a worthless man or in doing so viciously; but there is honor in sexually gratifying a good man in an honorable manner.	There is dishonor in yielding to the evil, or in an evil manner; but there is honor in yielding to the good, or in an honorable manner.
He who grants sexual favors to his male lover in the hope that he will be improved through the friendship shows himself to be virtuous, even though his lover proves to be a villain and to have no virtue.	He who lives for the sake of virtue, and in the hope that he will be improved by his lover's company, shows himself to be virtuous, even though the object of his affection be proved to be a villain, and to have no virtue.
As Pausanias says, It is honorable for a man to grant sexual favors to the good among men and shameful for him to grant them to the unbridled.	As Pausanias says, The good are to be accepted, and the bad are not to be accepted.

Through the nightly loving of boys a man, on arising, begins to see the true nature of beauty.

He who under the influence of true love rising upward begins to see that beauty is not far from the end.

Now I thought he was eager for my bloom of youth and I believed that it was a windfall and my marvelous piece of good luck that it should fall to me to sexually gratify Socrates in order to hear everything he knew.[212]

Now I thought he was seriously enamoured of my beauty and this appeared to be a grand opportunity of hearing him tell what he knew.[127]

It was because of distortions and coverups of this caliber that at the peak of its power in the early 1950's the Kinsey Research began a systematic retranslation of the classics from the original. This project and many others of more pressing significance were soon brought to a halt by a financial crackdown instigated by moralists who used a series of highly political maneuvers against Kinsey. It is important to see how these pressures worked, for the same ones and many of the same groups operate today to suppress truth and to control public opinion.

By the spring of 1950, the Kinsey Report (*Sexual Behavior in the Human Male*) had been out for two years. It had received the highest honors, with nearly unanimous acclaim from reviewers, including scientists in a dozen fields. And it had been recognized as the most extensive effort ever made to gather and present data on what people do sexually. (The casual reader could hardly master the Report with its 804 pages of intricate prose concerning 5300 males whose activities were charted in 335 graphs and tables; but then, neither did he have to, for the central findings were being restated throughout the popular press.) The effect was sensational—not only because of the surprisingly high figures on premarital, extramarital, and homosexual sex, but also because of the whole imprimatur of the study: It carried the direct backing of the National Research Council, Indiana University, the Rockefeller Foundation, and the list of close consultants read like a cross-section of American men of science.

Although Kinsey was very modest in his claims of accomplishment and leaned over backward to avoid drawing sweeping sociologic conclusions, the enormous prestige of his work drove his critics into a kind of hysteria. Dr. Harold Dodds, president of Princeton University, wrote a critique of the Kinsey Report for the *Reader's Digest* in which he compared the work to "toilet-wall inscriptions."[223] Behind the scenes, Dodds and a Baptist minister named Harry Emerson Fosdick organized public pressure against Kinsey's work. Clare Boothe Luce came before the National Council of Catholic Women to say, "The Kinsey Report, like all cheap thrillers, would fall into obscurity if so much attention was not paid to it."[200]

Nor did a handful of professionals in the field behave much better. Margaret Mead attacked Kinsey for not studying the "emotional meaning" of sex.[198] (She must have meant romantic love, since Kinsey was often eloquent on the emotional meaning of sex.) And Professor Helen Bond at Columbia University suggested that "there should be a law against doing research exclusively with sex."[199] The American Social Hygiene Association called a special conference to discuss the Kinsey Report (only negative comments were solicited) and its president, Dr. Walter Clark, explained to the assembly that he had deliberately not invited Kinsey because he thought his presence might "cramp the discussion."[198] In an especially bitter attack, Dr. A. H. Hobbs, Assistant Professor of Sociology at the University of Pennsylvania, charged that there must be something wrong with Kinsey's statistics[197] and that the prestige of the Rockefeller Foundation gave unwarranted weight to implications "that homosexuality is normal and that pre-marital relations . . . might be a good thing."

This clique of critics, operating against the mainstream of responsible scientific opinion, worked singly and together as well as openly and in secret against the *backers* of the Kinsey Research. Scores of letters of complaint poured in to the Rockefeller Foundation, to the National Research Council, to Indiana University, and to the legislature of Indiana (for its support of the university that supported Kinsey). When hostile critics such as Dodds, Hobbs, Fulton Oursler at the *Reader's Digest*, or Harry Emerson Fosdick at Union Theological Seminary would write a letter of protest to one of these groups, carbon copies were often sent to the others, and to congressmen as well.[141,217]

In one instance these efforts backfired. As a result of the protests and a certain hubbub in the press, the Indiana legislature formed a special committee to investigate the Research and invited Kinsey to speak to (and be questioned by) them. They were so impressed by this close-up view of the Kinsey Research that instead of cutting their support, they quickly approved an extra appropriation for a new building. But the Rockefeller Foundation and the National Research Council, intimidated in the face of challenge and fearful of political winds (especially from Washington), began to operate in various devious ways.[265]

As early as May, 1950, the National Research Council in response to underground pressures, but allegedly because of "critical questions regarding [Kinsey's] statistical analysis," asked the American Statistical Association to look into "the statistics used by Dr. Kinsey and his associates."[41] Because of the way this request was presented to the press, it immediately led to much derogatory publicity to the effect that the Kinsey Research findings were based on superficial data, and that they were statistically questionable—charges, by the way, which were so loudly made that to this day many professionals still believe them. But neither the Rockefeller Foundation nor the National Research Council spoke up to correct these abusive impressions, not even after they had received (early in 1952) a most favorable ASA evaluation.* Their disloyalty, both to the Kinsey Research and to their own stated aims, like other retreats of cowardice, was destined to buy them little safety, as they were soon to learn.

In 1952, as a defensive ploy, the Rockefeller Foundation privately asked Kinsey not to acknowledge its support in his forth-

---

*The final ASA evaluation (published in 1954 after the issue was past and much damage had already been done) was a model of caution and care. There were criticisms and suggestions of the sort that always arise after an initial research effort, but in every major respect the evaluation was tremendously supportive. The Kinsey Research results were ranked as the highest quality work ever done in the field. And as a final salute (p. 219) the entire research was characterized as "a monumental endeavor."[41]

coming book, *Sexual Behavior in the Human Female*.[217] Kinsey refused the request but the issue was soon made pointless anyway by a major assault against the Rockefeller Foundation. A group led by Hobbs loudly complained to Congress that "tax-free philanthropic and educational foundations are wielding powerful adverse effects on morality." This cry was taken up by Representative Carroll Reece (R., Tenn.) who, in 1953, formed a "House Committee to Investigate Tax-Exempt Foundations," consisting of himself, Angier L. Goodwin (R., Mass.), Jesse P. Woolcott (R., Mich.), Gracie Pfost (D., Idaho), and Wayne L. Hays (D., Ohio). When interviewed by the press, Reece was able to put his own motivations and those of other moralists in broad if loose group-language: "The Congress has been asked to investigate the financial backers of the institute that turned out the Kinsey sex report last August."

Thus began what was soon to become one of the most bizarre committee investigations ever undertaken by the Congress. The hearings began on May 10, 1954, and continued for sixteen sessions. Twelve witnesses ("handpicked," as Hays and Pfost later revealed) testified against the foundations, particularly the Rockefeller Foundation, and against the Kinsey Research. Hobbs had his day in court on May 19, during which he was allowed to raise the most spurious charges against the Kinsey Research—charges which, despite the protests of Hays and Pfost, were to go unchecked and unanswered. For as Reece had announced in advance, he had no intention of hearing Kinsey (or of hearing testimony from anyone else who might be familiar with the research).

Then, during the sixteenth session (June 17), a new set of remarkable events began. The twelfth witness was called, one who was supposed to speak against the foundations but, instead, proceeded to give evidence that, as Hays later said, "began to destroy with facts all the staff testimony." Reece was infuriated. He interrupted this witness in midstream, and from that moment forward, he closed all hearings to the public. In addition, he refused to hear *any* defense witnesses, even in private. He simply told the foundations they could write up sworn statements and mail them in, "if you want to." They wanted to all right—and they did—but their efforts were lost on Reece, for as Hays and Pfost said in a blistering 6000-word Minority Report: "There is no evidence that the Majority even read the Foundation Reports, let alone that they allowed them to influence the 'final conclusions' that were drawn before the hearings ever started." Hays and Pfost went on to describe the entire proceedings as "barbaric" and, in a final epithet, summarized the committee's report as "a crackpot view by persons who are ill with a fear sickness."[205]

Nor was this the end. The press was highly suspicious of all these goings-on and refused to let the matter drop. Why, for instance, had Representative Goodwin (whose vote had been crucial to the majority) sided with Reece, particularly since his vote contradicted some of his other public statements? At his home in Melrose, Massachusetts, *The New York Times* reached Goodwin to find out. Goodwin explained that he had neither read nor signed the Committee Report, and that he had lent his name *if and only if* a sizable list of exceptions and qualifications was included in the final report—qualifications which were not, in fact, included. On hearing this, parliamentarians in the House of Representatives then questioned the entire legitimacy of the Report, and Goodwin himself ended up pronouncing it *not* a majority opinion.[204] But nobody ever actually did anything about it. So the record stands to this day in its full illegality.

One might think that the Rockefeller Foundation would have gained encouragement, even courage, from all this. For while they had been denied a proper defense in front of Reece, much of their "position paper" found its way into press reports where, half by its own eloquence and the rest by Reece's patent foolishness, they had been thoroughly vindicated. (They ran little risk anyway, for it is in the very nature of foundations that they tend to be overly strict in their research demands, and are never radical, as Reece had tried to claim.) But one must think again, for events were about to take still another remarkable turn.

At the pinnacle of its success, the Rockefeller Foundation suddenly began to act as if it had taken over the ethics of Reece himself. It did an about-face and launched upon a series of cynical decisions and out-of-character shenanigans to spoil its own fine record and to accomplish exactly the aims for which

Reece and Hobbs had labored. This was all the more amazing, for during the battle with Reece, Dean Rusk, president of the Rockefeller Foundation, had made many highminded statements reiterating the guiding principles of the Foundation. He had said "the Foundation has always placed its confidence in [various] social and scientific studies which it has backed and which it plans to continue [to sponsor]," that it "does not intend to give up its intellectual freedom under government and [other kinds of] pressure," and that "the proper product of a grant is an intellectual achievement in which it is important to leave scientists and scholars unimpaired in their work," for "We believe that a free society grows in strength and in moral and intellectual capacity on the basis of free and responsible research and scholarship."[203] These were, indeed, high ideals and promises for the future, yet within a month—and almost certainly by the very day on which they were so reassuringly stated in public—the Foundation, in private, firmly decided to break them all.

This required several moves, all made in rapid succession. After having supported the Kinsey Research for twelve consecutive years with growing enthusiasm, the Rockefeller Foundation suddenly decided to discontinue its grant of $50,000 a year. At the same time, as if by some combination of apology and bribery, the Foundation quieted one of the noisiest groups of critics in its history by making one of the largest grants in its history—$525,-000 to Harry Emerson Fosdick's Union Theological Seminary, "to aid in the development of vital religious leadership."

The magnitude and transparency of this turnabout was hard to cover, but they did their best with tricky pieces of wording and outright misstatements: On August 24, when Dean Rusk announced the upcoming grants, it was explained that "Some of the projects formerly supported [by the Rockefeller Foundation], including that of Dr. Kinsey, are now in a position to obtain support from other sources." It was like throwing close friends out of the house during bad weather, saying they are now in a position to live where they choose. This move was a bit too obvious to go unnoticed by the press. Thus when *The New York Times* reported the Foundation's full statement, it interjected a reminder to the reader that three months earlier, Dr. Kinsey had, indeed, warned the American Psychiatric Association "that religious and other groups are exerting pressure on . . . the Rockefeller Foundation to end its support of [our] studies in human sexual behavior."[203] Clearly, more needed to be said, so within twenty-four hours another spokesman for the Foundation (Dr. Keith Cannon) explained that "the funds for Dr. Kinsey were dropped as of midsummer because [the Kinsey Research] did not request a renewal of support" and "the presumption was that Dr. Kinsey's work was now well endowed and did not need further help from the Foundation."

None of this was true. The Rockefeller Foundation had been in close contact with Kinsey at all times. No "presumptions" had to be made, nor were they made. The Foundation knew that the Kinsey Research had no endowment whatsoever. They also knew they were its main financial source and that it could not possibly continue its vigorous program without their support. And as for not receiving any request for renewal, the truth was that the request *had* been sent, despite the fact that a representative of the Foundation had explained to Kinsey that the central committee had already decided it was not politic for them to continue backing his work, and thus that they would be severing their connections with it and with him.[263,217]*

---

*There was much of significance in this whole relationship before the shadow of politics cast a pall over it. The Rockefeller Foundation deserves much credit for what it brought to Kinsey in the years before it lost sight of its own guiding principles. It not only supplied the money for the rapid expansion of the Kinsey Research, but bestowed a prestige and a recognition that brought to its doors the most distinguished professionals in the field—men such as George Corner, Robert Yerkes, Karl Lashley, Frank Beach, William Young and many more. In this heady atmosphere, the enormous talents of Kinsey flourished to give the Research unheard-of dimensions in perspective and scope. Besides the broad study of sexual behavior in American males and females, literally dozens of subprojects were simultaneously pursued. There was an extensive study of the differences between the sexes that so affect their psychology, their interaction, and thus their compatibility. There were studies of the sexual behavior of fourteen mammalian species, studies of human neurology and physiology, as well as ancient and modern cross-cultural surveys—including a detailed in-

With the fears and abandonment of the Rockefeller Foundation, the many attacks against the Kinsey Research had finally succeeded. Numerous projects had to be dropped and a carefully assembled staff of scholars and scientists to man the most ambitious project ever conceived in sex research began to dissolve—leaving a huge store of valuable materials and much of the world's classical literature clenched once again in the fist of prudery, where it still is.*

Homosexuality played a surprisingly important role in the fate of the Kinsey Research. For while it was only one of the six basic forms of sex considered, and represented only a fraction of the research effort, nothing so disturbed the critics nor brought them to such a fever pitch of hate as did the homosexual findings. Preachers, pundits, and prudes found much to lament, and a variety of ways to do the lamenting: Some questioned the scientific accuracy of the work—"homosexuality just can't be that prevalent." Others feared the sociological effects of even discuss-

---

vestigation of sex practices in pre-Columbian civilizations, and another to trace the shifts in Japanese mores over the last 400 years. There were legal experts to study such things as the relationship between a man's education and how he is treated by the courts, a bevy of translators to bring into English the first accurate record of important classical literature, and a project to collect an immense quantity of graphic materials for a study of certain subtle relationships between art and sex, and so on and on. Only a few outsiders knew of any of this, but the Rockefeller Foundation knew of it all and had been properly proud to support it for years.

*During an exhausting search for new backing, Kinsey's health suddenly began to fail; he died August 25, 1956. The Institute for Sex Research and its stores of untapped data still exist. But now under grants from the Department of Health, Education & Welfare, it is a quite different organization. Like much other human research dependent upon committee approvals from Washington, it has come under severe constraints. Gone is the knife-edge of inductive methodology that so distinguished Kinsey's work. The Institute with its largely new staff now emphasizes, as it must, established theory, hypothesis-testing devices and deductive methods—approaches which tend to dignify pre-existing assumptions. This shift is itself full of irony, for it is exactly in line with what Hobbs originally demanded and Kinsey *always* warned against.

ing such matters—"by talking about it you encourage it." But the most virulent resentments arose from the fact that sex, particularly homosexual sex, was dealt with without a word of moralizing—and worse still, that biological traditions were cited for it.*

In the final analysis, what is the meaning of all these attitudes and political events? Are the older examples to be discounted on the grounds that they would be unlikely to recur?—or in their essentials do they live on in ever-changing new forms? To the extent that they do, just how do they, and whom do they harm? Is one to lament the unlucky fate of a few individuals who now and again are crushed in the vise of local events?—or are there larger, more pervasive penalties to worry about? There certainly are, and a few of these come into view in answering a basic question: Why should anything as unobtrusive as homosexuality arouse as much concern as it does? On the surface there seem to be as many answers as there are critics, critics who sometimes feel an urge to defend the church, the home, society in general, or their own backyards. There are a few, always the most vociferous of the lot, who want to smite the homosexual dragon from without to keep from seeing it within. Many others find satisfaction in defending the mores, or in casting a loud vote for centerline norms. And yet, despite the strength of these and other moral interests, few if any public reactions against homosexuality are spontaneous. Most are either arranged or stage-managed by persons and factions who seldom care one way or the other about sexual matters, but who have set their sights on various kinds of political gains. Still, all such motivations seem either too local or too impersonal to account for the full thrust of excitements which have managed to drive the law into crime, the government into weird inconsistencies, the press into a fear of reporting, and the Navy into policies worthy of a common fool.

---

*Emotional reactions to the homosexual findings dominated every level of criticism, though they were frequently disguised as purely technical concerns. These emotions were what lay behind the insistence that the American Statistical Association should evaluate Kinsey's work. And when the ASA itself produced its final report, homosexuality was the only form of sex listed in the index of its 338-page report.[41]

Part of what needs to be accounted for is the fact that murder, graft, and a host of violent crimes, though strongly taboo, fail to stir the intensely personalized emotions that can still be aroused by the homosexual. A main reason seems to be that homosexuality can touch people, can involve them vicariously, in ways that serious offenses do not. Its individual actions include components common in everyone's behavior, here seen in a violational context. Thus, for most people, one of the most disturbing images in homosexuality is that of two men kissing, for it is easily imagined and sharply at odds with what is expected. The same thing is apparent in sex practices, too: Every kind of "penis use" as well as every expression of affection in homosexuality so duplicates an equivalent in heterosexuality as to be "brought home" to people in much stronger ways than some crime of violence which, however repugnant, contains actions unfamiliar enough to remain at a more comfortable distance. Thus, while homosexuality is not at all *ob*trusive, it can be exceedingly *in*trusive within people's imagination and expectancy.

In an example such as that of the Navy (or any other group where a cult of masculinity prevails), the shock of homosexuality lies not so much in its actions as in the idea that it is a violation of manly aggressiveness. For the armed services to really be able to accept the homosexual, they would either have to place considerably less emphasis than they do on a showy masculinity—or what is even less likely, arrive at the highly sophisticated realization that inversion is often not at all involved in homosexual contacts, and that even when it is, for a man to invert his role during sex does not imply an impaired aggressiveness at other times.

Finally, there is a more important set of reasons for homosexuality's arousing as much opposition as it does—reasons which have less to do with anything in this kind of sex than with the ogres it can raise near the philosophic base of heterosexuality. Not that heterosexuality needs the particular basis our society happens to rest it on, for it is and always will be the preference of most people. But in our society, it is hemmed in by a multitude of restraints that dampen the dignity of sex in all but a few forms. Even in the most conventional heterosexual settings, one violates basic codes by pursuing sex for fun, for variety, for conquest, and for still other "purely" erotic and personal desires. To do so is to hear charges of shallowness and adulteration—if not the adulteration of one's marriage then of love itself, frequently with lectures on what constitutes "mature" relationships. In short, the philosophic basis of our heterosexuality is still essentially ascetic, with the curse fully lifted off of sex when, and only when, it is transcended by affection and social commitments.

Very many people retain these attitudes and this whole way of viewing sex. If they have held to rigid sex codes, the loss of interest they have sustained in the bedroom has usually been made more tolerable by being rationalized—often with the idea that sex is not all that important anyway, and that through their privations they have earned moral credits and met family obligations. From this point of comparison, homosexuality not only seems personally unappealing (as "opposite" choices always are) but thoroughly contemptible, especially when pictured as lasciviously free. Yet even this image is bearable, so long as the sinners are suffering.

But it is quite another matter when an authoritative source (a Kinsey Report, a television documentary, or a social survey) suggests that a style of life contradictory to theirs not only works, but may even work better than their own for some people—people who, besides, are possibly neither sick nor sinners. Suggestions of this sort are generally *not* threatening to people who are fully gratified by heterosexuality, nor to others who are frank about their failures in it. But to the great mass of the population, taut with the rigors of conventionality and heavily invested in the symbols if not the letter of moral law, any suggestion of a fully acceptable homosexuality is worse than abhorrent. It is as if the very foundations of their beliefs are being threatened. Or is the threat mainly to their sexual rationalizations? In any event, the result is a fiercely dangerous set of emotions that has proved itself capable of corrupting every channel of enlightenment and of suppressing information that would ultimately be useful to everyone's understanding of himself and the world around him.

11

The Question of Psychotherapy

Almost from the moment homosexuality comes up for serious discussion, questions arise concerning the possibility of changing it via therapy. Such questions are reasonable and are worth considering, though they usually carry unfortunate underlying assumptions—that homosexuality is pathological, or the symptom of an illness—that in our society, at least, it arises from psychological disturbances—that there are psychotherapists who understand such matters and who, with the cooperation of the patient, can change his disposition. If the issues could be kept at this level, they would be fairly easy to deal with. One could straighten out the underlying assumptions, reword the central questions a bit, and then answer them.

But the sophisticated observer is not so easily satisfied; he knows how to ask very difficult questions about the "therapy" of "homosexuals." (The quotation marks already spell trouble; they mean that the frame of reference itself is to be examined.) He may ask at the outset: Why do most psychotherapists see homosexuality as a sickness to be cured (regardless of whether or not they make any claims of being able to cure it) while, on the other hand, most sex researchers do not raise the issue, and do not agree with it anyway? The question is surprisingly sticky, and more important than it may seem.

Part of the answer is that psychotherapy stems from a psychiatric tradition, one that has always tended to use society's view of expected behavior as a major reference point from which to measure deviations. Thus, therapists have tended to be ethnocentric, more than a little establishmentarian, and have frequently acted as the guardians of society. (The first job psychiatry ever had was to decide which crazy people should be kept locked up, and which were safe enough to let roam the streets.) Sex researchers, on the other hand, stem from a tradition comprised of wandering anthropologists (long suspected of being a bit disloyal to their home mores due to their cross-cultural interests) and a conglomerate of even worse "heretics" from the fields of biology, physiology, and other sciences—men whose objective observations have often been iconoclastic. With this in their background, sex researchers have frequently been accused (not too wrongly) of being socially unaccountable; that is, of caring little about the "immorality" their information might lead to, and perhaps even taking a certain delight in contradicting the mores. Indeed, they have been far more inclined to boil off the holy water than to place credence in the Wisdom of the Ages.

However, psychotherapy has more than its set of traditions to keep it continually referent to social norms. It deals with disturbed people whose behavioral problems invite both the therapist and the patient to hold a mental image of masses of ordinary people whose behavior is thought of as not only "normal" and largely uniform (as opposed to varying) but as well worth working toward. Fritz Fluckiger has described the attitudes exactly:

> The therapeutic situation is one in which the therapist and patient share certain social expectations. In the case of the homosexual patient, the shared expectation is most often that the patient ought to be heterosexual. His failure to meet this expectation is his "problem" or "symptom" to be treated—or at the very least, a "deficit" to be reduced.[67]

Certainly a therapist can hold these attitudes for reasons other than a devotion to conventional mores. Every example he sees may bear out what his training has led him to expect. Most homosexual patients display an array of disturbances, and most come for treatment at a time when they are experiencing a crisis of self-doubt. Not infrequently, a patient is in the throes of a major depression, highly articulate in damning his own life-style and unable to cite anything of value in it. Often he is in the midst of a broken love affair in which one or both partners are displaying various forms of hysterical behavior, emotional regressions, and the like. Of course, the same could be said of the heterosexual patient, except that his situation is one every therapist is familiar with and knows how to keep in perspective.

The whole problem of keeping the homosexual patient's disturbances in perspective is so marked that when sex researchers go into private practice (as they often do in later life) they almost invariably note that if they had seen homosexuality first and only in clinical examples, they would probably have agreed with the standard opinions. The same idea is often voiced in the shop-talk of therapists who are themselves homosexual—"What I heard from my H-patients this week alone would be enough to confirm every psychoanalytic theory in the book; no wonder everybody thinks as he does."

But of course "everybody" is not everybody. There are therapists who do not share the usual views of homosexuality, do not like healthy-sick formulations, and do not trust neatly put together portraits of doom. They know what is wrong with notions of "cure" and, in fact, would not consider trying to make basic changes in any established sexual pattern. A few of these clinicians are hardnosed pragmatists who have no time for the impossible. Others, by the sheer breadth of their experience (or from accidental examples that may have come before them) know what satisfactory homosexual life-styles look like and proceed to zero in on whatever the patient is doing to make his life dreary and dangerous.*

---

*While these therapists constitute a small minority, they hold an even lower profile in the field than their numbers might justify. By neither being organized nor speaking for any formal school of thought, they often come across as being without portfolio. Thus in public forums the orthodox therapist sounds as if he is speaking for his field and for society itself, while the views of liberal therapists tend to sound like individual opinions. Since

One might think a therapist's liberal attitudes would be met with open arms by the disturbed patient, but often they are not. Many patients have already thoroughly embraced conventional attitudes toward their "condition" and may be as little inclined to abandon these views as to have their troubles attributed to their own poor management. Thus the therapist who sides with a patient's homosexual urges (instead of joining him in lamenting his plight) often hears a storm of protest in which his professional competence is questioned even more by the patient than by colleagues who disagree with liberal views. However, this kind of protest is short-lived, for whether the patient is voicing society's argument in the private hope of losing it, or is more convinced of what he is saying, moral pretenses are no match for strong, persistent sexual motivations. To honor and to work toward reachable goals almost instantly dissolves depression, usually opening the door to a stream of small and larger successes.

But in most psychotherapy, conventional views predominate and there is not much success of any kind. In fact, the picture is worse than that. Homosexuality and psychotherapy have proved to be extremely bad for each other. Countless people who have brought homosexual problems to therapists have had cause to regret it. The price of the patient's not having had the clarity or intuition to leave immediately has been that he has almost certainly been headed toward some kind of disimprovement, usually in the form of sweeping new views of his "pathology" and even less self-acceptance than he started with. The squandering of time and money are pale penalties compared with the patient's heightened guilt feelings, his squelched *élan*, and other consequences of misdirection.

As if in retribution, homosexuality has damaged psychotherapy almost beyond its capacity to recover. The least of its punishments has been that by now there are thousands of people who, as a result of either observation or experience, are ready to

---

these impressions are in line with much public sentiment, they are likely to continue for a long time—despite the fact that the American Psychiatric Association has recently declassified homosexuality *per se* as an illness.

ridicule all therapy—casting aspersions not only on its validity but on its veracity. This scorn, along with doubts expressed in other quarters, has festered and has driven the most hidebound therapists into constantly reiterating their ideas on homosexuality in books, articles, and at professional conferences. And in reaction to this, a really major blow has been delivered to the whole field of psychotherapy: the thoroughgoing and quiet repudiation by scientists. For as sex researchers in biology and experimental psychology have heard more and more from conservative psychiatrists, they have come to be appalled by "the therapists," to shake their heads in despair over "the nonsense of applied psychology," and to think of therapy itself as a club of fools more to be left alone than argued with.

This is less an exaggeration than it may seem. A few years ago, a group of professors and graduate students at Yale University (from the departments of biology, zoology, and experimental psychology) decided to have some fun and at the same time to demonstrate to themselves and their students how far their combined disciplines have progressed. In particular, they wanted to show the contrast between what used to be thought about human instinct and what is now known. So as a group, and with a straight face, they invited a high-ranking member of the American Psychiatric Association (a man who was also president of the New York Psychoanalytic Society) to come speak to their combined departments on "The Vicissitudes of Human Sexual Development."[263]

The good doctor accepted the invitation and performed exactly as had been anticipated—only more so. After a few remarks about the fine application of Freudian theoretical constructs to the urgent work of curing patients, he began to outline in detail how Nature's procreative instinct expresses itself in the stages of a male child's development. He waxed eloquently on how a boy progresses from an oral to an anal and then finally to a phallic stage as he fights to leave his infantile ways behind him—to seduce his mother, wipe out his father, and failing this, to wait his turn to find an appropriate woman whose shyness whets his appetite, forcing some of his libido into affection (itself designed to keep him by his mate for later purposes of child care), thus guiding him to procreate and so to take his place in the scheme of things. Nicely woven into this theme were the variations of how the human instinct can fail to reach its appointed task if blocked by one of the homosexual deviations: phallic failure, narcissistic possession, oral or anal fixations—due if not to a boy's fear of placing his penis near the imagined teeth in the vagina, then to his being seduced by his mother, instead of vice versa.

The audience appeared to be spellbound, and in a sense, it surely was. At the end of the lecture, there was uproarious applause. The noted psychoanalyst seemed greatly pleased. One can only wonder what he would have thought if he had known that he had been welcomed as a voice from the past—and, in fact, that his honorarium had been paid from the graduate students' entertainment fund.

While elaborate pranks of this sort may be rare, it is undeniable that sex researchers from the scientific community maintain a profound and ongoing disrespect for therapists. Homosexuality is an especially irritating issue, not because it is of any special interest in itself but because, as one of the Yale psychologists put it, "It brings out the very worst in the psychiatric crowd." Apologists have suggested that while this alienation has grown in recent years (the two groups seldom share the same conference podiums as they once did), on a practical level, at least, the division is understandable. Indeed it is in one sense. Unlike the therapist, a biologist or experimental psychologist has next to nothing to say to the general public, or to any untrained audience. He is likely to know little and care less about patient-problems (least of all on the what-to-do-next level). He may know quite a lot about homosexuality (enough to reject the underlying assumptions in every psychiatric theory), but on the level that he operates he may doubt that it exists as an entity, and care too little of the matter to present any argument. If he were hit by the sort of question an anxious parent might ask, he would feel much like an African explorer who was suddenly called upon to explain a nuclear warhead to some native hovering over a pot of missionary stew.

On the other side of the earth live psychotherapists. They are in a very different position. Patients and the problems of patients are their business—so are worried parents, whose language they speak perfectly. There are few questions in sex and none in homosexuality for which they lack easily communicable answers. With these qualities and with plenty of eager, untrained listeners in an age of mass media, it is not surprising that they have come to have and to hold the respectful attention of a large audience. Viewed from this angle, what does it matter that they cut a shabby profile in the eyes of a few dozen specialists? A quick answer (besides the fact that it locks public opinion in a jail of ignorance) is that it quietly brings agony and corruption to therapy itself. And yet, the total picture so often combines calamity and innocence, it deserves to be seen in its most favorable light.

Most therapists do not write books or appear on television. They have no axe to grind in sustaining one theory over the next, or in winning public acclaim. For the most part, they are a composite of intelligent, kindly, personally quite nice (if sometimes a bit odd) men and women who seek more often than they find certain kinds of rewarding satisfactions in their work. Unlike what many of their critics believe, holding on to patients and collecting fees are not their main concerns. (The established clinician has plenty of both.) His pains and pleasures are elsewhere. His daily work requires a constant flow of attention and an interest in what he is doing—an outflow which is almost impossible to sustain without the hope and the prospect of improving the patient. Nothing disturbs a therapist more, or hits him harder where he lives, than feeling that his efforts are wasted, useless, hopeless. In seeing quite a lot of homosexuality (perhaps 10 to 20 per cent of his practice) it is important for him to work out his own positions. In hearing the patient's account, he needs to be able to make appropriate associations in his own mind as he restructures the local problem, or the whole problem, into one which is in some sense solvable.

Probably it would be correct to describe most therapists as being "for" anything that works. Initially at least, they do not care what kind of life a patient elects (or the margin by which he elects it), let alone what he does sexually. But most therapists are driven back toward formal interpretations of homosexuality by an unlucky combination of the patients they see and their own alienation from science. Unless they have already earned a reputation for accepting homosexuality (or at least leaving it alone) they will seldom get the kinds of clients for whom it is working at all well. But a far greater hazard is that most of the patients they do get are quite familiar with psychiatric ideas and have already translated their self-interpretations into these terms (which is one of their problems). Thus, one patient after the other presents a history of having a dominant mother, a weak or inattentive father, a package of early insecurities, and all the rest. Not infrequently, patients have worked out these versions of their lives with a certain microscopic precision, prefitting them into oedipal and fixation theories exactly—even to the point of making them fit the gaps the therapist is waiting to fill. Little wonder that the therapist who feeds at this incestuous banquet soon arrives at the groggy consolation that Freud was right about everything.

He unwittingly falls into this trap and into many another that line his path specifically because of his alienation from sex research. It is an alienation which has cost him his chance to be forewarned by many findings, among them, that dominant mothers and weak fathers correlate with nothing at all except each other—that cross-culturally and almost certainly in our society as well, a boy's closeness to his mother has a higher correlation with heterosexual than with homosexual outcomes[286]—that dreams characteristically take the shape most palatable to the anticipated listener[62]—that all preferences are fixations and that none is established without learned aversions[140]—that a young boy's awkwardness with (and disparagement of) females are among the highest prognosticators of his later attraction to them[82]—that the inversion-homosexual axis tends to be proportional to the strength of the "libido" and not to its weakness[4,69]—and so on and on to the utter embarrassment of every formal psychiatric theory without exception.

Thus from two sides—a technical naïveté, and the drab, sad, largely stage-managed reports of his patients—the average therapist is invited into the new trap of attempting to "cure" homosexuality, as opposed to attacking the neuroses and other disturbances which often accompany it.

The Cure Issue

There are no known "cures" for homosexuality, nor are any likely, since the phenomena which comprise it are not illnesses in the first place. Of course, the issue does not end here. Smoking and drinking are not illnesses either, but they can be stamped out by various means. With these and other considerations in mind, the Kinsey Research made a concerted effort over a period of years to find and evaluate the histories of people whose sex lives had changed either during or following therapy of any kind. None was ever found. Several psychoanalysts who were friends of the Research promised to send particular patients they were proud of having "cured" but none of these was ever forthcoming. After Kinsey's death, and to this day, Wardell Pomeroy (a long-time member of the Research and now a New York psychotherapist) has maintained a standing offer to administer the Kinsey Research battery to any person a therapist might send, and thus possibly validate a case of changed homosexuality. This offer has never had any "takers" except for one remarkable instance.

A New York psychiatrist who for a number of years has headed a large psychoanalytic research program on homosexuality—a man who has written an important book on the subject in which various percentages of changed cases were reported—did indeed make a definite commitment to exemplify these results. After several delays of several weeks each, the psychiatrist finally confessed to Pomeroy that he had only one case which he thought would qualify but that, unfortunately, he was on such bad terms with the patient he did not feel free to call him up.[219] One possible case?—then what about his 358-page book claiming from 19 to 50 per cent cures?[28] Whether or not it qualifies as an outright misrepresentation is, in part, a matter of definition. The psychiatrist did not actually say in his much-quoted book that he, personally, had cured anybody, nor did he claim to have actually seen or personally examined anybody else's successful results. There were numerous implications of a firsthand knowledge, to be sure (along with elaborate statistical citations) but legalistically speaking, the psychiatrist was, and is, in the clear. No doubt he was clear in his own mind, too—fully believing both what other psychiatrists reported and what he himself was able to make of these reports. In all this, he takes his place in a long tradition for this brand of reporting. Over the years there have been literally dozens of second-party accounts of "cured" homosexuality. Like the footprints of the Loch Ness monster, they very often appear, but without the presence of the elusive beast.

The efforts of the Kinsey Research to find people whose sexual response had changed as a result of therapy did manage to turn up a few instances worthy of mention, and in a few of these, the person was quite proud of the "progress" he or she had made. But on close examination all examples quickly failed to qualify. In most, it was a matter of sheer suppression—"I used to be a lesbian, but now I turn away when temptation knocks." Others were slightly more complicated, often involving a man's fantasying males during heterosexual intercourse, and the like. Once when Kinsey was in Philadelphia, a man phoned him at his hotel to say he had heard they were interested in people whose homosexuality had been changed by therapy, as his had been. Kinsey immediately arranged to take his history. The man explained that he had once been a very active homosexual but that, thanks to therapy, "I have now cut out all of that and don't even think of men—except when I masturbate."[141]

Actually, it is quite surprising that the Kinsey Researchers did not find *any* instances of people whose sexual responses were altered during therapy (and it surprised them, too). One would expect changes to occasionally occur by accident, if by nothing else. There are always a few people who are free to enter or to leave homosexual involvements by virtue of the fact that their preferences are not yet clearly defined. Others have clear-cut preferences which remain somewhat flexible due to a lack of aversion-reactions to their implied opposites; these individuals sometimes move back and forth across the heterosexual-homosexual line as a result of particularly good or bad experiences they have with members of either sex.

But, of course, the average therapist knows nothing of all this background. He does not realize that validated changes in homosexuality are nowhere to be found. And he certainly does not know that the most prestigious literature on the subject is all second-party reporting at best (if, indeed, it is not from still further back in some armchair). On the contrary, he finds himself surrounded by colleagues and by published accounts suggesting that such changes are feasible and are actually being made. Not infrequently he feels almost a professional obligation to be able to see what others see (something of an Emperor's New Clothes situation) and to be able to match their results, quite aside from the extent to which his own attitudes may press in the same direction.

Thus there are a great many therapists—including those who are wise enough to avoid the word *cure*, and who would not be fooled by the man from Philadelphia either—who feel the urge to launch major efforts to suppress and to change homosexual behavior. Their outlook and their level of sophistication vary considerably. More than a few have the notion that if they can get a patient to try out heterosexuality, he will "lose his fear of it," come to like it, and in that case the homosexuality will automatically disappear (shades, once again, of a "blocked" heterosexuality). Others know better than this, but nevertheless persistently aim at essentially the same target. In their view, the only really bad thing about homosexuality is its exclusivity, that it supposedly cuts a person off from general society and from the conventional experiences of hearth and home. In both of these positions, and in all gradations between them, the patient's marriage to a partner he cares about is considered the major breakthrough. (How interesting it is—and how alarming—that the risks and comforts of the spouse are never mentioned; the massive literature on how to alter homosexuality contains not a word on his or her behalf.)

But from the moment a therapist actually decides to turn a homosexual therapy situation into a theatre-of-change, he is in for trouble, and he knows it. He needs all the help he can get— much stronger stuff than his own convictions and a desire to keep up with his colleagues. He needs extensive cooperation from the patient, or as the literature so nicely puts it, the patient "must really *want* to change." Trouble is, virtually no patient ever starts out saying any such thing. The person who turns to therapy usually does so for help, not for a total remodeling job, and if he sooner or later does shift to an I-want-to-change position, it is a commitment made at some distance from the business of sex.* Thus the change-therapist must use his position of authority and various techniques at his command to undermine the basic validity of the homosexual alternative in order to make the heterosexual possibility appear to be the only solution to the patient's problem.

It is widely believed (especially by homosexuals) that such maneuvers are tolerated only by persons who feel very guilty over their homosexual involvements. Not quite so. Many change-therapists do not exactly announce their attitudes and intentions at the outset—and by the time the patient finds them out, he may be personally attached to the therapist, or deeply entangled in the "findings" in his own case. Furthermore, there are different kinds of guilt feelings, some of which have the effect of localizing the area of conflict. A person may have little concern over his sexual desires, and yet be alarmed by what these might "mean," or by what will happen to him later in life. With these kinds of concerns in the spotlight, a person may be in therapy for a year or more before fully realizing that the therapist has not been aiming at such twigs and branches, but has been sawing away at the trunk of his tree.

Even then, the basic techniques of the change-therapist are less than transparent to many patients. They may see him as an objective, friendly, nonjudgmental observer whose special skills allow him to peer below the surface and to make interesting connections. Frequently a patient is dazzled to find that bits and pieces of his behavior are interpretable as being richly complex

---

*The various surveys which have been conducted over the years have shown that from 90 to 96 per cent of homosexuals would not elect to change, even if they could do so by "pushing a button." These results prove neither that most of the individuals are pleased with their lives, nor that a few of them would like to change. The core issue is much more complex; it has to do with matters of component-thinking and intellectual honesty. In any event, it is highly questionable whether it is humanly possible for anybody to want what he does not want, and to genuinely want to not want what he does want, let alone to honestly desire both changes at once.

and wondrously systematized. He does not realize that the therapist, for his purposes, is not depending on these connections but is resting his case on far more mundane matters: the effects of certain policy positions, the more typical of which are these:

• If the patient is presently in a long-standing homosexual relationship, "analyze" any local conflict. Ask in detail what has happened to the intense sexual interest the partners started with; imply that in heterosexual relationships, sexual interest continues unabated until advancing age dissolves it. If, on the other hand, conflict arises in a relationship of short duration, point out that it is unrealistic to expect homosexual ties to last, since this kind of love is spurious make-believe, a counterfeit version of the real thing. (In this example and those that follow, the change-therapist's objectivity and his intellectual honesty may be questionable, but usually not his integrity; he often believes what he says, or at least he does not disbelieve it.)

• Point out that in the patient's present (or past) relationship, he has many times had flashes of hate for the partner, as well as thoughts that life would really be better without him. If the patient's response is "Yes! how did you know that?" then move in for the consolidation by explaining that even the best forms of homosexual attachment are inherently spasmodic and ready to break apart at the seams. However, if the patient is more sophisticated and has responded with something like "Of course I have felt daggers and have had the beautiful dream of total freedom; who hasn't?" then recover and take a new step, "Yes, every man has, but in heterosexuality not so often—and as you yourself have [previously] pointed out, homosexual affairs seldom last; I just want you to understand why."

• Adjust all interpretations to the fact that in most of his attachments the patient has been the one who pulled away from the partner, or vice versa. (Most people of any orientation fall into a pattern of either ending their relationships or of being left behind; relatively few mix these styles.) If the patient has usually been the one who first tires of a relationship, point out his unconscious motives in hurting people, or of constantly requiring new partners to assuage his self-doubts, to reaffirm his attractiveness, and the like. But if his partners have usually tired of him first, point out his overdependence, his appetite for masochistic suffering, the unavoidably shallow nature of all homosexual ties and the possibility that he is an "injustice collector" who thrives on his own defeats, or perhaps all of these interpretations interwoven to show the folly of his way of life.

• Use whatever the patient says of his doubts, hesitations, or guilt feelings to wipe out whatever hope he may still harbor of finding a satisfactory homosexual life. Agree with and elaborate all negative statements the patient may make about homosexuality, including those which are based on religious beliefs the therapist himself does not hold. For instance, if an orthodox Jew or strict Catholic centers his conflict around a particular edict, suggest that such moral standards are not just local rules but, in a sense, reflect the experience of mankind. (A few change-therapists throw in the notion that no society has ever approved of homosexuality and that homosexual "apologists" have fabricated or distorted the record of history—a suggestion that runs the risk that the patient just might know better.) Say or imply that much of the loneliness or isolation the patient feels is not of his own making, but is inherent in his life-style. When a patient expresses concern over getting older, point out that this will eventually leave him high and dry; conjure up an image of the old homosexual predator and make part of it fit. Repeatedly state the ravages of transiency and promiscuity in the lives of homosexuals. Point out that they must always contend with a separation between their sexual experiences, on the one hand, and their affectional and emotional experiences, on the other.*

But of all the individual traits of the homosexual which the change-therapist is able to exploit, probably none is more useful

---

*Ploys such as these and a host of others are part of the standard equipment of change-therapists. Many such techniques were assembled and published (along with detailed instructions on how to use them) by psychiatrist Lawrence Hatterer in 1970.[100] It is notable that a deliberate attempt to increase a patient's guilt is without precedent in the field. But neither this basic policy nor the use of overt misrepresentation (when "the ends justify the means") have yet been ruled on by the ethics committees of the American Psychiatric Association and American Psychological Association.

than a patient's special sexual preference. Since every grown male has at least a few fetishlike preferences, it is easy to weave these into a "dynamic pattern" that can greatly impresss the naïve patient. For instance, if he prefers partners who are shorter than himself and have prominent male features (perhaps a large penis and broad shoulders) then it can be "shown" that he is trying to repair his doubted masculinity by savoring the maleness of a partner whom he overpowers, perhaps as his father overpowered him, with numerous ramifications concerning how he wants to dominate, or to be dominated, or both. (Should there be a note of bondage in the picture such as fantasies of forcing the partner, or being forced by him, to do this or that, then the sky is the limit.) If the patient shies away from kissing his partners, this may "prove" that his main sexual motive is merely a power play—or if kissing is important, then it can be pointed out that he is seeking to treat his partner (or be treated by him) as his mother treated him (or should have) and so on. The pieces of "the puzzle" will fit together in a thousand ways to confirm absolutely any expectation.*

Among the very few homosexual patients who remain with a change-therapist over a considerable period of time, there are those who both believe what they hear and follow directions. This means, on the one hand, becoming sufficiently demoralized over his or her homosexuality to actively struggle against it and, on the other, to desperately try to build up a heterosexual response. Thus a new question arises: In these few cases where the treatment succeeds in its immediate goals, why is there still no final

---

*These various examples have been chosen from the relatively conservative repertoire of the ordinary change-therapist. The same kinds of interpretations have become phantasmagoric in the hands of a few psychiatrists who (for what appear to be serious personal reasons) have gone over the edge on "homosexual pathology." For instance, Irving Bieber has suggested that the odors a young child smells from his mother can trigger responses that cause him to stay away from women forever.[27] And Edmund Bergler has insisted that every homosexual motivation is externally self-destructive and internally superdynamic—for instance, that the man who places a penis in his mouth wants to do so because its relative shape and skin texture remind him of the gently rough and protruding nipple of his mother's breast to which he urgently wants to return, and so on.[24]

success? Answer: for the simple and not so simple reason that the adult human being's sexual response rests at bottom on a massive, cortically organized, sexual value system which is impervious to the trivial intrusions launched against it by what amount to social concerns (concerns which can muster their support from no more than a fragment of frontal lobe authority). The effort to wage this war is what George Weinberg has described as "an attempt to sink a battleship with a popgun."[271]

In the final analysis and in practical terms, it is still important to bear in mind the change-therapist's assumptions and his basic techniques—together they are what mislead him with a smattering of initial "changes" and a few brittle cases of rigid control, but in the end, leave him with not a single verifiable instance of record. And yet, at least his immediate future seems assured, for while he does not reach his goals, his efforts do gratify a variety of social and professional needs.

It is tempting at this point to turn the issue around and review the often excellent efforts of therapists who zero in on the homosexual patient's disturbances without trying to redirect his or her sexual proclivities. Such a review would be fair to the field, and it would be heartening, too. For while these therapists are in the minority, they still constitute a notable group of professionals, many of whom display an exceptional talent, humanity, and intellectual honesty. Yet, for reasons which may not be instantly apparent, to even sketch out their work would be a formidable undertaking. In examining the change-therapists, it was possible to quickly catch the flavor of their approach; they are quite tightly held together by a uniform set of underlying assumptions. But among the "liberal" therapists (even this label does not quite fit since the group contains extreme conservatives) there is not a single unifying assumption.

Take the matter of acceptance itself. A few therapists accept homosexuality because the results of their previous efforts to oppose it have made them wary of tampering with it. Others accept it much as they accept the phases of the moon. Still others grab the ball and run with it, glad to let out their stride in doing battle with particular sets of disturbances they have seen before in homosexual patients and have learned how to deal with. Across these groups, more than a few therapists feel that sexual matters *per se* will take care of themselves if improvements can be made in the patient's social integration and in his capacity to handle interpersonal problems. Others, in addition, go after a patient's hangups with a vengeance—"Make your sexual situations work, or all the success in the world won't be worth a damn."

Any therapist who fully accepts a person's basic sexual orientation has an enormous advantage; he can do what no change-therapist could ever get away with: He can zero in on particular trouble spots with a kind of flagrant brutality (actually, an affectionate abuse) to punch home a point with no risk of either drawing blood or arousing resistance—"That loose-wristedness you use when you're not being quite frank is murder; did you copy it from somebody or did you re-invent it?"—"Your hostility toward John is clear enough but to hold it back while expressing it gives your attitude a pinched, bitchy, faggoty quality; wouldn't it feel better to stab him a few times than to sting him to death with a swarm of bees?" Even a therapist who would never consider cartooning a patient's surface behavior (or even mention it) gains much leverage from fully accepting rather than privately lamenting the basic conditioning. The acceptance still manages to come across in ways that win confidence and allow the patient's problems to be dealt with on their own merits.

From these few examples it is clear there is wide diversity among liberal therapists and perhaps much to argue with besides, but there is also much that is elegant and useful in their work. At least they try to tune in on what is important in a person's homosexual involvements—the risks, penalties, and assets. Here, to be sure, there is plenty to work on, for while homosexuality's most commonly thought of drawbacks are seldom its most troublesome features, it does invite special problems.

The Real Trouble with Homosexuality

When people who are involved in homosexuality are asked to cite its disadvantages—those they have seen if not personally experienced—their answers are largely in line with public opinion. They point out that it can be inconvenient, that it makes a person's life harder to manage, that it can entail social complications and force a person to sail uncharted seas as he struggles to find his own way. Not infrequently, a person is shocked at first realizing his homosexual interests and may have to contend with guilt. Even when this is not a problem, he may feel obliged and hard put to keep this part of himself away from friends and relatives whom he knows are not prepared to understand it. Thus most people who are involved in homosexuality report having had a "rough time" adjusting to it, especially at first. And yet, it is probably fair to say that problems at these levels are generally overrated—not because they are any less disturbing than is commonly thought but they do tend to be temporary and relatively easy for a person to face and to grapple with.

In any case, there are other problems which can be far more troublesome—problems having to do with the management of aggression and, in some instances, a higher than average vulnerability to hysteria. Does this mean that homosexuality invites a person to be less forceful, less effective in expressing aggression, and perhaps less stable under conditions of stress? No and yes. In terms of the ordinary measures of ambition and "success" it is definitely not possible to say homosexual men and women are any more inclined to "fail" in life or to be squelched by it than anybody else. (Any such trend would be hard to detect anyway, since the attrition of human talents appears to be quite high in all segments of society.) Nor is it possible to say that in ordinary life situations the homosexual is any less effective than the heterosexual in handling friction and in modulating aggression. In fact, up to fairly high levels of stress it is probable that, like members of other integrated minorities, he is better than average in these respects.

But of course, it is not in the arena of daily interactions that the substance and stability of a person are put to the test. One is "tested" in moments of crisis and high stress—moments when he faces defeat, especially if he faces it more or less alone. No doubt this is why the homosexual is often particularly careful to maintain close friendships and meaningful social ties. Even so, the combination of his "difference" and the kinds of sharp challenges he faces from time to time give him an above-average chance to develop self-doubts and to be self-derogatory. Thus, for him to be "average" during periods of very high stress he generally needs to be much better than average at handling conflict and at mustering and managing aggression. (The word itself comes from a Latin root meaning a readiness to step forward.)

Or to put it the other way around, in situations of very high stress—perhaps a broken love affair or such defeats as being fired from an important job—the heterosexual is often able to retain his "aggressive protest" a bit longer. To the extent that he is able to view himself with conventional approval he may even be able to afford the luxury of feeling a righteous blamelessness. The homosexual, with his less conventional framework to fall back on, and frequently with a sharp awareness of his personal shortcomings, more easily loses his conviction of being justified—and along with it, much of his aggressiveness. Under particular kinds of stress he sometimes loses his whole sense of entitlement.

Many therapists have cited what the early analysts considered a "superego conflict" in accounting for the homosexual's special vulnerability to self-assaultive attitudes when under stress. (Since the comparison is between heterosexual and homosexual patients, the observation applies to nonpatients as well.) It is pointed out that in the course of growing up everyone has a set of conventional standards stamped into his head and that while a person may later ridicule these in the many places logic permits, and may consciously reject such standards as inapplicable to himself, nothing really erases those early traces. From this point of view, there is nothing contradictory or even very surprising in the fact that while the homosexual is often glad to be unconventional and may even take a certain pride in being independent and a free spirit, great stress can cause his superstructure of individuality to come unstuck, leaving him at the mercy of his originally learned standards. A simpler version of the same idea is that since a person's individualized self is what he lays on the line in most of his battles, it is naturally this part of him which is thrown into question in times of defeat, strengthening the hand of social opinion almost by default.

Perhaps these explanations "explain" what they are supposed to explain but they fail to account for the exceptions: the many instances in which people with individualized life-styles (homosexual or heterosexual) show little inclination to become self-critical in times of defeat. The innovator, the trail blazer, and the zealous reformer, for instance, are notoriously disinclined to turn against themselves under stress. On the contrary, they are often renewed by it. Perhaps these particular individuals, quite as public opinion has it, are aided by an exceptional forcefulness and "strength of character." But before too much of their unswerving stamina is attributed to their moral fiber, it should be understood that they are not alone. There are many other individuals of more ordinary temperament who, with nothing that qualifies as heroic fortitude, manage to live lives at some distance from the conventional mainstream without either falling apart or becoming self-destructive under stress. Where do they get their stability?

Sometimes they get it from possessing, or from being possessed by, a devotion, a commitment, or some other target of interest. It is quite significant that the particular item of focus need not have the breadth and substance of what a genius or crusader might choose—not at all. Since what is "doing the work" is the person's investment in his own obsession, neither the size of the target nor the value other people ascribe to it are of much consequence. Thus, as anyone can see, the person who is fascinated with something and is trying to do his best at it—be he an actor, a chef, a pianist or an expert at anything—finds in this focal interest a niche and a solace from which he is not easily dislodged.

But on close examination, it soon becomes clear that having an obsessional interest does not always bolster a person's ego. Neither does it necessarily supply resolve nor serve as a buttress against the impact of shock. But what it does do—often impressively for the homosexual—is to define a person's bailiwick and, in the process, give his ship a certain gyroscopic directionality, no matter how rough the seas. Undoubtedly this is why religious conversion (or a more personalized neurotic symptom) tends to hold a person together, often as well as does a fervent interest in being an artist or artisan.

Intuitively, it is easy to understand how having an obsessional focus of some kind reduces a person's vulnerability to hysterical scatter or to a breakdown. But exactly how does having a commitment to virtually anything manage to immunize him against depression and against the sting of personal rejection? When one asks the person who manages to stay secure in the face of adversity exactly how he does it, he usually grants all the credit to the obsession itself. The religious convert insists that his god saves him. The dedicated scientist says that his work is the only thing that counts and that lifts him out of his troubles. The politician bears up under stress in the name of his public obligation. And the concert pianist is amazed himself that his troubles vanish as he hovers over the keyboard. In these and in other such examples, is it a person's "outer focus" that lifts him out of himself and out of danger, as is often suggested? Absolutely not. The hypochondriac, the yogi, the member of a consciousness-raising group, and many a private patient in therapy use a certain "inner focus" to obtain essentially the same degree of dedication and stability.

Clearly, then, the direction of a focal interest does not matter. Its target and a person's dedication to it are what give him "something to hold on to" in times of stress. At this level of observation the idea is so familiar that almost everyone has heard it: that whatever hits a person cannot hurt him if he has an area of high investment, a personal talent or project, a steadying *raison d'être*. Thus it has become a cliché to hear a person say that what he or someone else needs is "something to get interested in." But the issue is so important it deserves to be stated and examined in a slightly more technical way: A focal interest safeguards the ego by compartmentalizing it, much as a warship that cannot be sunk by bombing and flooding only a few of its compartments.

Certainly there is nothing new about the process of compartmentalization. It is something most people use in everyday life. It is what allows a person to be relaxed and pleasant at home, though in serious trouble at work. It is what permits a person to surface his generous and kindly feelings toward a friend without having to bring up particular resentments he may also have.

(Only the wildest hysteric blabs out everything he thinks and feels.) And of course, compartmentalization is what permits a man to have a mistress or a male on the side, without necessarily being a Jekyll and Hyde.

In most such commonplace situations, a person's whole system may come tumbling down when the "walls" of his compartmentalization are breached. To keep something from the world or from someone else and then have it suddenly revealed can result in a person being badly shaken, both personally and in the estimation of others. And there are plenty of other situations in which a person's ego is crushed if the walls of his system were set up in the first place to protect only himself. As is often realized, the most steadying commitments are those designed to serve some outside person or cause, not merely self-protection. Thus the group leader, the Peace Corps worker, and many a private person who feels a responsibility to others can withstand a trauma or bypass a depression which could not have been coped with nearly as well under the aegis of self-preservation. One keeps seeing it on every side—in wartime, in family emergencies, and in the theatre where the actor easily lays aside a personal tragedy and arranges within himself to cry later "because the show must go on."

It is all true, and it is not true. The whole basic notion rests, as before, on the underlying assumption that in the process of compartmentalization, the *strength of the structure* resides not in its walls, but in the quality or nature of whatever is contained within the compartments—an idea which is definitely not true. In fact, to believe it for one moment is tantamount to believing that when "Jesus saves" it is Jesus who is doing the saving—or that the scientist's work is what saves him, or the pianist's piano him. If one steps back from the whole picture to take another look, certain new details begin to appear. A person's cohesiveness is sometimes rallied by little more than the expectation of others, or by an authoritarian command that he "pull himself together." The anxieties of a person who is frightened, "weak," or totally without any guiding commitment are sometimes held in check by an amulet, a charm, a rabbit's foot. At one level, hysteria is checked by a momentary holding-still, forced or voluntary—an observation which brings to mind that in India a newly captured, wild and nervous elephant can be literally tamed in twenty minutes by placing it between two old and quiet elephants that slowly and gently squeeze it from both sides.

If we now put all these images together, it will soon become apparent that the common denominator in a person's cohesion under stress is a certain confinement of attention, a walled-in control of anxiety, *not* the target item he may have (or think he needs) for that control. Or to put it the other way around, it is true that a directed aggression will hold a person together, so will a focal target, or the light from a distant star. But a far larger question is at last upon us: What holds a person together when Jesus doesn't do it, when there is no abiding interest, no *raison d'être*, no keyboard to hover over, no aches and pains to pander to, no guiding star, no niche sublime, no elephants that take their time nor lotus position to invite Nirvana from?

There is one thing left and, oddly enough, it is an element contained in all the rest. It is the ability of a person by still other means to hold in reserve a private sector of himself—a part set apart, a core untouched, a line unbent. And how can anyone retain such an unshaken core with no props (or as is more often the case, stay in control when he has had his props knocked out from under him)? The classical answer—that everyone needs a certain reserve of self-respect to "fall back on" in emergencies—will definitely not suffice. A person simply may not have much of what is commonly called self-respect in the first place, and even if he does, it may disappear at precisely the moment he needs it. No, the central problem in any crisis situation is not so much how to call forth strengths of "substance" but, rather, how to keep from being stampeded into joining the forces one finds lined up against him. Certainly he must not bow his head, run, or fight back in anger (for the reasons cited in Chapter 7); such tactics are not profitable for anybody, and for the homosexual they can be disastrous. But even the person who is not adept at any active ways of protecting himself may still have a surprisingly effective means of doing so "passively." He is often able to "hold together" under the most adverse conditions of stress by simply standing pat while, within his head, moving back an inch, a foot, or a mile (whatever it takes) from any constellation of untoward events to view them, in a sense, at a distance.

This mode of operating—a certain deliberate, internal retreat—occurs, for instance, when someone quietly surveys the havoc wrought in his life by a disaster or a series of unfortunate events without choosing to further honor the bad news by "living out" the alarm or depression that so seductively offers itself. As one patient put it, "When I'm really caught in some terrible situation, I find it strangely reassuring to just stand there and watch it rain on my parade." He might well have added that he seldom gets very wet by that method, and that he never experiences panic.

This deliberate, internal move-back—which at first glance appears to be such a plain-Jane device as to make one wonder how it works at all—on closer examination turns out to embody the central feature present in all the other "saving graces." It clearly shares the stand-aside-and-let-the-world-pass quality of the god-worships, the retreat quality of Nirvana, the distractional aspects of psychosomatic symptoms, the diversionary features of the lucky-charm-and-amulet group, and even the I-refuse-to-honor-my-own-pains quality of the devotionally committed scientist-pianist parameter. In short, it is a very powerful device indeed.*

---

*It is notable that this whole system—a kind of attentive nonparticipation in untoward events—borrows as much as it does from existential philosophy and Jungian psychology. From existentialism it borrows the pristine separatism of dealing with the events of circumstance apart from the entanglements of one's own personal and past associations. And it capitalizes on the truism that since a portion of oneself never invests in outside matters (the portion which comprises everyone's "existential aloneness") this portion, at least, is untouched by the fortunes of circumstance, and therefore can serve as a stable base from which one can simply watch the world pass—refusing to become involved in any of its seductions, least of all its trials and troubles.

And from Jungian psychology, the warning is heeded to steer clear of certain archetypes. For no matter how valid, how real and pressing a negative circumstance may seem to be, the central danger is not within the situation itself but in the lure of a Siren's call: the everpresent risk of being seduced into living out or playing out one of the classic archetypes—perhaps the role of a martyr, of a sinner, of a woefully depressed loser or whatever—not because any such role is implicit in the facts but because the events of circumstance have set the stage and dressed one for the part.

But in the final analysis, what do all these matters of self-control and of managing stress have to do with the homosexual's specific problems? Broadly observed, his problems are not at all unique. Certainly it is evident that, given the risks and traumas of life, nobody really manages to live safely and well without a structured and rewarding life-style backed up by a set of emergency controls for his protection during periods of very high stress. No doubt these requirements are doubly important to the homosexual—and for that matter, to anyone else whose position may at times imperil his balance, his assurance, and thus his loyalty to himself. It is here that the therapist who has managed to kick free of conventional thought patterns is sometimes able to be of great service to a troubled homosexual. But of course, there aren't many therapists and even if all of them were up to the task, their impact would be small. Thus for the most part, the homosexual, like everyone else, must seek his own salvation—and when he finds it he is as inclined as anyone to ascribe it none too accurately to his work, to his beliefs or to his particular something. No doubt a critical assessment of his or any other life-style ought to take into account both how well it rewards the individual (from his point of view) and how well it bears up under stress.

But all things considered, perhaps it would be just as well to measure the effectiveness of a person's adaptation by the ordinary criteria of whether it generally supports or generally dampens his vitality and his appetite for life. Viewed from this angle, homosexual adaptations clearly span an enormous range—from considerably worse to considerably better than average—with rather more individuals at both extremes than might otherwise have landed there. The reasons are not hard to find. People who are in any sense off-beat encounter more resistance, especially in the beginning, and tend to pay a higher-than-average price for their adaptive failures, while those who manage to make reasonable compensations are often able to use them as a launching platform for their ambitions and as a floor for their defeats.

12

Balancing the Equation

In the final analysis, what does it all mean?—or does homosexuality have any special meaning? Probably not. It is a fact of life; the rest is interpretation and consequence. But it would be useful to see it in balance and to approach a number of broad questions which have not yet been dealt with. What kind of entity is homosexuality, and what are its prospects? Is it likely to increase or decrease? For the persons involved in it, it usually entails certain kinds of risks and social pressures which would not otherwise be faced. When these drawbacks are avoided or turned to some advantage, is this merely a clever or lucky adaptation, or is there something else involved? And what about everybody else?—does it offer anything to them? In short, when is homosexuality productive, or merely a disturbance to the tranquillity of conventional expectations? And finally, what lessons does it teach, and who can benefit by them?

If the prospects of homosexuality are to be guessed at, it is useful to see it in perspective. First, is there any substance to the notion that it is increasing? As a general observation, probably not. But the idea has a long and curious history. In the fifth century B.C., Plato was convinced that homosexuality was increasing, as were many other scholars in the remaining centuries of a society in which an exclusive heterosexuality was almost certainly unusual. The early Christian and Jewish writers held the same conviction during times when homosexuality was certainly decreasing. (No doubt the decrease was largely due to religious pressures, though there were other reasons, too. Rigid new laws against infanticide began to save female infants and equalize the male-female ratio, permitting and encouraging the heterosexual rate to rise.)

In recent centuries, seemingly every period of evangelical fervor as well as every other climate of alarm over "moral decay" has sponsored renewed claims of an increasing homosexuality, but without evidence of any real change. Thus, in the three generations of subjects examined by the Kinsey Research there was no trend either up or down. A sharp increase in sexual freedom during the 1920's increased various sex rates but homosexual and heterosexual activities evidently went up together, leaving the ratio unchanged. Is this what has happened to a further extent in recent years? Probably so, though there are no firm data to prove it and thus to hold in check the distortions of perception which forever arise from what might be called an "aging effect." That is, as people get older they begin to see and hear more of homosexuality than when they were younger and more naïve—the "increase" being an increase in their own awareness rather than any change in reality. Not even the homosexual observer is immune to this tendency, and if he happens to become increasingly moralistic with advancing age and the loss of his own potency, he may then be struck by the "sexual excesses" of youth, as was the case with Plato.

Of course, there is always the possibility that a liberal trend such as is presently evident in our society, if it were to continue, might lead to deeper and more fundamental changes than those of the 1920's. Besides bringing people out of the closet and increasing sex rates, it could conceivably alter the mores markedly by relaxing sexual attitudes and by further reducing the age at which overt experience begins. Supposedly, an early permissiveness is arousing to youngsters and opens the door to a number of possibilities, including homosexuality, which they would not otherwise have known about or felt so free to try out in their formative years. Perhaps the number of homosexual contacts would be increased, along with a few instances of permanent conditioning from these contacts. But it would be at least equally reasonable to expect heterosexual patterns to be established sooner and more firmly than ever before—in theory, reducing homosexuality. In addition, there are perhaps a dozen minor influences which are also capable of exerting pressure in one direction or the other. Could some combination of these seriously affect the heterosexual-homosexual balance? Nobody knows. But remembering that the groundwork for homosexuality involves the establishment of a sexual value system which usually predates puberty, often by many years, the prediction offered here is that the frequency of homosexuality will remain unchanged.

It is often thought that with or without any basic change in the heterosexual-homosexual balance, a general reduction in sexual prohibitions might tend to increase bisexuality. Not likely. Any significant rise in bisexuality is virtually ruled out for males unless they happen to have one of its special supports (early bisexual practice, or a particular brand of *machismo*). Otherwise, the polarizing tendency of male sexual conditioning soon elaborates a fairly exacting choice while rapidly building up aversions to any and all competing alternatives. A similar selectivity is evident in women, too, though it is frequently not as rigidly guarded by polar aversions. Thus, among present-day "swingers" and a variety of other experimentalists, less than 1 per cent of the men move over to engage in homosexual contacts, even momentarily, while 64 per cent of the women do so with ease.[2] Whether these women are typical of others, and whether most of them would want to step over the boundaries of heterosexuality purely on their own and without the presence of a male who is "turned on" by female-female contacts (as many men are) are matters which are relevant to the future of female bisexuality. But in view of the wide breach which tends to exist between the capacity for a response, on the one hand, and a definite motivation to use it, on the other, the best guess is that bisexuality, too, will fail to increase significantly.

Consequences for the Individual

As long as there are social pressures against homosexuality it will undoubtedly continue to present a variety of adaptational problems to those who are involved in it. The casual observer is convinced, and is likely to stay convinced, that these problems are inevitably burdensome. Interestingly enough, most homosexuals agree, for while more than 90 per cent do not regret their sexual orientation (and would not elect to change it, remember, even if they could do so by "pushing a button") about an equal proportion definitely "would not recommend it" for others.

This near-contradiction raises a number of questions. Is the homosexual's lack of regret merely a defensive rationalization of some sort? Or is it that for a person to wish away a major element in his or her make-up is practically equivalent to self-eradication? Perhaps both of these components are present, but something is to be said for the fact that most of a male's sharpest adaptational problems hit him soon after he realizes his sexual proclivities, usually before he is grown, and are solved for better or for worse within a reasonably short period of time. In any case, a person tends to become heavily invested in the kinds of rewards he has learned to pursue and is then usually quite satisfied with his own life—though when he looks back at the bumps in the road he has traveled he does not recommend it for others.

All this is clear enough when a person is generally pleased with his life, or even when he is merely able to see his present and future as more rewarding than his past. But what is not so clear is how the homosexual who has not made a very successful adaptation remains, in a sense, loyal to his way of life. How is it that he, too, seldom regrets it and is usually able to view it as worthwhile? Or to sharpen the question: When a person allows so many of the possible penalties of homosexuality to find their way into his life that he is plagued by a host of pains and frustrations, how is he able to still hear the music over all the background noise?

Essentially the same questions concerning the difference between a person's real and apparent satisfactions commonly arise in heterosexuality, too, though here they tend to be hidden behind conventional stereotypes. The Kinsey Research once started out to rate the happiness of marriages but quickly had to abandon the effort in the face of the most obvious contradictions. A man or woman would often describe a stormy home situation, sometimes bitterly complain of one incompatibility after the other, and yet insist that the marriage was "better than average" or even "very happy." There were staggering contradictions in the other direction, too. Often a man would laud his wife, praise his children, and otherwise describe an excellent home situation—only to add, "but if I had it to do over, I wouldn't marry." Such examples certainly reflect the labyrinthine nature of human ambivalence, but the core problem is larger still. It has to do with the whole question of how a person deals with the negative components, the resistances, he encounters—both those in his path as he pursues "happiness" and those that are stirred up by his reaching it.

It is possible to penetrate quite a distance into such matters, though not quite to the core of them, with a dozen different observations, all true. It is true, for instance, that people often voice the negative aspects of their lives as a way of discharging complaints, or of cashing in on them for sympathy. Members of minority groups seem to be especially adept at this but they are not alone. Many other people, too, know how to hide their secret delights behind a posture of travail—either to assuage the envy and anger of others, or to ward off any bolts of lightning that jealous gods might throw. Moreover, the very parts of a person's life that may seem most lamentable to an outside observer are often the parts the individual himself likes the best, or else has become inured to and thus well-calloused against. Even when ongoing discomforts are very real, many people consider them a fair price for moments of exquisite pleasure. And when actual enjoyments are in short supply, fantasy can sometimes bridge the gap—as when a person imagines that the right lover or a future success of some kind will lift him out of his present situation. It may all be an illusion, of course, but it is still the opposite of being disillusioned. It is notable that almost regardless of whether or not the homosexual has yet managed to solve his particular problems, he often considers it a piece of good fortune that he has not fallen into a conventional heterosexual life. From his point of view, to know what will *not* work for him and to have avoided it is itself worth something—quite as the heterosexual, regardless of whether he is satisfied with his lot or not, is glad to not be homosexual.

Are these rational compensations and tricks of the mind all that comprise the homosexual's adaptation? If they were, then he would certainly be in trouble, for it would mean that he would have only commonplace tools with which to meet both his share of common problems plus all his special problems besides. This, of course, is exactly the predicament he is widely thought to be in and sometimes is. But more often, he largely escapes the expected penalties and not infrequently is able to reap special advantages from his position for reasons that have nothing to do with homosexuality *per se*—reasons which are implicit in the nature of human gratification itself. As long as a person fits neatly into most of the conventionalities of his social milieu, a localized area of alienation (homosexuality, Jewishness, or whatever) not only delivers less than its proportional amount of hindrance, it often produces drive and even gusto. Is this because people who have a particular vulnerability tend to overcompensate for it? That may be part of the answer, but the rest has to do with the fact that all satisfactions exist in, and only in, the wake of an immediately displaced barrier, be it one of privation, alienation, isolation, or any other tension that urgently requires reduction. This becomes obvious from a detailed look at the quiet rewards of comfort, contentment, and the gentle flow of friendly exchanges. But the principle is brought into especially sharp focus in sexual examples where, in fact, the intensity of every pleasurable experience is rigorously proportional to the resistance against it.

Consequences for Society

Depending on a host of personal and situational considerations, homosexuality may be good, bad, or indifferent for the individuals who are involved in it. But society as a whole undoubtedly benefits from it. Of course its drawbacks also cost something. That homosexuality raises the level of neurosis in many of its participants, and that it seriously disturbs a few others, are facts which, though localized, do ultimately amount to social liabilities. And more than a few observers would include on the list of liabilities the fact that the very existence of homosexuality disrupts the uniformity of society, amounting to a source of worry and conflict that would not otherwise exist. But in the eyes of sex researchers and a number of other social analysts, there is much more to be gained than lost from homosexuality. Its penalties, after all, affect relatively few people, while the understandings which can be gleaned from it are useful to everybody.

In fact, sex researchers find homosexuality exceptionally useful. As a demonstration of many kinds of conditioning (and much else in learning theory) it is interesting in its own right. And of course, its male-male and female-female combinations tend to concentrate—and thus bring into easy view—both the biological and the socially derived gender-differences between men and women. Often the findings have an immediate, practical use—for example, in marriage counseling, where quite a few of the problems men and women have with each other are best solved by what has been gleaned from lesbian relationships. (From a study of lesbians came the discovery that female sexuality is "wired for continuity" and is most easily disturbed by precisely the sorts of momentary interruptions most men make in abundance, usually without awareness of exactly what they are doing, let alone its consequences.) And male homosexuality is a veritable gold mine of information, so extensive that it has hardly begun to be tapped. It is replete with examples that cast light on such hard-to-get-at matters as the relationship between how a sexual contact is terminated (how the partners "get out of bed," so to speak) and how quickly, if at all, a man will regenerate a sexual interest in the same partner.

But beyond the laboratory of sexual and social research, does homosexuality make any direct contributions to society?—a question that used to be in hot debate. Homosexuals of the Victorian era—and their successors until fairly recent times—insisted, no doubt defensively, that all sorts of famous persons (artists, inventors, explorers, and geniuses in general) were homosexual, and by implication, that their contributions were due in part or in whole to this fact. Of course the counterargument was deafening: That the homosexuals were greatly exaggerating, "to hear them tell it, everybody (especially everybody who's anybody) is homosexual"—that they were obviously and desperately searching for social justification—and anyway, the homosexual who happens to be talented achieves whatever he achieves in spite of and not because of his sexuality. The whole argument has virtually died out in recent decades, no doubt partly by having become a dated cliché, and the rest by the disappearance of the prize: In an age of counter-culture, it is hard to find a Leonardo da Vinci and harder still to see him as any champion, living as he probably does on a grant from the Department of Health, Education & Welfare.

But what was the truth of the argument and what relevance did it have? The truth was that everybody was right, but in another sense, not quite right. The homosexual was certainly looking for self-justification (a search more damaging to him than the value of anything he may have found), but he was not greatly exaggerating. It is hard to find an instance of any public figure ever having been falsely labeled homosexual, and yet nothing is easier than to find notable examples that were missed. But of course, this still does not answer the question, So what? And what about the other charge, that the gifted homosexual's accomplishments are achieved in spite of and not because of his sexuality? Is there any way to reconcile these claims? Yes there is—provided one is prepared to accept a measure of truth on both sides, and to realize that what is true of the exceptional individual may not apply to others who share his tastes.

Right off, it is apparent that if 3 or 4 per cent of the total population is homosexual, and only a small fraction of 1 per cent, one in hundreds, can qualify as a "special achiever," then most people, including most homosexuals, are not outstanding. (Incidentally, quite the same "base-rate problem" applies to every specific occupation, leading to the interesting little conundrum that almost everyone ends up doing what he is doing against a sizable initial probability that he would do exactly that.) Moreover, it is probable that nearly all occupations are pursued by people who share no common central trait, least of all one related to their sexual orientation.

Nevertheless, there are a number of fields in which just such a connection is undeniable. Among the examples easiest to find (and hardest to fully understand) are those in which homosexual personnel clearly predominate in a particular art or science. In a field that requires a certain delicacy, it often seems logical to the casual observer (though less so to the sex researcher) that most of the men should be homosexual. One theory is that the heterosexual male's "toughness" and/or his fear of being too fully attuned to what is graceful or "soft" almost dispositionally rules out his becoming, say, a ballet dancer, a fashion designer, or an interior decorator, leaving such fields primarily to those who have less interest in maintaining a he-man image. Perhaps so, to some extent, but such theories are contradicted by many examples. In a music school, for instance, why should the violinists rarely be homosexual, while the students and teachers who specialize in certain keyboard instruments, and not in others, are predominantly so? Nobody knows. But it is clear that much more than accident is involved when frequency rates jump from less than 4 per cent to as much as 90 per cent, and then back again as one crosses professional lines. And to make the puzzle all the more formidable, the same sorts of contrasts occur within science and technology. In medicine, for instance, surgeons as a group are undoubtedly at least as heterosexual as the general population, and yet there are a few surgical specialties in which homosexual personnel clearly predominate—for reasons which, again, are not understood.

About the only firm conclusion is that there are indefinable lines of "connective relevance" between the homosexual matrix and what a number of occupations in Western society happen to require. Thus, it has to be admitted that society, as it is presently constituted, gains something from particular homosexual contingents which is not as readily available from heterosexual personnel.

But the issue is still understated. It is probably safe to say that the places within the structure of society where the homosexual has his most important impact are not those in which he predominates, but those in which his particular viewpoint simply extends the parameters of a field. Painting and sculpture are not arts in which he is overly represented and yet he makes important contributions to them. Science offers impressive examples, too. There is no indication that homosexuality is much if any more frequent in anthropology, for instance, than it is in any other discipline. And yet, a few of the contributions made by the field-anthropologist who happens to be homosexual are exceptional— not because his work is better or worse than that of anybody else, but simply because of his slightly different standpoint. In the first place, his basic life-style sometimes makes it easier for him to pick up and travel and to spend protracted periods of time in Timbuktu. He appears to be especially sensitized to sexual and to homosexual elements in a foreign milieu, and is often remarkably adept at making his informants feel at ease in discussing such matters. (When he has this ability, perhaps his very interest makes him seem nonjudgmental. Or is it that his relatively peripheral position in his own society makes him come across to the natives as less formidable?) Of course, much of his special information is lost when he chooses to leave it out of his formal reports, as is often the case, but a portion of it still seeps through to the scientific community where sex researchers, in particular, are greatly enlightened by it.

Admittedly, there is a problem of balance in these kinds of examples. Often the specialist who happens to be homosexual is so orthodox in his work and in his approach to it that there are few places for his particular angle of view to show up, or to make much difference if it does. But orthodoxy is not the only thing that will save his work. There is also a degree of commonality in what the trail blazer and the exceptional individual manage to accomplish. For while homosexuality may alter a person's viewpoint, cause him to "hear a different drummer," and sometimes to march off in unusual directions, if he finds anything worth having he ultimately brings it back to us all. It is a principle that operates over the entire span from the lowliest minutiae to the heights of poetic expression. Thus, once upon a time when a stealthy European homosexual made a lifelong collection of male and female toilet-wall inscriptions and later gave it to Kinsey, it became a cornerstone in the foundation of modern concepts of gender-response. And at the other extreme, when Michelangelo poured his concentration of care and of eroticized passion into such figures as his statue of David, he did something more than express his particular genius (and in the eyes of psychologists, inscribe his own sexual history in stone). He made it possible for a viewer who has not the slightest sexual response to males to ride in on the sculptor's eye, to see what he saw, and to glimpse an image of man he could not possibly have seen on his own.*

In one sense, such examples are a bit off the point. For while it is true that society often benefits from the output of exceptional individuals, the prize goes to diversity itself. A certain leeway for differences, including sexual differences, is what best nurtures talent when there is any—and when there is none, there is still much to be gained from granting a measure of credence to every cast of mind from the roughneck to the ribbon clerk. By making room for the eccentric, for the semiconformist, and for the exercise of everpresent personal peculiarities, a respect for diversity greatly improves the tone and quality of everyday life. (That it works against the sameness of conventionality seems by itself worth the price.) On every side, it opens the door to the kinds of individuality that constantly suggest new approaches to common problems. It even serves the rigid conformist by supplying him with rejectable alternatives—the pushoffs by which he keeps himself on his own track. But certainly the main beneficiary is the person who is able to accept fairly sharp differences in others, not by merely tolerating them but by finding common denominators within himself: He attains what is undoubtedly a superior ethic, and in the process, escapes the tyranny of having to ride herd on his own conformity.

---

*Not too surprisingly, in art as in everything else, a highly polarized interest usually costs something. Michelangelo's female figures are disappointing, to put it mildly; he lavished all his genius on males. To touch these heights with the female form, one must turn to heterosexual artists such as Bernini, often at the price of then having to abide relatively inferior males. In theory, it might be expected that the best artists would come from a bisexual contingent and thus be able to cross gender-lines with ease but, in practice, it seldom works out that way. It is hard to find any artist of rank who does male and female figures, especially nudes, with equal facility. Evidently, a certain singularity of commitment is related in some way to the intensity that exceptional achievements require.

Of course, this is not the whole picture. It is a set of observations that largely supports the liberal's point of view, and it really is the key to individuality and to personal freedom. But if human differences are to be respected, this includes a respect for the position of people who want no such freedom, who find their own variations alarming (not to mention those of others), and who find great solace in conventions and in conforming to them. Have they no right to despise the homosexual and to find his ways repugnant?—of course they have. (And since their attitudes amount to feeling-states that are part of their own conditioning, they may have no alternative anyway.) But it is a right which stops short of their taking action on it. From the moment an angry conservative hurls a stone, he violates at least a few of his own principles and human decency besides—and the same goes for the liberal who fires back.

People who hold the liberal position like to believe that the conservative's views carry their own punishment: "When a person deprecates others, he ultimately hurts himself." It is a noble sentiment, one that longs for a kind of automatic justice, but it is also a bias and an imperfect description of what happens in reality. The person who disparages the homosexual may not only "get away" with his attitude, he may reap various rewards from expressing it. There is much to be savored in righteous indignation, and it can be a way of reassuring himself and others about his own "normality." Not infrequently, he improves his standing with those who agree with him, usually a clear majority.

Thus, people as far apart as the archconservative and the extreme liberal find ways to cash in on their viewpoints—viewpoints that in each case swing on the issue of diversity, and rest on considerably more than matters of individual psychology. Just what they do rest on is of much importance in any final assessment of homosexuality.

The conservative position has its roots in the stable stuff of religious beliefs, social traditions, and the quieting reassurances of a uniform standard of behavior. The liberal position, on the other hand, is always short on these particular reinforcements. Whether its adherents come across as rebellious iconoclasts or as gentle peacemakers in search of a larger commonality, it has little backing from any of the classical traditions. But what it does have to an almost embarrassing degree is an ever increasing validation from the natural sciences. Into the liberal column lands most of the fallout from biology, zoology, sociology, and a dozen other disciplines. Most (though not quite all) of what is learned about man from a careful study of his nature and origins tends to underline his diversity, usually at the expense of his social traditions.

Not that this means conservatism will ever lose its almost singlehanded control of the mores. Even when religious and social dogmas undergo radical change, there are other motives for conservatism which tend to keep it at the helm, and that promise never to let it disappear. These stem, in part, from what Kinsey has called "the clustering tendency of living organisms"— a clustering which causes single-cell animals to hover together, causes birds to flock and fish to swim in schools. This tendency to cluster becomes greatly elaborated in human psychology where it induces an urge for a degree of closeness and like-mindedness that far exceeds what can be attained by mere proximity and cooperation. A sharable similarity is needed. Thus all societies tend to resist diversity and to seek a relatively narrow uniformity, especially in the emotion-laden matters of sex. Usually this is accomplished by setting up quite restrictive mores which are then the business of conservatism to police. But it is noteworthy that even the most permissive societies frown on the individual who stands apart.

And yet there is so much innate diversity in man that most people find themselves facing a disquieting, guilt-inviting disparity between what they want to do and to avoid, on the one hand, and what society and perhaps their own expectations call for, on the other. Anyone can see the homosexual's conflict here; he runs all the risks of standing apart unless he reduces them by maintaining quite a few firm ties to the social cluster. But what are not so easy to see are the dangers that lie on the other side: the risks that are run by anyone who too wholeheartedly or too unwarily embraces conventionality—risks made all the more insidious by their low profile. From a conventional position especially, it is tempting to abhor divergence, to overseek the unity of mass accord, and thus slip toward those rigors of conformity that slowly crush all pluck and enterprise. No doubt there are those who would say this overstates the case. People of every disposition seem ready to believe that the good life is easily attained by various presumed others whose appetites are thought to be fully satisfied by conventional fare, conventionally attained. This belief, this abiding faith in the mores, is poles apart from the none too cheerful conclusion suggested here: that both a high and a low conformity are about equally restricting to individual liberty and to one's freedom to use it. Certainly, in practice, nobody could deny the truth of Thoreau's observation, "Most men lead lives of quiet desperation."

In the final analysis the central question is: Who among us all of every class and ilk escape these somber tidings, as many manage to? Surely the answer is clear: Any person who is able to honor both the elements of his own diversity and those of common cause—that is, to grant to Caesar what is Caesar's and to himself what is his own.

Miscellanea

You don't seem to use the word or even the idea of latent homosexuality—why not?

Because the term is virtually undefinable unless one assumes that the individual has in some sense already eroticized at least a few attributes found in same-sex partners, or is otherwise "ready" to respond to them—and in that case, the person firmly meets either the homosexual or bisexual definition. To fail to so classify such a person on the grounds that, like the heterosexual, he or she does not *practice* homosexuality, would be equivalent to confusing a Trappist monk (who takes an oath of silence) with a deaf mute.

Do homosexual men hate (or dislike) women?

Not as much or as often as heterosexual men do. Kinsey estimated that no less than two-thirds of heterosexual men "don't like" women, though I have forgotten the criteria he used. And for the same reasons, it is *men* that homosexual males have trouble liking.

On the other hand, in the case of particular gender-related annoyances there is an element of truth in what you suggest. The heterosexual male has a relatively high threshold of irritability in contending with an attractive woman's slowness, perhaps as she readies herself to go out, or takes a moment too long to drive off from a toll-booth. (Eros carries a measure of forgiveness.) There are role-elements in the picture, too—not always as crude as a man's feeling reinforced by aiding a "helpless" woman with her flat tire. In many of those jungle-type movies made in the 1930's there are scenes in which a small group of people, including one beautiful woman, are running to escape the natives, but of course she sprains her ankle or otherwise slows up the group to everyone's peril. Such scenes tend to "make sense" to heterosexual males, annoy homosexual males, and are often extremely irritating to adequacy-minded lesbians.

I think you give a false picture of homosexuality. Why do you hardly mention the many ways people can have their lives ruined by it?

Yes, the horses that people ride to hell on are numerous, and are no doubt more numerous in homosexual than in heterosexual life-styles. But it is hard to glean basic information from extremely negative or positive examples. Both extremes have been somewhat understated here.

You often seem to side with the Devil on moral issues, and yet you embrace a number of ethical ideas; why this inconsistency?

Since there are fundamental differences between morals and ethics, this is no inconsistency. Morals bestow their allegiance on social rules and habits of thought. They are essentially provincial and vary from one neighborhood to the next—becoming a crazy-quilt of contradictions in most cross-cultural comparisons. Ethics, on the other hand, tend to bestow their allegiance on such things as kindness and fair play. They vary hardly at all from one society to the next.

Some women prefer the company of homosexual men and sometimes want to marry them. Is this because they are afraid of other men?

Hardly. I know of no examples in which anybody ever urgently wants something because they are afraid of something else, least of all its competing alternative. Many women especially like homosexual males because they feel better treated, better understood, better liked, or more respected by them—as is often the case. And yet mateships which grow out of these relationships are usually a disaster. Eros requires an underlay of antagonism. From such tensions in the bedroom, one can struggle toward smooth compatibilities in the living room, but this is a one-way street that cannot be traveled in the other direction.

At a medical conference, I heard a well-known sex researcher say that homosexuality is unknown in some societies, as evidenced by their having no word for it in their language—which societies?

The doctor you heard is not a sex researcher. He is a psychoanalyst who writes extensively on the subject, and he is quite wrong. Language "blanks" are no indication of anything. There is no word in French for "sexual intercourse," but that doesn't mean they never heard of it. Homosexuality has been found in every carefully studied society in the world, though there are large variations in its frequency and matrix. Incidentally, it tends to be especially prevalent in the handful of societies which have no word for it.

Why is it that many homosexual men tend to "make the most of their looks" while many lesbians seem to be careless about matters of "beauty"?

Because in subtle and not so subtle ways, most people's style of self-presentation is geared to the anticipated market. And since the "male eye" tends to be highly visual and symbolic in its response— i.e., attuned more to surface features than to "deeper values"—homosexual men and heterosexual women have to take this into account.

In several places you mention the fatigue element in love or sexual relations, and how short-lived high romance is. That seems to be true of most people but I have never wanted a serious relationship to end.

That is because your partners have always begun to tire first, probably due to overaccessibility and faulty closure-habits on your part. On correctly perceiving their increased resistance at the first sign of trouble, you will have found that your interest has been maintained or has even increased. There are no exceptions to the law of fatigue, especially where accessibility is high. You will find that your partners have all reduced their accessibility and all the more rapidly if, at the first sign of trouble, you have leaned forward instead of slightly leaning back in some way.

Don't some scholars feel that the whole homosexual thing in Ancient Greece has been greatly exaggerated, perhaps by a handful of ancient writers whose own tastes became overly represented in the surviving literature?

Yes, this is a notion which is often expressed, but not by persons who are well informed. In the first place, our record of ancient times is not from a "handful" of contributors but from literally hundreds of writers, scholars, and historians. However, on the theory that all these documentors might still have been reflecting only an upper-class view, perhaps the strongest indication of a popular acceptance of homosexuality is found in the scribblings of ordinary citizens. That is, the penchant men of all ages and classes had for inscribing the names of their lovers on everything in sight—walls, doors, columns, basins, footstools, altars, chests, bags, discus rims, and just any stone protruding from the ground. It was some workman, not a poet, who cast his sentiments into immortality by scratching on a common brick, "Hippeus is beautiful, or so it seems to Aristomedes."[55]

Why is lesbianism relatively rare cross-culturally?

We don't absolutely know that it is—due to a shortage of female investigators and its low profile where it does exist. But probably it is less common, since female sexuality tends to be both less insistent and less "initiating" than that of males.

Are you absolutely sure the use of the word camp *dates back only to the early* 1930's?

No, not absolutely. A theatre tradition says that it does, and a number of seventy- and eighty-year-old informants could not remember having heard it before that time, but your doubt is quite reasonable. Most words in homosexual argot date surprisingly far back. *Mary* was in use in the early 1700's; so were *queer* and *queenly*. Homosexual extractions of buggery date to the eleventh century. And *blow job*, which now implies nothing about the sex of the performer, was originally entirely homosexual and was in use at least as far back as the fifth century B.C.

In accounting for bisexuality especially, why get into the complications of considering value systems and the like? Wouldn't it have been simpler to say that man is basically a bisexual creature who, as a result of various individual and social influences, is inclined to develop a taste for either sex, or for both?

Yes, it certainly would have been simpler. And when the theory is stated with the breadth and precision you have put into it, it makes no mistakes and quite properly respects the whole fact of man's "psychosexual neutrality at birth." The fatal weakness in the basic-bisexuality-of-man theory is that it implicitly predicts that homosexuality will flourish where there are minimal restrictions against it—which, in reality, is a sometimes-thing at best. Worse still for the theory and its prediction, the very lowest frequencies of homosexuality occur in societies which exert few restrictions against it, or none at all. Thus, to account for these and all other variations without running into heterosexual, homosexual, or bisexual contradictions, it was necessary to explore value systems, how particular kinds of partners become eroticized, the buildup of aversion reactions, etc.

What is Aversion Therapy?—I keep hearing it can change homosexuality.

Aversion Therapy is the name applied to no less than six different systems for trying to make a homosexual male "averse" to male partners. Most of these techniques involve showing a picture of a nude male to a man at the moment he is given an electric shock, or an instant before he is thrown into drug-induced convulsions or vomiting. Although most such procedures have been carried out in respectable-sounding institutions both in Britain and the United States, they are a professional embarrassment and a laughingstock. They usually entail giving the patient a number of jolts (at least one a day) until he says he is "cured"—often to a doctor who is at that moment ready to order another needle or electric shock should the patient say he is not cured.

A variation of this technique is to put the patient in a dark room, instructing him to masturbate to orgasm and at that moment shout "ready," at which time the doctor throws a switch that lights up a picture of "a beautiful girl." In an especially amusing example reported from an Italian clinic, the patient is subjected to several weeks of harsh treatment, after which he is brought in to sit across the table from an old doctor with a long beard who proceeds to show him nude pictures of "beautiful boys." Midway through the series, the doctor reaches under the table and feels the patient's penis to see if it is getting hard. Evidently none ever did; he reports 100 per cent cures.

As a man who is very much "with" women in their struggle to be recognized as essentially equal in all matters, I'm troubled by statements which imply that particular differences in the reactions of men and women are founded in biology. Couldn't such differences be traced almost entirely to training, role-learning, and other sociological influences?

There are several tests for whether a behavioral trend is basically biological, or could be grounded in social influences alone. If it is cross-cultural, it is likely to be fundamental—quite definitely so if it is a gender-difference that is also evidenced among lower mammals. In instances where the trait or trend is distinctly human (such as the sexual "focality" of men vs. the "peripherality" of women) it is sure to reflect a fundamental difference between the sexes if 1) it is clearly evident cross-culturally, and 2) if it is rarely or never contradicted in any society.

If you are "troubled" by the thought of there being basic differences between the response characteristics of the sexes, you are probably assuming that the traits of one of them are "better" than the other's—which may very well be true for you. But on balance, probably most people would agree: *vive la différence.*

In your analysis of homosexuality you use neither the phrase nor the concept of a disturbed sexual identity. But wouldn't you agree that problems of sexual identity are sometimes uppermost?

I've never seen even an approximate instance of it. In the first place, all notions of a confused sexual identity assume from the outset a marked effeminacy in males. And yet it is precisely in effeminate males that one finds something close to the opposite of any such confusion: In the Machover Figure-Drawing Test (the most powerful projective technique for studying such matters) it becomes immediately clear that the effeminate male has, if anything, a sharper-than-average awareness of gender-related items.[166] Thus despite his mixture of male and "female" characteristics, he is far from confused about them. It's the outside observer, looking at him, who gets confused.

My wife and I feel very close to several friends who happen to be homosexual, but we are put off by large groups of homosexuals and really hate some of the effeminate ones. Is this because of something we are doing, or they are doing?

Probably neither. Many people quickly become satiated with any homogeneous group—even one that shares as little as a single point of view—be they central Europeans, Baptist ministers, or all one's own relatives at a family reunion.

And if it's any comfort to you, I've never met anybody who wasn't practically allergic to at least one (or some combination) of the effeminacies.

It is hard to believe that sexual contacts between women can be as effective as you say; what can a lesbian possibly do with her partner that a kind, loving, and educated man cannot?

Kiss a single breast for a solid hour and thoroughly enjoy it.

The "focality" of male sexuality is such that it requires a more or less continual shifting of the target-area. (At his slowest-best, a man still has to move through the orchard too fast to pick all the apples off any single tree.) Male arousal generates prostatic secretions which can be contained by the control sphincters only a relatively few minutes. A man must then either ejaculate fairly promptly, or be able to enjoy the kinds of interruptions which repeatedly break his arousal and permit him to rebuild it again. His female partner may adjust to this and may especially enjoy the latter alternative, but she can never bask in a two- or three-hour steady-climb cycle with a man as she might with a woman. Not that matters of technique are all that important. The impact of a sexual experience nearly always owes more to the rightness of the partner and to the "chemistry" of the situation.

Is an "aversion to implied opposites" the only thing that stabilizes an exclusively heterosexual or homosexual orientation?

Strictly speaking, no. The Institute for Sex Research has in its files a motion-picture record of a male porcupine that responds only to other males—suggesting that a "one track" conditioning can be sustained on its own without the build-up of any specific aversion to other alternatives. But the human mind is so inclined to think in categories and to build up aversions to nonchosen alternatives that such aversions are almost certain to be (or to become) involved in every ongoing exclusivity-of-taste.

Does homosexuality have any broad sociocultural effects?

Probably so, although none of these is firmly established, let alone well understood. In societies in which homosexuality is prevalent, it seems to increase intramural aggression between males who are at medium distances from each other (i.e., just over the river, just over the hill, just across the bay, etc.), while tending to reduce their aggressiveness at very close and at very distant ranges. If future research ever validates this trend, it would suggest an underlying psychological similarity, and thus a connection, between such things as the frequency of the Peloponnesian wars, and the fact that the notably homosexual tribes of South America speak more than half of the world's languages. (In all of Eurasia—from Europe to Asia and from Siberia to India—there are only 17 basic language groups. But in the South American jungles alone, there are more than 120 such groups.)[1]

If you could wave a magic wand that would affect nobody now alive, but which would eliminate homosexuality in future generations, would you do so?

Certainly not. For while it is always tempting to opt for any kind of uniformity which would automatically reduce human conflict, only a fool would reach into some giant computer that nobody understands and start yanking out transistors.

Reference Notes

1. American Museum of Natural History, Department of South American Ethnology, Personal communication.
2. Bartell, G., *Group sex: A scientist's eyewitness report on swinging in the suburbs*. New York: David McKay, 1971.
3. Beach, F. A., Sex reversals in the mating pattern of the rat. *Journal of Genetic Psychology*, 1938, Vol. LIII, 329–334.
4. Beach, F. A., Female mating behavior shown by male rats after administration of testosterone propionate. *Endocrinology*, 1941, Vol. XXIX, 409–412.
5. Beach, F. A., Analysis of factors involved in the arousal, maintenance and manifestation of sexual excitement in male animals. *Psychosomatic Medicine*, 1942, Vol. IV, 173–198.
6. Beach, F. A., Bisexual mating behavior in the male rat: Effects of castration and hormone administration. *Physiological Zoology*, 1945, Vol. XVIII, 391–402.
7. Beach, F. A., Evolutionary changes in the physiological control of mating behavior in mammals. *Psychological Review*, 1947, Vol. 54, 297–315.
8. Beach, F. A., A Review of physiological and psychological studies of sexual behavior in mammals. *Physiological review*, 1947, Vol. XVIII, 240–307.
9. Beach, F. A., *Hormones and behavior*. New York: Hoeber, 1948.
10. Beach, F. A., Sexual behavior in animals and men. *The Harvey Lectures*, 1948, 254–280. Springfield, Ill.: Charles C. Thomas, 1950.
11. Beach, F. A., A cross-species survey of mammalian sexual behavior. In P. H. Hoch and J. Zubin (Eds.), *Psychosexual development in h. .lth and disease*. New York: Grune and Stratton, 1949.
12. Beach, F. A., The snark was a boojum. *American Psychologist*, 1950, Vol. 5, 113–127.
13. Beach, F. A., The descent of instinct. *Psychological Review*, 1955, Vol. 62, 401–410.
14. Beach, F. A., Factors involved in the control of mounting behavior by female mammals. In M. Diamond (Ed.), *Perspectives in reproduction and sexual behavior*. Bloomington: Indiana University Press, 1958.
15. Beach F. A., Biological bases for reproductive behavior. In W. Etkin (Ed.), *Social behavior and organization among vertebrates*. Chicago: University of Chicago Press, 1964.
16. Beach, F. A., Experimental studies of mating behavior in animals. In J.

Money (Ed.) *Sex research: New developments*. New York: Holt, Rinehart and Winston, 1965.

17. Beach, F. A. (Ed.), *Sex and behavior*. New York: John Wiley and Sons, 1965.
18. Beach, F. A., Locks and beagles. *American Psychologist*, 1969, Vol. 24 (11), 971–989.
19. Beach, F. A. and Holz-Tucker, M., Effects of different concentrations of androgen upon sexual behavior in castrated male rats. *Journal of Comparative Psychology*, 1949, Vol. XLII, 433–453.
20. Beach, F. A. and Jaynes, J., Effects of early experience upon the behavior of animals. *Psychological Bulletin*, 1954, Vol. 51, 239–263.
21. Beach, F. A., Rogers, C. M., & LeBoeuf, B. J., Coital behavior in dogs: Effects of estrogen on mounting by females. *Journal of Comparative and Physiological Psychology*, 1968, Vol. 66, 296–307.
22. Becker, H. S., *Outsiders*. New York: Free Press, Macmillan, 1963.
23. Beigel, H. G. (Ed.), *Advances in sex research*. New York: Hoeber, 1963.
24. Bergler, E., 1000 *Homosexuals*. Paterson, N.J.: Pageant, 1959.
25. Berndt, R. M. and Berndt, C. H., *Sexual behavior in western Arnhem Land*. New York: Johnson Reprint, Viking Fund Publications in Anthropology, No. 16, 1963.
26. Best, E., *The Maori*. London: H. H. Tombs, Ltd., 1924.
27. Bieber, I., Olfaction in sexual development and adult organization. *American Journal of Psychotherapy*, 1959, Vol. 13, 851–859.
28. Bieber, I., *Homosexuality: A psychoanalytic study of male homosexuals*. New York: Basic Books, 1962.
29. Bogoras, W., The Chukchee. *Memoirs of the American Museum of Natural History*. New York: Vol. XI, 1904–1909.
30. Bossu, J. B., *Travels through that part of North America formerly called Louisiana*. London: T. Davies, 1771. 2 vols.
31. Bowie, T., Brendel, O. J., Gebbard, P. H., Rosenblum, R., Steinberg, L. (Ed. by Bowie, T. and Christenson, C. V.), *Studies in erotic art*. New York: Basic Books, 1970.
32. Browne, L., *This believing world*. New York: Macmillan, 1942.
33. Burton, R., *The erotic traveler*. New York: Putnam, 1967.
34. Carneiro, R. L., Personal communication.
35. Carpenter, C. R., A field study in Siam of the behavior and social relations of the gibbon (Hylobates Lar). *Comparative Psychological Monographs*, 1940, Vol. XVI, 1–212.
36. Carpenter, C. R., Sexual behavior of free-ranging rhesus monkeys (Macaca Mulatta): periodicity of estrus, homosexual, autoerotic and nonconformist behavior. *Journal of Comparative Psychology*, 1942, Vol. XXXIII, 143–162.
37. Catlin, G., Illustrations of the manners, customs, and condition of the North American Indians. Cited by E. Westermarck, *The origin and development of the moral ideas*. London: Macmillan, 1908.

38. Christenson, C. V., *Kinsey, a biography*. Bloomington: Indiana University Press, 1971.
39. Churchill, W., *Homosexual behavior among males*. New York: Hawthorn Books, 1967.
40. Cline, W., *Notes on the people of Siwah and El Garah in the Libyan Desert*. General Series in Anthropology, No. 4. Menasha, Wisc.: George Banta, 1936.
41. Cochran, W. G., Mosteller, F., and Tukey, J. W., *Statistical problems of the Kinsey Report*. Washington, D.C.: American Statistical Association, 1954.
42. Cole, M., Gay, J., Glick, J. A., and Sharp, D. W., *The cultural context of learning and thinking*. New York: Basic Books, 1971.
43. Cooper, J. B., An exploratory study on African lions. *Comparative Psychology Monographs*, 1942, Vol. XVII, 1–48.
44. Coopersmith, L. J., Personal communication.
45. I Corinthians 6:9.
46. Cory, D. W. (Ed.), *Homosexuality: A cross-cultural approach*. New York: Julian Press, 1956.
47. Czaplicka, M. A., *Aboriginal Siberia*. Oxford: Clarendon Press, 1914.
48. Deacon, A. B., *Malekula, a vanishing people in the New Hebrides*. C. H. Wedgwood (Ed.). London: Routledge & Sons, 1934.
49. Deuteronomy 23: 17, 18.
50. Davenport, W., Social structure of Santa Cruz Island. In W. Goodenough (Ed.), *Explorations in cultural anthropology*. New York: McGraw-Hill, 1963.
51. Davenport, W. (and P.), Sexual patterns and their regulation in a society of the Southwest Pacific. In F. A. Beach (Ed.), *Sex & behavior*. New York: John Wiley & Sons, 1965.
52. Devereux, G., Institutionalized homosexuality of the Mohave Indians. In H. Ruitenbeek, *The problem of homosexuality in modern society*. New York: Dutton, 1963, 183–226.
53. Diethelm, O., *Treatment in psychiatry*. Springfield, Ill.: Charles C. Thomas, 1950.
54. Driver, S. R., *A critical and exegetical commentary on Deuteronomy*. Edinburgh, 1895.
55. Durant, W., *The life of Greece*. New York: Simon and Schuster, 1939.
56. Ecclesiastes 7:26.
57. Ellis, A., *Homosexuality: Its causes and cure*. New York: Lyle Stuart, 1965.
58. Ellis, H., *Studies in the psychology of sex*. New York: Random House, 1936. 2 vols.
59. Ellis, W., *Polynesian researches*. London: Fisher, Son, and Jackson, 1830, Vol. 1, 246–258.
60. Eglinton, J. Z., *Greek love*. New York: Oliver Layton Press, 1964.

61. Epstein, L. M., *Sex laws and customs in Judaism*. New York: Block, 1948.
62. Farber, L. H. and Fisher, C., An experimental approach to dream psychology through the use of hypnosis. In S. S. Tomkins (Ed.), *Contemporary psychopathology*. Cambridge, Mass.: Harvard University Press, 1943.
63. Festinger, L., *A theory of cognitive dissonance*. Stanford, Calif.: Stanford University Press, 1957.
64. Firth, R., *We, the Tikopia*. London: Allen & Unwin, 1936.
65. Fisher, P., *The gay mystique: The myth and reality of male homosexuality*. New York: Stein & Day, 1972.
66. Fluckiger, F. A., Research through a glass darkly: An analysis of the Bieber study on homosexuality. *The Ladder*, 1966, Vol. X, Nos. 10, 11, 12.
67. Fluckiger, F. A., *Criteria for treatments in homosexuality*. Unpublished.
68. Fluckiger, F. A. Some basic issues of scientific method in sex research. Unpublished, 1975.
69. Ford, C. S. and Beach, F. A., *Patterns of sexual behavior*. New York: Harper & Bros., 1951.
70. Fox, R., The evolution of human sexual behaviour. In *The New York Times Magazine*, March 24, 1968.
71. Freud, S., Three contributions to the theory of sex. In A. A. Brill (Ed.-Trans.), *The basic writings of Sigmund Freud*. New York: Modern Library, 1938.
72. Freud, S., *Collected papers*. J. Riviere. (Trans.) London: Hogarth Press, 1946, 5 vols.
73. Freud, S., Letter to an American mother. *American Journal of Psychiatry*, 1951, Vol. 107, 786. (Letter sent by mother to Kinsey in 1948.)
74. Furer-Haimendorf, C. von. *The Chenchus*. London: Macmillan, 1943.
75. Gage, M. J., Women, church and state. Cited in E. Westermarck, *The origin and development of the moral ideas*. London: Macmillan, 1908.
76. Gagnon, J. and Simon, W. (Eds.), *Sexual deviance*. New York: Harper & Row, 1967.
77. Gajdusek, C. D., *New Guinea journal 1906-1970*. Bethesda, Md.: National Institutes of Health, 1971.
78. Gebhard, P. H., Situational factors affecting human sexual behavior. In F. A Beach (Ed.), *Sex & behavior*. New York: Wiley & Sons, 1965.
79. Gebhard, P. H., Sexual motifs in prehistoric Peruvian ceramics. In T. Bowie and C. V. Christenson (Eds.), *Studies in erotic art*, New York: Basic Books, 1970.
80. Gebhard, P. H., Interview material. In A. Karlen, *Sexuality and homosexuality: A new view*. New York: W. W. Norton, 1971.
81. Gebhard, P. H., Incidence of overt homosexuality in the United States and Western Europe. In J. M. Livingood (Ed.), *National institute of mental health task force on homosexuality: Final report and background papers*. Washington: U.S. Printing Office, Pub. No. HSM 72-9116, 1972.

82. Gebhard, P. H., Gagnon, J. H., Pomeroy, W. B., and Christenson, C. V., *Sex offenders*. New York: Harper & Row, 1965.
83. Genesis 3:16.
84. Gerassi, J., *The boys of Boise*. New York: Macmillan Co., 1966.
85. Gichner, L. E., *Erotic aspects of Chinese art*. Washington: Author, 1957.
86. Gifford, E. W., *Tongan society*. Bulletins of the Bernice P. Bishop museum, Vol. LXI, 1929.
87. Gillin, K., The Barama River Caribs of British Guiana. In *Papers of the Peabody Museum of American Archaeology and Ethnology*. Cambridge, Mass.: Harvard University, Vol. XIV, No. 2, 1936.
88. Gittings, B. B., The homosexual and the church. In R. Weltge (Ed.), *The same sex*. Philadelphia: Pilgrim Press, 1969.
89. Gittings, B. B., *A gay bibliography*. Philadelphia: Task force on gay liberation, American Library Association, 1974.
90. Glass, S. J., Deuel, H. J., and Wright, C. A., Sex hormone studies in male homosexuality. *Endocrinology*, 1940, Vol. 26, 590–594.
91. Goffman, E., *Stigma: Notes on the management of spoiled identity*. Englewood Cliffs, N. J.: Prentice-Hall, 1963.
92. Goy, R. W., Experimental control of psychosexuality. In G. W. Harris and R. G. Edwards (Eds.), *A discussion on the determination of sex*. Philosophical Transactions of the Royal Society. London, Series B, 1970, Vol. 259, 149–162.
93. Goy, R. W., Bridson, W. E., and Young, W. C., Period of maximal susceptibility of the prenatal female guinea pig to masculinizing actions of testosterone propionate. *Journal of Comparative and Physiological Psychology*, 1964, Vol. 57, 166–174.
94. Green, R. and Money, J. (Eds.), *Transsexualism and sex reassignment*. Baltimore: Johns Hopkins Press, 1969.
95. Gregory of Tours (Saint), *Opera omnia*. Migne, J. P., Patrologiae cursus, Vol. 21, Paris, 1849. Cited by E. Westermarck, *The origin and development of the moral ideas*. London: Macmillan, 1908.
96. Grinnell, G. B., *The Cheyenne Indians: Their history and way of life*. New York: Cooper Square Publishers, 1962. 2 vols.
97. Hamilton, J. E., The southern sea lion (Otaria Byronia DeBlainville). *Discovery Reports*, 1938, Cambridge University Press, Vol. VIII, 268–318.
98. Hampson, J. L. and Hampson, J. G., The ontogenesis of sexual behavior in man. In W. C. Young (Ed.), Vol. 2. *Sex and internal secretions*. Baltimore: Williams & Wilkins, 1961.
99. Hart-Davis, R., *The letters of Oscar Wilde*. New York: Harcourt, Brace & World, 1962.
100. Hatterer, L. J., *Changing homosexuality in the male*. New York: McGraw-Hill, 1970.
101. Henry, G. W., *Sex variants: A study of homosexual patterns*. New York: Hoebner, 1941. 2 vols.
102. Henry, G. W., Personal communication.

103. Henry, J., *Jungle people: A Kaingáng tribe of the highlands of Brazil.* New York: Vantage Books, 1941.

104. Herskovits, M. J., *Dahomey: An ancient West African Kingdom.* New York: J. J. Augustin, 1938.

105. Hess, E. H., Seltzer, A. L., and Shlien, J. M., Pupil response of hetero-sexual and homosexual males to pictures of men and women. *Journal of Social and Abnormal Psychology,* 1965, Vol. 70, 165–168.

106. Hill, W. W., The status of the hermaphrodite and transvestite in Navaho culture. *American Anthropologist,* 1935, Vol. 37, 273–279.

107. Hirschfeld, M., *The sexual history of the World War.* New York: Cadillac, 1946.

108. Hooker, E., A preliminary analysis of group behavior of homosexuals. *Journal of Psychiatry,* 1956, Vol. 42, 217–225.

109. Hooker, E., The adjustment of the male overt homosexual. *Journal of Projective Techniques,* 1957, Vol. 21, 18–31.

110. Hooker, E., Male homosexuality in the Rorschach. *Journal of Projective Techniques,* 1958, Vol. 22, 33–54.

111. Hooker, E., What is a criterion? *Journal of Projective Techniques,* 1959, Vol. 23, 278–281.

112. Hooker, E., Male homosexuality. In *Taboo topics,* N. L. Farberow (Ed.). New York: Atherton Press, 1963.

113. Hooker, E., An empirical study of some relations between sexual patterns and gender identity in male homosexuals. In J. Money (Ed.), *Sex research: New developments.* New York: Holt, Rinehart & Winston, 1965.

114. Hooker, E., Male homosexuals and their 'worlds.' In J. Marmor (Ed.), *Sexual inversion.* New York: Basic Books, 1965.

115. Hooker, E., The homosexual community. In J. H. Gagnon and W. Simon (Eds.), *Sexual deviance.* New York: Harper & Row, 1967.

116. Hooker, E., Homosexuality. In *International encyclopedia of the social sciences.* New York: Macmillan Co., 1968.

117. Hoffman, M., *The gay world.* New York: Basic Books, 1968.

118. Holmberg, A. R., *Nomads of the long bow.* New York: Natural History Press, 1969. (Paperback only; Smithsonian hardback was expurgated.)

119. Holroyd, M., *Lytton Strachey.* New York: Holt, Rinehart & Winston, 1967. 2 vols.

120. Hornblower, G. D., Letter to *Man.* London: *Man,* August, 1927.

121. Howitt, A. W., On some Australian ceremonies of initiation. *Journal of the Royal Anthropological Institute of Great Britain and Ireland.* London: 1884, Vol. 13.

122. Humphreys, L., *Tearoom trade.* New York: Aldine, 1970.

123. Hyde, M. H., *A history of pornography.* New York: Farrar, Straus and Giroux, 1964.

124. Hyde, M. H., *The love that dared not speak its name.* Boston: Little, Brown, 1970.

125. Institute for Sex Research. Unpublished data.

126. Jorgensen, C., *Christine Jorgensen: A personal autobiography*. New York: Eriksson, 1967.
127. Jowett, B., (Trans.), *The works of Plato*. New York: Tudor Publishing Co., undated.
128. Joyce, M. (Trans.), Symposium. In E. Hamilton and H. Cairns (Eds.), *Plato: the collected dialogues*. Pantheon Books, 1961.
129. Junod, H. A., *The life of a South African tribe*. London: Macmillan, 1927.
130. Kagan, J., and Beach, F. A., Effects of early experience on mating behavior in male rats. *Journal of Comparative and Physiological Psychology*. 1953, Vol. 46, 204–208.
131. Kameny, F. E., Gay is good. In R. Weltge (Ed.), *The same sex*. Philadelphia: Pilgrim Press, 1969.
132. Kameny, F. E., Personal communication.
133. Karlen, A., *Sexuality and homosexuality: A new view*. New York: W. W. Norton, 1971.
134. Kemp, R. K. and Lloyd, C., *Brethren of the coast: Buccaneers of the south seas*. St. Martin's Press, 1960.
135. Kensinger, K. M. (Ed.), *Marriage practices in lowland South America*. In press.
136. Kensinger, K. M., Personal communication.
137. Kinsey, A. C., Homosexuality: Criteria for a hormonal explanation of the homosexual. *Journal of Clinical Endocrinology*, 1941, Vol. 1, 424–428.
138. Kinsey, A. C., Comments on the history of sex research. In K. M. Bowman, O. S. English, M. S. Guttmacher, A. C. Kinsey, K. A. Meninger, N. Reider, and R. W. Laidlaw, Psychiatric implications of surveys on sexual behavior. *The Psychoanalytic Review*, 1956, Vol. 43, 471–500.
139. Kinsey, A. C., Notations in Europe. *Private diary* (unpublished). The Institute for Sex Research, 1956.
140. Kinsey, A. C., Unpublished notes on the sexual behavior of young children.
141. Kinsey, A. C., Personal communication.
142. Kinsey, A. C., Pomeroy, W. B., and Martin C. E., *Sexual behavior in the human male*. Philadelphia: Saunders, 1948.
143. Kinsey, A. C., Pomeroy, W. B., Martin, C. E., and Gebhard, P. H., Concepts of normality and abnormality in sexual behavior. In P. H. Hoch, and J. Zubin (Eds.), *Psychosexual development in health and disease*. New York: Grune & Stratton, 1949.
144. Kinsey, A. C., Pomeroy, W. B., Martin, C. E., and Gebhard, P. H., *Sexual behavior in the human female*. Philadelphia: Saunders, 1953.
145. Kinsey, A. C. and Dellenback, W. H., Observations and motion picture documentations at the Oregon state agricultural college farm. Cited in W. B. Pomeroy, *Dr. Kinsey and the Institute for Sex Research*. New York: Harper & Row, 1972.
146. Khun De Prorok, B., *In quest of lost worlds*. New York: Dutton, 1935.
147. Kroeber, A. L., *Anthropology*. New York: Harcourt, Brace, 1948.

148. La Barre, W., The Aymara Indians of the Lake Titicaca Plateau, Bolivia. *Memoirs of the American Anthropological Association*, 1948, No. 68.

149. La Salle, R. R. de, *An account of Monsieur de La Salle's last expedition and discoveries in North America*. New York: Collections of the New York Historical Society for the year 1814, Vol. 2, 1814.

150. Landtman, G., *The Kiwai Papuans of British New Guinea*. London: Macmillan, 1927.

151. Lane-Poole, S., The speeches and table-talk of the prophet Mohammad. Cited in E. Westermarck, *The origin and development of the moral ideas*. London: Macmillan, 1908.

152. Layard, J., *Stone men of Malekula*. London: Chatto & Windus, 1942.

153. Lea, H. C., *The inquisition of the middle ages* (abridged). New York: Macmillan, 1961.

154. Lehrman, D. S., Hormonal regulation of prenatal behavior in birds and infrahuman mammals. In W. C. Young (Ed.), *Sex and internal secretions*. Baltimore: Williams & Wilkins, 1961. 2 vols.

155. Leviticus 18:22.

156. Levy, R. I., *Tahitians: mind and experience in the Society Islands*. Chicago: University of Chicago Press, 1973.

157. Lewis, M., and Clark, W., *The journals of Lewis and Clark*. Boston: Houghton Mifflin, 1953.

158. Licht, H., *Sexual life in ancient Greece*. New York: Barnes & Noble, 1963.

159. Linton, R., Marquesan culture. In A. Kardiner (Ed.), *The individual and his society*. New York: Columbia University Press, 1939.

160. Linton, R., *The tree of culture*. New York: Knopf, 1955.

161. Livingood, J. M. (Ed.), *National institute of mental health task force on homosexuality: final report and background papers*. Washington: U. S. Government Printing Office, Pub. No. HSM 72-9116, 1972.

162. Lorenz, K., *Evolution and the modification of behavior*. Chicago: University of Chicago Press, 1965.

163. Lorenz, K., *On aggression*. New York: Harcourt, Brace & World, 1966.

164. Lowie, R. H., *Primitive society*. New York: Liveright, 1947.

165. Macdonald, J., East Central African customs. *Journal of the Anthropology Institute*, Vol. 22. London: 1893.

166. Machover, K., *Personality projection in the drawing of the human figure*. Springfield, Ill.: Charles C. Thomas, 1949.

167. Maclean, P. D., New findings relevant to the evolution of psychosexual functions of the brain. In J. Money (Ed.), *Sex research: New developments*. New York: Holt, Rinehart & Winston, 1965.

168. Malinowski, B., *The sexual life of savages in Northwestern Melanesia*. New York: Harcourt, Brace & World, 1929.

169. Marks, I. M., Aversion therapy. *British Journal of Medical Psychology*, 1968, Vol. 41, 47-52.

170. Marmor, J., (Ed.), *Sexual inversion: The multiple roots of homosexuality*. New York: Basic Books, 1965.

171. Marmor, J., Notes on some psychodynamic aspects of homosexuality. In J. M. Livingood (Ed.), *National institute of mental health task force on homosexuality: Final report and background papers*. Washington: U. S. Government Printing Office, Pub. No. HSM 72-9116, 1972.

172. Masters, W. H. and Johnson, V. E., *Human sexual response*. Boston: Little, Brown, 1966.

173. Masters, W. H. and Johnson, V. E., *Human sexual inadequacy*. Boston: Little, Brown, 1970.

174. Maugham, R., *Journey to Siwa*. New York: Harcourt, Brace, 1950.

175. Maurer, D. W., Homosexual argot. Plagiarized by Legman as Slang Vocabulary. In G. W. Henry, *Sex variants*. New York: Hoeber, 1941.

176. McGuire, R. J. and Vallance, M., Aversion therapy by electric shock: a simple technique. *British Medical Journal*, 1964, Vol. 1, 151.

177. Mead, M., Cultural determinants of sexual behavior. In W. C. Young (Ed.), *Sex and internal secretions*. Baltimore: Williams & Wilkins, 1961.

178. Merker, M., *Die Masai*. Cited in C. Ford and F. A. Beach, *Patterns of sexual behavior*. New York: Harper & Bros., 1951.

179. Migeon, C. J., Rivarola, M. A., and Forest, M. G., Studies of androgens in transsexual subjects, effects of estrogen therapy, *Johns Hopkins Medical Journal*, 1968, Vol. 123, 128–133.

180. Money, J., Sex hormones and other variables in human eroticism. In W. C. Young (Ed.), *Sex and internal secretions*. Baltimore: Williams & Wilkins, 1961.

181. Money, J., Psychosexual differentiation. In J. Money (Ed.), *Sex research: new developments*. New York: Holt, Rinehart & Winston, 1965.

182. Money, J. (Ed.), *Sex research: New developments*. New York: Holt, Rinehart & Winston, 1965.

183. Money, J., *Sex errors of the body*. Baltimore: Johns Hopkins Press, 1968.

184. Money, J., Sexual dimorphism and homosexual gender identity. *Psychological Bulletin*, 1970, Vol. 74, 425–440.

185. Money, J., Pubertal hormones and homosexuality, bisexuality, and heterosexuality. Appendix B in J. M. Livingood (Ed.), *National institute of mental health task force on homosexuality: Final report and background papers*. Washington: U.S. Government Printing Office, Pub. No. HSM 72-9116, 1972.

186. Money, J., Personal communication.

187. Money, J., and Ehrhardt, A., *Man & woman, boy & girl: The differentiation and dimorphism of gender identity from conception to maturity*. Baltimore: Johns Hopkins University Press, 1972.

188. Murdock, G. P., *Social structure*. New York: Macmillan, 1949.

189. Murphy, G. and Murphy, L. B. (Eds.), *Asian psychology*. New York: Basic Books, 1965.

190. Musil, A., *The manners and customs of the Rwala Bedouins*. New York: Charles R. Crane, 1938.

191. New York *Post*, May 1, 1942.
192. New York *Post*, May 5, 1942.
193. New York *Post*, May 6, 1942.
194. *The New York Times*, May 20, 1942.
195. *The New York Times*, May 21, 1942.
196. *The New York Times*, October 6, 1942.
197. *The New York Times*, March 7, 1948.
198. *The New York Times*, March 31, 1948.
199. *The New York Times*, April 1, 1948.
200. *The New York Times*, September 16, 1948.
201. *The New York Times*, May 20, 1954.
202. *The New York Times*, June 7, 1954.
203. *The New York Times*, August 5, 1954.
204. *The New York Times*, August 25, 1954.
205. *The New York Times*, December 20, 1954.
206. Nichols, J. and Clarke, L., *I have more fun with you than anybody*. New York: St. Martin's Press, 1972.
207. Nimuendaju, C., *The Apinaye*. Catholic University of America, Anthropological Series No. 8, 1939.
208. Parker, W., *Homosexuality: A selective bibliography of over 3000 items*. Metuchen, N. J.: Scarecrow Press, 1971.
209. Patai, R., *The Arab mind*. New York: Charles Scribner's Sons, 1973.
210. Pearson, H., *Oscar Wilde: His life and wit*. New York: Harper & Brothers, 1946.
211. Pfaff, D. W., Central implantation and autoradiographic studies of sex hormones. In J. Money (Ed.), *Sex research: New developments*. New York : Holt, Rinehart & Winston, 1965.
212. Plato. *Works of Plato*. Incomplete translations of Plato, Institute for Sex Research. Bloomington, Indiana, Unpublished, 1952.
213. Pomeroy, W. B., Human sexual behavior. In N. Farberow (Ed.), *Taboo Topics*. New York: Atherton, 1963.
214. Pomeroy, W. B., *Boys and sex*. New York: Delacorte, 1968.
215. Pomeroy, W. B., Homosexuality. In R. Weltge (Ed.), *The same sex*. Philadelphia: Pilgrim Press, 1969.
216. Pomeroy, W. B., *Girls and sex*. New York: Delacorte, 1969.
217. Pomeroy, W. B., *Dr. Kinsey and the Institute for Sex Research*. New York: Harper & Row, 1972.
218. Pomeroy, W. B., The diagnosis and treatment of transvestites and transsexuals. *Journal of Sex & Marital Therapy*, 1975, Vol. 1, No. 3.
219. Pomeroy, W. B., Personal communication.
220. Pool, J. J., Studies in Mohammedanism. Cited in E. Westermarck. *The origin and development of the moral ideas*. London: Macmillan, 1908.
221. Rattray, R. S., *Ashanti*. Oxford: Clarendon Press, 1923.
222. Read, K. E., *The high valley*. New York: Charles Scribner's Sons, 1965.
223. *Reader's Digest*, September, 1948.

224. Rechy, J., *City of night*. New York: Grove Press, 1963.
225. Regelson, R., Up the camp staircase. *The New York Times*, March 3, 1968.
226. Reik, T., *Masochism in modern man*. New York: Farrar & Rinehart, 1941.
227. Reik, T., *A psychologist looks at love*. New York: Farrar & Rinehart, 1944.
228. Reik, T., *The psychology of sex relations*. New York: Farrar & Rinehart, 1945.
229. Reik, T., *Myth and guilt: The crime and punishment of mankind*. New York: George Braziller, Inc., 1957.
230. Reichel-Dolmatoff, G., *Amazonian cosmos: The sexual and religious symbolism of the Tukano Indians*. Chicago: University of Chicago Press, 1971.
231. Rovere, R. H., *Senator Joe McCarthy*. London: Methuen & Co., 1960.
232. Ruitenbeek, H. M. (Ed.), *The problem of homosexuality in modern society*. New York: E. P. Dutton, 1963.
233. Saghir, M. T. and Robins, E., *Male and female homosexuality*. Baltimore: Williams & Wilkins, 1973.
234. Schneebaum, T., Notes on an isolated tribe of the Amarakaire. Department of South American Ethnology, American Museum of Natural History. Unpublished, 1958.
235. Schneebaum, T., *Notes and observations on Mashco Amarakaire and Huachipairi*. Unpublished.
236. Schneebaum, T., *Keep the river on your right*. New York: Grove Press, 1969.
237. Schneebaum, T., *Notes from Far-Eastern travels*, 1971–1972. Unpublished.
238. Scott, J. P. and Fuller, J. L., *Genetics and the social behavior of the dog*. Chicago: University of Chicago Press, 1965.
239. Secor, N. A., A brief for a new homosexual ethic. In *The same sex*. R. W. Weltge (Ed.), Philadelphia: Pilgrim Press, 1969. ·
240. Seidenberg, R., *Marriage in life and literature*. New York: Philosophical Library, 1970.
241. Shadle, A. R., Copulation in the porcupine. *Journal of Wildlife Management*, 1946, Vol. X., 159–162.
242. Shadle, A. R., Smelzer, M., and Metz, M., The sex reactions of porcupines (Erethizon D. Dorsatum) before and after copulation. *Journal of Mammalogy*, 1946, Vol. XXVII, 116–121.
243. Simon, W. and Gagnon, J. H., Homosexuality: The formulation of a sociological perspective. In *The same sex*. R. W. Weltge (Ed.). Philadelphia: Pilgrim Press, 1969.
244. Smith, A. H., The proverbs and common sayings of the Chinese. Cited in E. Westermarck, *The origin and development of the moral ideas*. London: Macmillan, 1908.
245. Socarides, C., *The overt homosexual*. New York: Grune & Stratton, 1968.

246. Sonnenschein, D., Homosexuality as a subject of anthropological inquiry. *Anthropological Quarterly*, 1966, Vol. 39, 73–82.

247. Sontag, S., Notes on camp. *Partisan Review*, Vol. 31, 515–580.

248. Sorenson, A. P., Jr., Linguistic exogamy and personal choice in the Northwest Amazon. In K. M. Kensinger (Ed.), *Marriage practices in lowland South America*. In press.

249. Spemann, H., *Embryonic development and induction*. New Haven: Yale University Press, 1938.

250. Stevenson, I., and Wolpe, J., Recovery from sexual deviations through overcoming non-sexual neurotic responses. *American Journal of Psychiatry*, 1960, Vol. 116, 8, 737–742.

251. Steward, J. H. (Ed.), *Handbook of South American Indians* (7 vols.). Washington: Issued as Bulletin 143, Smithsonian Institution, Bureau of American Ethnology, U. S. Government Printing Office, 1946–1957.

252. Stone, C. P., A note on 'feminine' behavior in adult male rats. *American Journal of Physiology*, 1942, Vol. LXVIII, 39–41.

253. Szasz, T., *The myth of mental illness*. New York: Hoeber, 1964.

254. Szasz, T., Legal and moral aspects of homosexuality. In J. Marmor (Ed.), *Sexual inversion*. New York: Basic Books, 1965.

255. Szasz, T., *The manufacture of madness*. New York: Harper & Row, 1970.

256. Taylor, G. R., *Sex in history*. New York: Vanguard, 1960.

257. Tertullian, Q. S. F., De praescriptionibus adversus haereticos. Cited in E. Westermarck, *The origin and development of the moral ideas*. London: Macmillan, 1908.

258. Tiger, L., *Men in groups*. New York: Random House, 1969.

259. *Time*, December 12, 1955.

260. I Timothy 2:14.

261. Tinbergen, N., The evolution of signaling devices. In W. Ekin (Ed.), *Social behavior and organization among vertebrates*. Chicago: University of Chicago Press. 1964.

262. Tripp, C. A., Who is a homosexual? *Social Progress: A journal of church & society*, 1967, Vol. 58, 2, 13–21.

263. Tripp, C. A., Author present.

264. Tripp, C. A., Private survey.

265. Tripp, C. A., Direct observation.

266. Turnbull, C. M., *The forest people*. New York: Simon & Schuster, 1961.

267. Turnbull, C. M., *Wayward servants*. New York: Natural History Press, 1965.

268. Turnbull, J., *A voyage round the world in the years 1800-1804*. London: A. Maxwell, 1813.

269. Underhill, R., *The social organization of the Papago Indians*. New York: AMS Press (Columbia University, Contributions to Anthropology series), 1969, Vol. 30.

270. Ward, W., A view of the history, literature and religion of the Hindoos.

Cited in E. Westermarck, *The origin and development of the moral ideas*. London: Macmillan, 1908.

271. Weinberg, G. H., *Society and the healthy homosexual*. New York: St. Martin's Press, 1972.

272. Weinberg, G. H., *The action approach: How your personality developed and how you can change it*. New York: St. Martin's Press, 1974.

273. Weinberg, M. S. and Bell, A. P., *Homosexuality: An annotated bibliography*. New York: Harper & Row, 1972.

274. Weinberg, M. S. and Williams, C. J., *Male homosexuals*. New York: Oxford University Press, 1974.

275. Westermarck, E., *The origin and development of the moral ideas*. London: Macmillan, 1906–1908. 2 vols.

276. Wright, J. (Trans.), Lysis, In E. Hamilton and H. Cairns (Eds.), *Plato: the collected dialogues*. New York: Pantheon Books, 1961.

277. Whiffen, T., *The North-West Amazons*. London: Constable & Co., 1915.

278. Whiting, J. W. M., *Becoming a Kwoma*. New Haven: Yale University Press, 1941.

279. Whiting, J., Kluckhohn, R., and Anthony, A. The function of male initiation ceremonies at puberty. In E. E. Maccoby, T. M. Newcomb, and E. L. Hartley (Eds.), *Readings in social psychology*. New York: Holt, Rinehart & Winston, 1958.

280. Williams, C. J. and Weinberg, M. S., *Homosexuals and the military*. New York: Harper & Row, 1971.

281. Williams, F. E., *Papuans of the Trans-Fly*. Oxford: Clarendon Press, 1936.

282. Wolfenden, J., *Report of the committee on homosexual offenses and prostitution*. New York: Stein & Day, 1963.

283. Wolpe, J., *Psychotherapy by reciprocal inhibition*. Stanford: Stanford University Press, 1972.

284. Wright, L. B., *Gold, glory and the gospel*. New York: Atheneum, 1970.

285. Wysor, B., *The lesbian myth*. New York: Random House, 1974.

286. Yale Cross-Cultural Index. New Haven: Yale University Library.

287. Yerkes, R. M., *Chimpanzees*. New Haven: Yale University Press, 1943.

288. Yerkes, R. M., Personal communication with Alfred C. Kinsey.

289. Young, W. C. (Ed.), *Sex and internal secretions*. Baltimore: Williams & Wilkins, 1961.

290. Young, W. C., The hormones and mating behavior. In W. C. Young (Ed.), *Sex and internal secretions*. Baltimore: Williams & Wilkins, 1961.

291. Young, W. C., Goy, R. W., and Phoenix, C. H., Hormones and sexual behavior. In Money, J. (Ed.), *Sex research: New developments*. New York: Holt, Rinehart & Winston, 1965.

292. Zuckerman, W., *The social life of monkeys and apes*. London: Kegan Paul, Trench, Trubner, Ltd., 1932.

Index